Instructor's Resource Manual

to Accompany

Information Technology for the Health Professions

Third Edition

Lillian Burke

Barbara Weill

Upper Saddle River, New Jersey

Pearson Education Ltd., *London*
Pearson Education Australia Pty. Limited, *Sydney*
Pearson Education Singapore, Pte. Ltd.
Pearson Education North Asia Ltd., *Hong Kong*
Pearson Education Canada Inc.
Pearson Educación de Mexico, S.A. de C.V.
Pearson Education—Japan, *Tokyo*
Pearson Education Malaysia, Pte. Ltd.
Pearson Education, Upper Saddle River, New Jersey

10 9 8 7 6 5 4 3 2 1
ISBN-13: 978-0-13-514604-0
ISBN-10: 0-13-514604-6

Contents

Short Syllabus

Week 1: Chapter 1

Week 2: Chapters 2 and 3

Week 3: Chapter 4

Week 4: Chapter 5

WEEK FIVE: TEST ON CHAPTERS 1–5

Week 6: Chapter 6

Week 7: Chapter 7

Week 8: Chapter 8

Week 9: Chapter 9

WEEK TEN: TEST ON CHAPTERS 6–9

Week 11: Chapter 10

Week 12: Chapter 11

Week 13: Chapter 12

WEEK FOURTEEN: FINAL EXAM

Suggested Syllabus and Lecture Notes

WEEK ONE: Read Chapter One

Chapter 1 Introduction to Information Technology—Hardware, Software, and Telecommunications

SUGGESTED LECTURE NOTES—This chapter is for students who do not have a firm grasp of the technology underlying the contributions of information technology (IT) to health care. The instructor may choose to skip it or spend some time on it.

An introduction to computer literacy and computers in health care.

Introduction

- Computer literacy—ability to use computers, discuss them intelligently (know what hardware and software are and what a communications network is), make use of the Internet.
- Information technology includes computers, computer literacy, and the Internet.
- Computer—an electronic device, operating according to instructions stored in its memory that can accept data as input, process it, produce information as output, and store the results. Computers are fast, reliable, and (because they can be programmed) flexible.
  - *It is especially crucial for allied health students to have knowledge of computers and networks now because of the push to make the use of the electronic health record (EHR) and integrated hospital information technology systems universal by 2014.*

Computer Classifications

- Supercomputer—largest and most powerful at any time; scientific applications like weather forecasting and simulations
- Mainframe—used by large institutions (businesses, hospitals, and universities); powerful, multiuser computer; many users access mainframe through terminals; used for data processing tasks, for example, generating a payroll, processing insurance claims
- Minicomputer—scaled down multiuser computer
- Microcomputer (PC and desktop)—single user; used by individuals
- Personal digital assistants (PDAs) are small handheld computers and are used throughout the health care system for references, to gather information, and to write prescriptions.
- Embedded—single-purpose computer on a chip inside appliances or human beings, where they may be used to regulate a heartbeat or dispense medication among other uses.

Data representation: Inside a computer, everything is represented by patterns of binary digits (bits).

Hardware

Input Devices

- Keyboards
- Direct-entry devices
- Scanning devices include the optical mark recognition, optical character recognition, barcode scanner, MICR, and Kurzweil scanner
  - *Radio frequency identification (RFID) tags can be implanted in patients, contain medical history, and send out radio waves.*
  - *Pointing and drawing devices include the mouse, trackball, joystick, touch screen, and pen-based input*
  - *Cards include smart cards, which include a microprocessor and can hold some information; optical cards that can hold a great deal of information*
  - *Sensors collect data directly from the environment and digitize it*
  - *Vision input through cameras*
  - *Speech recognition*
  - *Human biology input*

Processing Hardware and Memory

- Processor (system unit)
  - *Central processing unit (microprocessor)*
    - Control unit
    - Arithmetic logic unit

      [Note: Microprocessors differ in speed, which depends on clock speed (measured in megahertz) and word size, and is related to the size of memory.]
- Memory (primary storage)
  - *Read only memory (firmware) holds start-up instructions; permanent*
  - *Random access memory holds the program you are working with, your work, and parts of the operating system.*
    - Temporary
    - Measured in bytes, kilobytes, megabytes, and gigabytes

Output Devices

- Hard copy
  - *Printers*
    - Impact (dot matrix)
    - Nonimpact (ink-jet and laser)
  - *Plotters*
- Soft copy
  - *Monitor*
  - *Voice synthesis*
- Secondary storage (permanent—more or less)
  - *Magnetic media*
    - Diskette
    - Hard disk
    - Tape
  - *Optical media (laser burns pits in a plastic disk; pits are zeroes and lands are ones)*
    - CD-ROM, CD-R, CD-RW
  - *Solid-state memory devices—Flash memory; high capacity*

Software

Software (programs) give the computer line-by-line instructions on how to do something; it is the software that makes the computer such a flexible tool.

System Software

- Operating system (communicates with hardware, monitors the computer's operations, manages processor resources, memory, input and output, and provides the user interface). Parts of the operating system must be booted for computer to do anything.
- Utilities (screen savers, virus detectors, and automatic backup)

Application Software

- Word processors for text documents
- Spreadsheets for math
- DBMS for organizing huge amounts of data
- Communications for networking
- Graphics
- Specialized packages, specifically created for medical offices

Networking and Telecommunications

Introduction

- Connectivity—the fact that computers can be linked for sending and receiving data
- Telecommunications—involves telephone lines in the linking of computers

Media (data must follow some path between connected computers)

- Connections can be high bandwidth or low bandwidth, wired or wireless
- Hospitals use fast T1 lines

Protocols—technical standards that govern the exchange of data

Networks (allow the sharing of hardware, software, and data)

- Classified by size: LANs, WANs, personal networks using Bluetooth—links your cell phone, pacemaker, and so on
- Expansion of wireless technology: cell phones, GPS, Wi-Fi, PDAs

The Internet

- History (ARPANet—1969)
- Internet protocols: transmission control protocol/Internet protocol (TCP/IP)
- Services: exchange of text, data, programs; research; e-mail; MEDLINE
- World Wide Web—part of the Internet that allows the linking of multimedia documents (Web sites); you must have an Internet connection and software called a browser (Windows Explorer or Netscape Navigator)
- Finding information
  - *Every document has an address (uniform resource locator) that you can enter if you know it.*
  - *Browsing: start anywhere and click on links to other sites*
  - *Search tools*
    - Search engines (Ask and Google) allow the user to enter a search expression and finds documents with the matching phrase.
    - Subject guides or directories (Yahoo) organize information into categories.
- Evaluating information
  - *There are no standards governing the quality of information on the Internet. Much of it is unreliable.*
  - *Some questions to ask when judging reliability of information:*
    - Is the site maintained by an educational (.edu), nonprofit (.org), or government (.gov) institution? Is it maintained by an individual (address may include ~)? Is the site maintained by a commercial organization (.com) that is trying to sell you something?
  - *Be careful of conflicts of interest on any site. For example, much of the drug budget for the FDA comes from the drug companies it regulates. Some people might consider this a conflict.*
  - *Does the page have an author?*
  - *Has the page been updated recently?*
  - *Does the information make sense and can it be supported by other sources?*

WEEK TWO: Read Chapters Two and Three

Chapter 2 Medical Informatics: The Health Information Technology Decade

SUGGESTED LECTURE NOTES—Discuss the contributions of medical informatics. Is the computerization of all medical information by 2014 realistic given the cost, lack of infrastructure, and resistance of various people?

Medical Informatics

Medical informatics has many definitions. The common emphasis in all definitions is on the use of technology to organize information in health care.

- It focuses on improving diagnostic images, improving image-guided and minimally invasive surgery, developing simulations, developing low-cost diagnostic tests, treating physical handicaps, providing consumers with information, coordinating international medical reporting, developing and improving information systems, and developing decision-support systems.
- Subspecialties include bioinformatics, dental informatics, nursing informatics, and public health informatics.

The Health Information Technology Decade

- The U.S. government is attempting to make the EHR and e-prescribing universal by 2014. It is calling 2004–2014 the Health Information Technology (HIT) decade.

HIPAA: A Brief Introduction

- HIPAA was passed by the U.S. Congress and signed into law in 1996. Its goal was to make health insurance portable from one job to another and to secure the privacy of medical records.

The Patient Information Form

- Includes personal, medical, and insurance information

The Paper Medical Record

- The traditional patient record was on paper, stored in one doctor's office. One of the problems with paper records is that they may be illegible, which can lead to serious errors in diagnosis, treatment, and billing. There is only one copy of a paper record leading to difficulty in sharing patient information.

The Electronic Medical Record

- Encouraged by HIPAA, and the federal government, the electronic medical record (EMR) is very slowly replacing the paper record.

The Electronic Health Record

- The information on a patient's EMR will form the basis of the electronic health record (EHR).
- It is an electronic record of patient health information generated by one or more encounters in any care delivery setting, and it includes information from all the health care providers and institutions that give care to the patient.
- Ideally, the EHR is not the property of any one institution or practitioner.
- Eventually, it must be interoperable nationally and internationally.

Regional Health Information Organizations (RHIOs)

- Regional cooperation is being fostered through the establishment of regional health information organizations (RHIOs) in which data could be shared within a region. It is a first step toward national interoperability.

The Indian Health Service Electronic Health Record

- The Indian Health Service of the Department of Health and Human Services of the federal government has developed an electronic health record with a graphical user interface, which interacts with the Resource and Patient Management System (RPMS) database of health care applications.

Computer Information Systems in Health Care

- Computerized information systems are used in some hospitals and other health care facilities to help manage and organize relevant patient, financial, pharmacy, laboratory, and radiological information. To receive the full benefits of computer technology, each of these separate information systems needs to be linked under the hospital information system (HIS).
- Very few hospitals have reached this point of computerization.
- HIS needs to integrate the administrative and clinical functions in a hospital. Ideally, the HIS includes clinical information systems, financial information systems, laboratory information systems, nursing and pharmacy information systems, picture archiving and communication systems, and radiology information systems.

Does Computerization Improve Patient Outcomes?

- Not enough providers are using the EHR to see the full benefit of computerization, and an editorial in *Health Affairs* asserted that more testing is needed.

Introduction of Computer Systems

- Studies that do exist suggest that the most successful systems are created with the participation of those who will use them. Systems imposed from above are not as readily accepted.

Chapter 3 An Introduction to the Administrative Applications of Computers: Accounting

SUGGESTED LECTURE NOTES—Emphasize the varied administrative programs. Have students search the Web for "medical administrative software." Discuss the differences between a medical office and other offices; emphasize bucket billing.

Medical Informatics

- Clinical applications—direct patient care
- Special-purpose applications—education, pharmacy
- Administrative—office and materials management, scheduling, accounting, and financial applications
- Telemedicine—delivery of health care over telecommunications lines; includes clinical, special-purpose, and administrative applications

Administrative Applications (Earliest Applications)

- Programs designed to computerize administrative functions in a health care environment
- Allow organization of patient data, case data, provider data
- Enable electronic scheduling and electronic progress notes and create lists of codes for diagnosis, treatment, and insurance
- Allow bucket billing (billing one insurer after another until the patient is billed)
- Organize information in a relational database
  - *Each type of information is organized in its own table.*
  - *Tables can be linked.*

Database

A database is an organized collection of data created and maintained by software called database management software (DBMS)

- A file holds related information on an entity
- A file can hold many tables, each holding related information
- A record holds information on one item in the table
- A field is a piece of information in a record
  - *A key field uniquely identifies a record*

Coding and Grouping

- DRG holds diagnostic codes
- CPT holds procedure codes
- ICD holds disease codes
- MEDCIN codes symptoms, history, examinations, tests, diagnosis, and treatment
- SNOMED provides a common language
- LOINC standardizes laboratory and clinical codes
- NDC codes drugs

Accounting

- Transactions—charges, payments, and adjustments
- Case—condition that brings a patient to the doctor's office

Insurance

- Indemnity (fee-for-service) plans
- Health maintenance organizations
- Preferred provider organization
- Government insurance: Medicare, Medicaid, CHAMPVA, CHAMPUS, TRICARE, Workers' compensation
- Claim (request for payment from an insurer)—submitted electronically through a clearinghouse or on paper
  - *An explanation of benefits (EOB) is a response to a paper claim*
  - *An electronic remittance advice (ERA) accompanies a repose to an electronic claim*
  - *Balance or bucket billing*

Accounts receivable (any invoices or payments)

- Superbill (encounter form)—list of diagnoses and procedures common to a practice
- Reports—procedure day sheet, payment day sheet, patient day sheet, practice analysis report, patient aging report

WEEK THREE: Read Chapter Four

Chapter 4 Telemedicine

SUGGESTED LECTURE NOTES—Telemedicine continues to expand. Have students research the expansion, the licensing problems, and the reciprocal licensing agreements between states. Have students discuss the uses of telepsychiatry (referring to the selected reading).

- Telemedicine uses computers and telecommunications lines to deliver health care at a distance.
- Telemedicine may use store-and-forward technology to transmit still images or interactive videoconferencing for real-time consultation.
- Any medical information can be transmitted as e-mail or video, using technologies from plain old telephone service to dedicated high-speed lines.

- The uses of telemedicine continue to grow in part because the U.S. Department of Veterans Affairs (VA) has adopted telehome care, in part because more insurers cover it, in part because of the growing prison population; telemedicine has been used in prisons for years.
  - *Subspecialties: teleradology (radiological images), telepathology (microscopic images), teledermatology (skin conditions), teleophthalmology (eye care), telecardiology [most often second opinions for emergency rooms (ERs) for suspected heart attacks], teleneurology including telestroke and the treatment of epilepsy, and telehome care, using remote monitoring devices*
- Internet-based services can connect patients wearing pacemakers to their doctors.
- Bluetooth technology can connect various devices, so that, for example, when the pacemaker senses a dangerous event, the cell phone automatically calls 911. Telephone-based heart monitors are being used in Japan.
- Telemedicine is particularly important when time is a consideration; telestroke patients can be evaluated by experts miles away to see if they need tPA (a clot busting drug that needs to be administered within a few hours of a stroke).
- Teleneurology uses e-mail and videoconferencing, so that a neurologist can diagnose at a distance. Teleneurology is also making referrals using e-mail. Video can be used to study gait.
- Telepsychiatry is used where there are few psychiatrists but is not appropriate for all conditions.
- Remote monitoring devices make it possible for patients to be monitored at home.
- New experimental devices embed sensors in wearable fabric.
- Telehome care involves a link between the patient's home and a hospital or central office that collects the data. Equipment is installed in the patient's home. Using it, the patient can telecommunicate vital signs to a nurse at a distant location and can also speak to the nurse. Telehome care has been found to cut rehospitalizations and ER visits and to reduce hospital stays.
- Telemedicine in prisons is cost-effective, enhances security, and improves medical care.

Other Uses of Telemedicine

- Baby CareLink
- RetCam to diagnose retinopathy of prematurity
- Treatment of Alzheimer's (using motion detectors to monitor patients)
- In daycare
- Teletrauma in Vermont
- Telemedicine is also used in weight management, pain management, spinal cord injury, and podiatry. Teleoncology systems are helping cancer patients avoid lengthy trips to the doctor and feel more secure because they have a twenty-four-hour link to health care.
- SATELLIFE delivers information to health care workers in remote areas.
- Telenurses and doctors are using the eICU Smart Alerts® to monitor intensive care patients from afar and send alerts to the ICU personnel.
- In July 2006, the FDA approved a wireless electronic capsule to help diagnose stomach disorders.
- Telenursing involves teletriage and the telecommunication of health-related data, the remote house call, and the monitoring of chronic disease.
- For telemedicine to fulfill its promise, certain technical, legal, insurance, and privacy issues need to be addressed and an appropriate telecommunications infrastructure must be in place.
  - *In addition, legal issues such as licensing, medical liability, insurance, and privacy concerns need to be addressed.*

WEEK FOUR: Read Chapter Five

Chapter 5 Information Technology in Public Health

SUGGESTED LECTURE NOTES—Discuss the place of computers and information technology (IT) in public health. Discuss Hurricane Katrina as a natural and human-made disaster; as a public health issue.

- Public health deals with the health of a whole community. Public health can save more lives than medicine. Understanding the epidemiology of a disease can lead to prevention through public health measures like providing a cleaner, healthier environment (including taking steps against global warming), providing better sanitation, the distribution of information, and the development of vaccines.
  - *The field of public health also includes the use of tobacco, planning for natural and human-made disaster, and identifying and containing epidemics.*
  - *Public health refers to the health of the whole community; social inequality is one determinant of health. Therefore, diminishing inequality within society can be seen as a public health measure.*
- Public health informatics supports public health practice and research with information technology.
- Epidemiology is the study of disease by collecting and analyzing statistical data.
  - *Computers are helpful in collecting and organizing worldwide data (or community or national data).*
- IT plays a role in infection control by helping with surveillance, monitoring, and reporting the spread of a disease, by identifying organisms and patients, and by spotting trends.
  - *Identifying an epidemic means counting the "extra" cases.*
  - *Computers can create models of how a disease may spread, given air travel and climate, the supply of drugs, and the existence of vaccines; prepare what-if simulations changing variables, using computational models.*
- Before computers, before any understanding of the germ theory, statistics and public health measures stopped epidemics (Jenner and small pox; Snow and cholera).
  - *Reappearance of "conquered diseases" in the late twentieth and early twenty-first centuries (polio)*
- The flu pandemic of 1918–1919; public health measures had little effect.
- New diseases continue to appear and challenge public health authorities: Ebola, AIDS, SARS, bird flu, West Nile virus, mad cow.
- Office of the National Coordinator for Health Information Technology (ONCHIT) proposes a national interoperable network to gather and disseminate information.
  - *PDAs are being used in the developing world to help gather disease information (SATELLIFE).*
  - *In the United States, the National Electronic Disease Surveillance System (NEDSS) (part of the Public Health Information Network) will be a national electronic surveillance system allowing epidemics to be identified quickly. Eventually, it would automatically collect data in real time.*
  - *Several software tools are available to map and predict disease spread.*
    - MIDAS is a U.S.-funded plan for researchers to use computers to model diseases.
    - WHONET is a microbiology information system that is used to monitor antibacterial resistance.
- Global warming: The scientific consensus is in. Our planet is warming, and we are helping to make it happen by adding more heat-trapping gases, primarily carbon dioxide (CO_2), to the atmosphere.

  - *Global warming may have a devastating effect on human health and life including more intense heat waves leading to more heat-related deaths; an increase in asthma and eczema; more intense storms; an increase in flooding of major rivers; an increase in pollution, drought, and forest fires; the destruction of crops; and the destruction of wildlife habitats.*
  - *One of the concrete steps that could be taken to slow global warming is cutting carbon dioxide emissions.*
- Hurricane Katrina flooded New Orleans both because it was a "monster hurricane" and because the levees failed; this should not have been surprising. Computers are used to model various hurricanes and their paths and effects. In 2004, "in an exercise simulating a direct hit by a slow-moving category 3 hurricane [using 2 different models], both models showed that the levees would not prevent flooding in New Orleans."
  - *An adequate public health plan could have been in place before the storm: evacuation plans; the designation of shelters provided with adequate food, clean water, medications, and vaccinations; plans to get all the people to those shelters; plans to clean up and rebuild the city.*
  - *However, after the hurricane, many were "stranded without basic human necessities and exposed to human waste, toxins, and physical violence." Many shelters lacked electricity and air conditioning.*
- Public health involves the protection of the health of whole populations.
  - *Epidemics (which can become pandemics) also require world cooperation.*
  - *Global warming requires a global response.*
  - *Computers can model diseases and natural disasters, so that adequate public health responses are in place before disaster strikes.*

WEEK FIVE: Test on Chapters One to Five

WEEK SIX: Read Chapter Six

Chapter 6 Information Technology in Radiology

SUGGESTED LECTURE NOTES—Emphasize the improvements in imaging technology over the past century and how this has impacted on disease. Discuss interventional radiology.

- Computer-based imaging techniques use computers to generate pictures of internal organs of the body. A digital image is an image in a form computers can process and store, that is, in bits.
  - *Even older technologies (X-ray and ultrasound) are now computer based.*
    - X-ray used for broken bones, in mammography.
    - Ultrasound uses sound waves to produce a real-time image of a moving fetus.
  - *Newer imaging techniques*
    - Computerized tomography (CT)—uses X-rays and digital technology to produce a cross-sectional image of the body
    - Magnetic resonance imaging (MRI)—produces images of soft tissue within the body that could not be pictured by traditional X-rays. MRIs can produce images of the insides of bones. MRI machines use computers and a very strong magnetic field and radio waves to produce pictures.
      - *fMRI—identifies brain area by function by sensing small changes in oxygen use*
      - *Diffusion tensor imaging—shows the white matter of the brain, the connections between parts of the brain, so that these are not damaged during surgery*
    - Single photon emission computed tomography (SPECT)—shows movement

- Positron emission tomography (PET)—uses radioisotope technology to create a picture of the body in action
  - *Accurate diagnosis of breast cancer*
  - *Measure an esophageal cancer patient's response to chemotherapy and radiation therapy before surgery. PET scans can detect metastases that other imaging techniques could not see.*
  - *Can show the functioning of the brain by measuring cerebral blood flow*
- DEXA scans (bone density tests)
- Other imaging technology: LUMA cervical imaging system to help detect cervical cancer. Innova digital flat panel biplane imaging system that can be used for many interventional, image-guided procedures.

- Picture archiving and communications systems (PACS)—"a system that transmits, stores, retrieves, and displays digital images . . . and communicates the information over a network." PACS is a server.
- Digital imaging and communications in medicine (DICOM) is the standard communication protocols of imaging devices.
- Interventional radiology
  - *Stereotactic radiosurgery (gamma knife)—noninvasive treatment of brain tumors*
    - Cyber knife noninvasive treatments of other tumors
  - *Nonsurgical repair of some thoracic abnormalities*
  - *The gamma knife is also being used to treat neuralgia, intractable pain, Parkinson's, and epilepsy*
  - *Radiofrequency ablation (RFA) can be used on cancerous tumors of the liver or lungs.*
  - *Interventional radiology is also used in the treatment of blocked carotid arteries in patients who do not exhibit stroke symptoms; the use of an improved embolization procedure to treat and reverse male infertility. Lasers are being used to treat children with painful vascular malformations.*
  - *Interventional radiology is being tested as a treatment for uterine fibroids with a 92 percent success rate.*
- The improvement in imaging techniques has made surgery more precise and has reduced the need for exploratory surgery.

WEEK SEVEN: Read Chapter Seven

Chapter 7 Information Technology in Surgery—the Cutting Edge

SUGGESTED LECTURE NOTES—Discuss how students feel about surgeons who are machines, not human beings.

Computer-Assisted Surgery

- Surgical planning: virtual reality; virtual environments help teach and plan surgeries
- Minimally invasive surgery (MIS)
  - *Endoscope projects an image of the surgical site onto a monitor*
  - *MIS is performed through small incisions leading to less pain and shorter recovery time*
  - *Surgeon sees image on a monitor. It is image directed.*
  - *Endoluminal surgery—done through natural orifices*
- Robots
  - *Used to hold endoscopes*
  - *Used to "decide" if tissue is normal*
  - *Used in many surgeries*
  - *ROBODOC—in hip replacements*
  - *AESOP—first FDA-cleared surgical robot; holds endoscope—one arm*
  - *ZEUS—minimally invasive microsurgery*

- *DaVinci—minimally invasive heart surgery—mimics surgeon's hand motions; used to repair an inborn condition called atrial septic defect. In 2005, daVinci was approved for gynecological procedures; cleared for heart surgery in 2004; used in prostate surgery.*
- *MINERVA—stereotactic neurosurgery*
- *HERMES—FDA-cleared system software that connects operating room hardware into a voice-controlled network, from lighting to robots.*
- *In March 2005, a six-day-old baby was successfully operated on by robots to repair a congenital hernia—the youngest patient to undergo robotic surgery!*

Currently attempts are being made to create smaller surgical robots.

- Augmented reality—provides surgeons with a look inside the body, projected onto the outside of the body
- CAVEman—new four-dimensional model of the human body
- Telepresence (distance) surgery: gall bladder surgery (2001), prostate surgery (2002), surgery to correct acid reflux (2003); first developed by NASA
- Lasers: different wavelengths do different things and are used to destroy cancer cells, used in LASIK (eye surgery) and in other surgeries, changes the shape of the cornea.

NASA Extreme Environment Mission Operation (NEEMO)

- NEEMO 7 and 9 included doctors, but no surgeons. NEEMO 12 crew conducted advanced medical experiments using robotic telesurgery. The major purpose of these projects is to enable astronauts to be operated on in space from earth using wireless technology and robotics.

The Operating Room of the Future

- Images from all sources will be integrated and available to surgeons and other personnel.
- Information displayed includes a patient's vital statistics, allergies, the whereabouts of operating room (OR) personnel.
- In some ORs of the future, all personnel including doctors are identified and their movements tracked by RFID tags.

WEEK EIGHT: Read Chapter Eight

Chapter 8 Information Technology in Pharmacy

SUGGESTED LECTURE NOTES—Discuss with students how the Human Genome Project is leading to the development of new medications. Discuss with students ways to decrease medication errors in the United States.

- IT affects all aspects of pharmacy (drug design, testing, and administering).
- The U.S. Food and Drug Administration (FDA) is supposed to oversee the safety and effectiveness of medications.
  - *Since the 1992, passage of Prescription Drug User Fees Act (PDUFA) renewed in 1997, 2002, and 2007, which requires drug companies to pay fees to support the drug review process and also to pay annual fees, more and more of the FDA budget has come from private companies.*
    - Between 1998 and 2005 user fees doubled; they now comprise over 50 percent of the FDA's drug review budget.
    - Congressional oversight has declined since 1992.
    - Some of the FDA's advisory panels have ties to the drug industry.
  - *Two percent of the drugs on the market have not been reviewed by the FDA.*
- Computers are being used to help design and test new drugs. Genetic tests can be used to determine an individual's response to a specific medication.

- Biotechnology sees the human body as a collection of molecules and seeks to understand and treat disease in terms of these molecules.
  - *Developing drugs by design requires mapping the structure and creating a three-dimensional graphical model of the target molecule.*
- The application of information technology to biology is called bioinformatics.
- The development of new medications is becoming more dependent on knowledge of genes. The Human Genome Project (HGP) mapped the human genome.
  - *HGP attempted to understand the molecular bases of genetic diseases.*
  - *By 2006, several genes related to disease had been identified and dozens of drugs have been approved.*
  - *Antisense technology attempts to shut off disease-producing genes.*
  - *RNAi is a process that cells use to turn off genes. The attempt at developing drugs based on RNAi holds some promise.*
  - *In 2006, a synthetic molecule that caused cancer cells to self-destruct was developed. However, it has not been tested.*
  - *Stem cells are cells that can develop into different types of body cells; theoretically, they can repair the body.*
- Software can help simulate drug trials.
- The Physiome Project is an international project seeking to create mathematical models of human organs. Mathematical models may in the future allow the testing of drugs, tailoring a drug to a person, and practice of surgery.
- Computers are used to help the FDA speed clinical trials.
- Pharmacies inside and outside the hospital can be computerized.
- Introducing computers into any aspect of prescription entry, the filling of orders, and dispensing of medications appear to lead to a decrease in medication errors. However, there are errors caused by computerization.
- Community and centralized hospital pharmacies that computerize use robots to dispense medication. The system should be connected to a database to allow the computer to warn of possible drug interactions, allergies, and incorrect dosage. Barcodes are used to identify medications.
- Some computerized hospital pharmacies are using point-of-use dispensing of drugs—a decentralized automated system.
- Intravenous administration errors are very serious. Two new safety technologies being introduced in 2006 are barcode medication administration (BCMA) and smart infusion systems with dose error reduction systems (DERS).
- RFID tags can be used to identify drugs. Unlike barcodes, RFIDs do not have to be scanned by hand; RFID readers can be embedded anywhere and automatically read the RFID tag.
- Telepharmacy involves using a computer, a network connection, and a drug-dispensing unit to allow patients to obtain drugs outside of a traditional pharmacy, at, for example, a doctor's office or clinic.
- Some medications can currently be delivered on a surgically implanted chip.

WEEK NINE: Read Chapter Nine

Chapter 9 Information Technology in Dentistry

SUGGESTED LECTURE NOTES—Discuss how changing demographics have impacted on dentistry.

- Dental informatics—combines the use of computers with dentistry
  - *Eighty-five percent of dental offices make some use of computers.*
- Special purpose applications: education
  - *Computer-generated treatment plans to educate patients.*

  - *Simulations for training dentists*
    - Virtual dentist's office
- Administrative applications
  - *Electronic appointment book, electronic accounting software, dental record*
  - *Electronic dental chart*
    - Standardized, easy to search, and easy to read. It will integrate practice management tasks (administrative applications) with clinical information.
- The effects of changing demographics on dentistry
  - *Combination of an aging population who keep their teeth and children whose teeth are cared for means dentists are filling fewer cavities in children; they are treating older patients who have different dental problems.*
  - *Despite the general improvement in dental health, there is an epidemic of decay among poor children.*
- Clinical applications
  - *Computerized instruments*
    - Fiber-optic camera
    - Ultrasonic instruments used in endodontics (treats diseases of the pulp)
    - Electronic probe used in periodontics (treats diseases of the gums)
    - Lasers and digital cameras in cosmetic dentistry
    - WAND™ includes a microprocessor that measures tissue density; this insures a steady flow of anesthetic.
  - *Endodontics treats diseases of the pulp.*
  - *Periodontics treats diseases of the gums.*
    - Periodontal disease is caused by bacteria.
    - Sequence of the genome associated with the pathogen causing gum disease has been identified.
    - Gum disease is related to heart disease, premature birth, cancer, and diabetes.
    - Voice-activated charting is beginning to be used.
  - *Cosmetic dentistry uses bonding, implants, orthodonture, and virtual reality images.*
  - *Diagnosis*
    - Expert systems or clinical decision-support systems (EXPERTMD) and online databases
    - X-rays
    - Digital X-rays (less radiation, immediately developed, and seen on a monitor)
    - Electrical conductance
    - Light illumination
      - *Fiber-optic transillumination*
      - *DIFOTI®*
      - *Intra-oral fiber-optic cameras*
  - *Lasers—depending on the wavelength of the light, lasers can do different things: drill teeth, reshape gums, whiten teeth*
  - *Minimally invasive dentistry—emphasis on prevention*
  - *Surgery*
    - The newest techniques use interventional radiology: radiosurgery is a technique that uses radio waves instead of knives. It is used for the following procedures: cosmetic surgery (to heat bleaching agents), gum surgery, root canal therapy, the removal of a muscle that grows between the two front teeth, and biopsies.
- The growth of specialization—the percent of dentists who are specialists is expected to rise.
- Teledentistry allows dentists to consult with other dentists, specialists.

WEEK TEN: Test on Chapters Six to Nine

WEEK ELEVEN: Read Chapter Ten

Chapter 10 Informational Resources: Computer-Assisted Instruction, Expert Systems, Health Information Online

SUGGESTED LECTURE NOTES—Discuss how you would check the accuracy of information.

- Educational resources on the Internet
  - *The Visible Human—computerized library of human anatomy at the National Library of Medicine.*
  - *Explorable Virtual Human is being developed. It will include authoring tools that engineers can use to build anatomical models that will allow students to experience how real anatomical structures feel, appear, and sound.*
  - *The Vesalius Project (Columbia University) is creating these three-dimensional models (called maximal models) of anatomical regions and structures to be used in teaching anatomy.*
  - *The Virtual Human Embryo is digitizing some of the 7,000 human embryos lost in miscarriages, which have been kept by the National Museum of Health and Medicine of the Armed Forces Institute of Pathology since the 1880s.*
- Computer-assisted instruction
  - *Drill and practice for skills requiring memorization*
  - *Simulation software*
    - ILIAD
    - ADAM
    - Virtual reality simulators are particularly useful in teaching procedures that are guided by haptic clues
      - *Used to train surgeons to perform minimally invasive operations*
    - Human patient simulators are programmable mannequins on which students can practice medical procedures.
- Distance learning
- Decision-support (expert) systems: an expert system (or computerized decision-support system) is an attempt to make a computer an expert in one narrow field.
  - *MYCIN*
  - *Internist*
  - *POEMS*
  - *Databank for cardiovascular disease*
- Health information on the Internet
  - *Tens of millions of people logging on to the Internet are looking for health-related information. Advantages: cheap and easy way to get information leading to well-informed patients*
  - *The digital divide means that access to computers and the Internet is not distributed equally in society; many people do not have access to the Internet.*
  - *About 100,000 health-related Web sites, most with no quality control leads to misinformation.*
  - *Reliable sites: those maintained by federal government (http://www.nih.gov) like the MEDLARS databases, including MEDLINE. Other reliable sources: CINAHL for allied health professionals; the Virtual Hospital. (Even reliable sites may contain dated and unreliable information.)*
  - *AMA guidelines for judging information: check the source, check the financing, check the latest update, does it refer to outside print sources. If a site is trying to sell you a miracle cure that sounds too good to be true, it probably is. Do not believe anything with the words*

"scientific breakthroughs," or miraculous, or claims of a conspiracy of the medical establishment. Less than 25 percent of sites offering health info meet these minimal standards.

- *Support groups on the Web can offer community, support, and advice (Starbright World), but the anonymity can also lead to fraud.*

- E-mail
  - *Used by 15 percent health care providers and consumers to communicate with each other (although 90 percent consumers want it)*
    - Advantages: less intrusive than a telephone call, allows time to compose thoughts and put them on paper. Leaves a hard copy record. Doctors who use e-mail say it gives patients the sense that they can contact the doctor at any time; there has never been a suit based on e-mail.
    - Disadvantage: lack of security and confidentiality. According to doctors who will not use it, paper trail can lead to suits; takes up extra time.
    - Suggested guidelines from one practice that invites patients' e-mail
      - *Inform patients—who will read the e-mail, likely response time, what will and will not be discussed via e-mail (e.g., psychiatric diagnosis, HIV test results, or work-related injuries will not be discussed).*
- Computers and psychiatry
  - *First uses of computers in psychotherapy were in testing.*
  - *Other uses are in self-help Internet sites, computer-administered therapy, virtual reality therapy*
  - *Web-based depression and anxiety test was found effective in diagnosing anxiety disorders and depression.*
  - *Programs that are effective include Fear Fighter for phobias and panic; BTSteps for OCD; Cope and Overcoming Depression Course for depression; Balance for general anxiety disorder.*
  - *Internet therapy (Interapy) for those suffering from post-traumatic stress disorder according to self-reports.*

WEEK TWELVE: Read Chapter Eleven

Chapter 11 Information Technology in Rehabilitative Therapies: Computerized Medical Devices, Assistive Technology, and Prosthetic Devices

SUGGESTED LECTURE NOTES—Discuss the advantages and disadvantages of using computerized medical devices.

- Computerized medical instruments are "electronic devices equipped with microprocessors [which] provide direct patient services such as monitoring . . . [and] administering medication or treatment." They are both more accurate and more reliable than their predecessors.
  - *Computerized drug delivery systems are used to give medications.*
  - *Computerized monitoring systems collect data directly from patients via sensors.*
    - Physiological monitoring systems analyze blood
    - Arrhythmia monitors monitor heart rates
    - Pulmonary monitors measure blood flow through the heart and respiratory rate
    - Fetal monitors measure heart rate of the fetus
    - Neonatal monitors monitor infant heart and breathing rates
    - Monitoring devices may or may not be linked to a network.
      - *Standalone devices include intravenous (IV) pumps, electrocardiogram (ECG) and cardiac monitors, defibrillators, temperature pulse respiration (TPR), and blood pressure monitors.*
      - *Networked equipment is most common in emergency rooms, operating rooms, and critical and intensive care units.*

- *Several computerized devices are used in optometry/ophthalmology for vision testing, early diagnosis of macular degeneration, glaucoma, cataracts, and diabetic retinopathy.*
  - A newly developed type of glasses (which include a computer) may improve vision in people with tunnel vision.
  - The FDA has approved the testing of retinal implants, but they have not yet been approved as of 2006.
  - Software developed in France can calculate the dimensions for glasses that will maximize the amount of light transmitted to any part of the retina that is still functioning.
  - A prototype of smart glasses, developed at the University of Arizona, will soon be able to automatically change focus.
  - In 2007, P2, an integrated system that will automate the examination and treatment of the eye, will be introduced.

- Adaptive or assistive technology makes it possible for people with disabilities to exercise control over their home and work environments.
  - *Devices are being developed that help people adjust balance.*
  - *Smart wheelchairs can climb stairs and find their way in a crowd.*
  - *Computer technology can help those with impaired vision, hearing, speech, and mobility.*
    - People with impaired vision can use speech-recognition systems as input and speech synthesizers for output.
    - Brain input systems are being developed for people who lack the muscle control to use alternative input devices.
    - A new portable speech-synthesizing device that uses a digital camera and a handheld organizer has been developed. The device takes a picture of the written text and scans and reads it.
    - Other alternate input devices include
      - *Head mouse*
      - *Puff straws*
      - *Eye movement*
- An augmentative communication device is any device that helps a person communicate.
- Environmental control systems help physically challenged people control their environments.
- Prosthetic devices replace natural body parts or organs with artificial devices.
  - *Myoelectric limbs—artificial limbs containing motors and responding to the electrical signals transmitted by the residual limb to electrodes mounted in the socket now contain microprocessors.*
- Other prosthetic devices include
  - *A knee socket has been developed that includes a computer chip that allows patients to walk naturally.*
  - *Energy-storing feet*
  - *C-leg or computerized leg. It includes a prosthetic knee and shin system controlled by a microprocessor.*
- A digital hearing aid (essentially a tiny computer), which can be programmed to meet individual needs and adjust to background noise, helps some hearing-impaired people. So does the cochlear implant.
  - *The newest hearing aids (2006) include "digital processing and directional microphones."*
- Computerized functional electrical stimulation (CFES or FES) directly applies low-level electrical stimulation to muscles that cannot receive these signals from the brain.
  - *It is now used to strengthen paralyzed muscles with exercise.*
  - *It can be used to simulate a full cardiovascular workout for people who are paralyzed.*
  - *FES even makes it possible to restore movement to some limbs paralyzed by stroke and spinal injury.*

  - *FES is used in many implanted medical devices, including pacemakers and implantable cardioverter defibrillators.*
  - *A breathing pacemaker controls breathing by sending electrical impulses to the phrenic nerve.*
  - *An implanted device reduces seizures in people with epilepsy by delivering electrical signals to the brain.*
  - *Osseointegration involves using titanium. The human tissue grows around the implant, so that the implant is more integrated with the human body.*
  - *Pacemakers for the brain are being tested for treatment of bipolar disorder and depression.*
  - *Electronic stimulation is also being used to prevent chronic pain.*
  - *A neuroprosthesis—uses "low levels of electricity in order to activate nerves and muscles in order to restore movement" to paralyzed limbs (when it is switched on).*
  - *Neuromove and Biomove 3000 are for stroke patients. Both devices help to stimulate the muscles to avoid atrophy and increase both range of motion and blood circulation. The devices help to communicate with paralyzed muscles through electrical stimulation of the brain.*
  - *"BrainGate Neural Interface System," for ALS (Lou Gehrig's disease), is in clinical trials. The system involves implanting a chip in the brain that will convert brain cell impulses to computer signals.*
  - *Neuromodulation is a new field that may help treat disorders of the central nervous system including chronic pain.*
  - *There are some risks posed by implanted devices:*
    - Blood clots
    - Infection
    - Rejection
- Computers are used in rehabilitation
  - *HELEN (HELp Neuropsychology) contains diagnostic analyses for stroke patients. HELEN also contains a rehabilitative module.*
  - *FES has been used for many years in several forms of rehabilitation.*
  - *Virtual reality is being used experimentally to help people with amputations control phantom pain.*
  - *Vision replacement therapy (VRT) retrains the brain of stroke victims who have lost their vision. Using dots on a computer screen, the aim is to stimulate peripheral vision.*

WEEK THIRTEEN: Read Chapter Twelve

Chapter 12 Security and Privacy in an Electronic Age

SUGGESTED LECTURE NOTES—Discuss the relationship between privacy and security. Does the loss of privacy make us more secure?

- Privacy has many aspects. Among them is the ability to control personal information and the right to keep it from misuse.
- Security measures attempt to protect computer systems, including information, from harm and abuse; the threats may stem from many sources including natural disaster, human error, or crime including the spreading of viruses.
- Protection may take the form of anything from professional and business codes of conduct, to laws, to restricting access to the computer.
- Computer technology has led to new forms of crime. Crimes involving computers can be crimes using computers and/or crimes against computer systems.
  - *Software piracy*
  - *Theft of services*
  - *Theft of information*

- *Fraud*
- *Spread of viruses*
- *Identity theft*
- *Other threats to computer systems*
    - Spyware is software that can be installed without the user's knowledge to track their actions on a computer.
    - Adware may display unwanted pop-up advertisements displayed on your monitor; it may be related to you the sites you search on the Web or even the content of your e-mail.
    - A fraudulent dialer can connect the user with numbers without the user's knowledge.
    - Keylogging can be used by anyone to track anyone else's keystrokes.
    - Malware includes different forms of malicious hardware, software, and firmware.

- Security measures
    - *Internal codes of conduct (self-regulation)*
    - *Audit trails*
    - *Encryption*
    - *Laws*
        - Fair Credit Reporting Act
        - Federal Privacy Act
        - Health Information Portability and Accountability Act
        - Online Privacy Protection Act
    - *Restricting access*
        - Personal identification numbers (PINs)
        - Biometrics—fingerprinting, retina or iris scan, biometric keyboards, lip prints, facial thermography, body odor sensors, voice recognition, DNA
    - *RFID tags*
    - *Backscatter X-ray machines to search air travelers (also known as the virtual strip search)*
    - *Firewalls*
- Privacy
    - *Computers and networks allow personal information to be centralized and gathered easily.*
    - *As an employee*
        - E-mail (at work) is not private.
        - Background checks
    - *Real ID Act of 2005 "directly imposes prescriptive federal driver's license standards" by the federal government on the states*
        - Requires every American to have an electronic identification card
        - State Departments of Motor Vehicles (DMV) must share all the information in their databases with all other state DMV's databases. This creates a huge database.
        - A new threat to personal privacy may come from implanted RFID tags (Verichips).
- Databases—an electronic database is an organized collection of data that is easy to access, manipulate, search, and sort.
    - *Government databases*
        - Federal government: FBI, Internal Revenue Service, Social Security Administration, Department of Defense, The National Directory of New Hires, Census Bureau, Department of Health and Human Services.
            - *Only the federal government has some restrictions on how it uses information although this may be weakened by the USA Patriot Act and the Homeland Security Act.*
                - These acts give law enforcement greater power to demand information and limit Congressional oversight.
                    - *Homeland Security is now sharing data with the Centers for Disease Control (CDC) in violation of its own agreement with the European Union (EU).*

- Some states and municipalities are putting all their records online.
- The Real ID Act of 2005 will (if successful) establish a distributed database containing every person in the United States.

■ *Private databases—private organizations keep computerized databases of employees and potential customers. Hospitals keep records of patients.*

- Medical Information Bureau is composed of 650 insurance companies. Its database contains health histories of 15 million people. It is exempt from HIPAA.
- Credit bureaus—credit history and credit report. Your credit report is used as a basis for granting or denying you a credit card, or mortgage, or car loan.
- Data warehouses exist for the sole purpose of collecting and selling personal information. They sell information to credit bureaus and to employers for background checks.

■ *Databases and the Internet—computerized files are kept on networks; many of these networks are linked to the Internet. The information includes highly personal data such as Social Security numbers, dates of birth, mother's maiden name, and unlisted phone numbers.*

- Privacy, security, and health care

  ■ *Health Insurance Portability and Accountability Act (HIPAA) of 1996*

  - By encouraging the use of the electronic medical record and facilitating the sharing of medical records among health care providers, it can assure continuity of care and thus save lives.
  - However, the more easily your records are available, the less secure they are. Medical information can be used against you.
  - All patients have the right to see their medical records and request changes; patients will have some knowledge of the use of their medical records and must be notified in writing of their providers' privacy policy.
  - The regulations cover "[a]ll medical records and other individually identifiable health information used or disclosed by a covered entity in any form, whether electronically, on paper, or orally. . . ."
  - In 2006, enforcement of HIPAA is lax.
  - Under both HIPAA and the Patriot Act, there are many circumstances that allow police access to your medical records without a warrant.

    ■ *HIPAA requires that you be informed in a general way how your records may be used without consent. However, you do not have to be notified of any specific sharing of your information, and further the USA Patriot Act does not allow you to be told.*

  - HIPAA requires that e-mail be secured by either by using encryption or controlling access. HIPAA specifically discusses privacy issues of telemedicine, including the presence of nonmedical personnel (e.g., camera people and other technicians) and the fact that the more stringent privacy protection (federal or state) has precedence.

  ■ *As research focuses on genetics and an individual's genetic probability of developing certain diseases, privacy issues arise.*

  ■ *The problems of protecting private medical information may multiply if all medical and health records are digitized and put online under a national system proposed by the Health Information Technology Decade. Security breaches are common.*

WEEK FOURTEEN: Final Exam

Suggested Web Projects

(Chapters 2–12)

Open your Web browser and use a search engine (such as Google™ or Yahoo!™) to conduct research using the guidelines listed below.

CHAPTER 2

1. Search for definitions of medical informatics (there are many).
2. Look for the latest information on HIPAA.

CHAPTER 3

1. Search for "medical office management" software to see how many programs exist to computerize administrative tasks in a health care environment.

CHAPTER 4

1. Find the latest legislation affecting telemedicine at http://tie.telemed.org/legal/articles.asp. Summarize the legislation.
2. Find the latest report to Congress on telemedicine at http://tie.telemed.org/legal/articles.asp. Summarize the report.

CHAPTER 5

1. Do a search to find the latest information on New Orleans after Katrina.
2. Do a search to find the latest information on one of the "new" diseases that threaten public health (SARS, bird flu, Ebola virus, or mad cow disease).

CHAPTER 6

1. Use PubMed (http://www.ncbi.nlm.nih.gov/PubMed/) to search MEDLINE for information on the use of PET scans in the management of invasive breast cancer. Write a paragraph on what you find.
2. Search MEDLINEplus for interventional radiology (stereotactic neurosurgery).

CHAPTER 7

1. Search to find pictures of AESOP and ZEUS on the Web. Print them.

CHAPTER 8

1. Go to http://www.healthieryou.com/complete.html and NCBI.gov to finc recent information on the Human Genome Project. Write a paragraph abou the most recent developments.

CHAPTER 9

1. Look at the *Journal of the California Dental Association, CDA Journal,* http:// www.cda.org/search/?q=teledentistry, to find information on teledentistry Write a paragraph on the most recent developments in teledentistry.
2. Find information on evidence-based decision making in dentistry in *Journal of Contemporary Dental Practice,* http://www.thejcdp.com/search/index.htm Describe evidence-based decision making.

CHAPTER 10

1. Find the latest information on the Visible Human at Fact Sheet, The Visible Human Project, http://www.nlm.nih.gov/pubs/factsheets/visible_human html Briefly describe what you found.
2. Go to http://www.ncbi.nlm.nih.gov/PubMed/. Do a search on the use of computers in psychiatry. Do the same search using MEDLINEplus (medlineplus gov). Briefly describe what you find using MEDLINE and what you find using MEDLINEplus.

CHAPTER 11

1. Search to find out the newest information on
    a. Pacemakers for the brain
    b. Augmentative communications devices
    c. The use of computers in rehabilitation

Write a paragraph on each. Cite you sources.

CHAPTER 12

1. Go to www.aclu.org for the latest information on HIPAA and the USA Patriot Act
2. Go to http://www.epic.org/privacy/medical for recent information on laws effecting the privacy of medical information.
3. Go to http://www.epic.org for new information regarding privacy on com puter networks.

CHAPTER 1

Introduction to Information Technology—Hardware, Software, and Telecommunications

CHAPTER OUTLINE

LEARNING OBJECTIVES

Upon completion of this chapter, you will be able to

- Define information technology, computer, and computer literacy and understand their significance in today's society.
- Describe the classification of computers into supercomputers, mainframes, microcomputers, minicomputers, personal digital assistants (PDAs), and embedded computers.
- Differentiate between hardware and software and discuss the different hardware components of a computer.
- Describe the difference between system and application software, know what an operating system is, and know what various application programs are used for what tasks.

- Discuss the significance of connectivity and networking.
- Discuss the recent expansion of the uses of wireless technologies including cell phones, Global Positioning System (GPS) technology, and PDAs with Internet access.
- List the components necessary for telecommunications to take place.
- State the uses of telecommunications and networking.

KEY TERMS

application software
arithmetic-logic unit
ARPAnet
automatically recalculated
binary digits (bits)
biometrics
Bluetooth
booted
cell phone
central processing unit (CPU)
communications software
compact disks (CDs)
computer
computer literacy
connectivity
control unit
database management software
digital video disks (DVDs)
digitize
direct-entry devices
electronic spreadsheets
embedded computer
expansion boards
expansion slots
extranet
firewall
graphical user interface
hard copy
hardware
Healthfinder
information technology (IT)
input devices
Internet
intranets
keyboards
local area networks (LANs)
magnetic disk
main circuit board (or motherboard)
memory
monitors
mouse
network
open architecture
operating system
optical disks
output devices
personal digital assistants (PDAs)
plotters
ports
printers
processing unit
processor
program
protocols
PubMed
radio frequency identification (RFID) tags
random-access memory (RAM)
read-only memory (ROM)
scanning devices
search engine
secondary storage devices
sensor
soft (digital) copy
software
solid-state memory devices sensor
system software
system unit
telecommunications networks
transmission-control protocol/Internet protocol (TCP/IP)
uniform resource locator (URL)
user interface
Web browser
Web sites
wide area networks (WANs)
Wi-Fi
word processing software
World Wide Web (WWW) or Web

DISCUSSION QUESTIONS

1. Why is it necessary for a future health care professional to be familiar with computer technology?
As a future health care professional, familiarity with information technology (IT) is crucial. As in other fields, the basic tasks of gathering, allocating, controlling, and retrieving information are the same. The push to use IT in all aspects of health care, from the electronic health record (EHR) to integrated hospital information technology (HIT) systems makes it crucial for health care professionals to be familiar with basic computer concepts. Computers are used in every specialty from psychiatry to surgery. Personal digital assistant

(PDAs) are used throughout the health care system. Physicians can write prescriptions on PDAs, consult online databases, and capture patient information and download it to a hospital computer. PDAs can hold reference manuals. They are also used in public health to gather information and help track diseases and epidemics. Administrative tasks in medical offices are being computerized. Supercomputers are used in research. The embedded computer is a single-purpose computer on a chip of silicon, which is embedded in anything from appliances to humans. An embedded computer may help run your car, microwave, pacemaker, or watch. A chip embedded in a human being can dispense medication among other things.

2. Discuss computer hardware. Define computer, hardware, input devices, processing hardware, secondary storage, and output hardware.
   The physical components of a computer are called hardware. Input devices function to take data that people understand and translate those data into a form that the computer can process—that is, ons and offs. Input devices can be divided into two categories—keyboards and direct-entry devices. Once data is inside the computer, it is processed. Processing hardware is the brain of the computer. Located on the main circuit board (or motherboard), the processor or system unit contains the central processing unit (CPU) and memory. The CPU has two parts: the arithmetic-logic unit, which performs arithmetic operations and logical operations of comparing; and the control unit, which directs the operation of the computer in accordance with the program's instructions.

   The CPU works closely with memory. The instructions of the program being executed must be in memory for processing to take place. Memory is also located on chips on the main circuit board. The part of memory where current work is temporarily stored during processing is called random-access memory (RAM). It is temporary and volatile. The other part of memory is called read-only memory (ROM) or firmware. Output devices translate the language of bits into a form humans can understand. Output devices are divided into two basic categories: those that produce hard copy, including printers and plotters, and those that produce soft (digital) copy, including monitors. Magnetic disk and magnetic tape and optical disks are used as secondary storage media. Magnetic media (disk, diskette, tape, and high-capacity Zip disks) store data and programs as magnetic spots or electromagnetic charges. High-capacity optical disks (compact disks [CDs] or digital video disks [DVDs]) store data as pits and lands burnt into a plastic disk. Solid-state memory devices include flash memory cards used in notebooks, memory sticks, and very compact key chain devices; these devices have no moving parts, are very small, and have a high capacity.
3. Discuss the use of RFID tags in human beings.
   Radio frequency identification (RFID) tags are now used to identify anything from the family dog to the sponge the surgeon left in your body, by sending out radio waves. One medical insurance company is conducting a two-year trial with chronically ill patients who will have an RFID the size of a grain of rice implanted. The RFID will contain their medical histories. It transmits 30 feet without the person's knowledge.
4. Distinguish between system software and application software.
   System software consists of programs that let the computer manage its resources. The most important piece of system software is the operating system. The operating system is a group of programs that manage and organize resources of the computer. It controls the hardware, manages basic input and output operations, keeps track of your files saved on disk and in memory, and directs communication between the CPU and other pieces of hardware. It coordinates how other programs work with the hardware and with each other. Operating systems also provide the user interface—that is, the way the user communicates with the computer.

   Application software allows you to apply computer technology to a task you need done. There are application packages for many needs. Word processing software allows you to enter text. Electronic spreadsheets allow you to process numerical data. Database management software permits you to manage large quantities of data in an organized fashion. Communications software includes Web browsers, such as Internet Explorer. These programs allow you to connect your computer to other computers in a network.

5. Define connectivity and telecommunications network. What are the advantages of connectivity?
   The fact that computers can be connected is referred to as connectivity. Connectivity greatly enhances the power of your computer, bringing immense stores of information to your fingertips and making it possible for you to interact with people around the world. Connectivity is the prerequisite for developing the field of telemedicine. Computers and other hardware devices that are connected form what is called a network. Networks come in all sizes, from small local area networks (LANs), which span one room, to wide area networks (WANs), which may span a state, nation, or even the globe, like the Internet and World Wide Web. Networks can be private or connected via telephone lines, making them telecommunications networks. Given the right mix of hardware and software, computers are connected globally. Connectivity gives you access to all the information on the computers and networks you are connected to.
6. Define broadband and low bandwidth. How are both used in health care settings?
   Communications can be high bandwidth (broadband or high speed) or low bandwidth (slow). Most hospitals use broadband connections such as dedicated T1–T3 lines. A slow dial-up connection, however, may be used for sending e-mail and attachments.
7. Define Bluetooth.
   Bluetooth technology is used to create small personal area networks. Bluetooth is a wireless technology that can connect digital devices from computers to medical devices to cell phones. For example, if someone is wearing a pacemaker and has a heart attack, his or her cell phone could automatically dial 911.
8. Discuss the expansion of the use of wireless technology.
   During the last few years, the use of wireless technologies has expanded. Cell phones, global positioning system (GPS) technology, and PDAs with Internet access have become commonplace. In places without electricity and without landlines, wireless networks using cell phones and PDAs are both bringing health information to people and gathering information to track the spread of disease. Wi-Fi is a wireless technology that allows you to connect, for example, a PDA (and other devices) to a network (including the Internet) if you are close enough to a Wi-Fi access point.

   The most common wireless device is the cell phone. The use of GPS technology, which can pinpoint your location to within several feet, is widely available.
9. Define and discuss the Internet.
   The Internet (short for interconnected network) is a global network of networks, connecting innumerable smaller networks, computers, and users. It is run by a committee of volunteers; no one owns it or controls it. The Internet originated in 1969 as ARPAnet, a project of the Advanced Research Projects Agency of the U.S. Department of Defense. The Department of Defense was attempting to create both a national network of scientists and a communications system that could withstand nuclear attack. The network was, therefore, to be decentralized, forming a communications web with no central authority. The protocol that eventually governed ARPAnet and continues to govern the Internet today is public domain software called transmission-control protocol/Internet protocol (TCP/IP).
10. Using information from the reading by Pogue, discuss speech-recognition technology.
    The newest speech-recognition software is easy to use and accurate. It does not need to be trained to your voice as older programs did. As you correct its few errors (by voice), the software gets even more accurate. The software uses context clues to try to distinguish between words that sound the same (e.g., bare and bear). Eventually, the program approaches 100 percent accuracy.

IN THE NEWS

Like Having a Secretary in Your PC

by David Pogue

TESTING, testing, one two three. Is this thing on?

Well, I'll be darned. It's really on and it's really working. I'm wearing a headset, talking, and my PC is writing down everything I say in Microsoft Word. I'm speaking at full speed, perfectly normally except that I'm pronouncing the punctuation (comma), like this (period).

Let's try something a little tougher. Pyridoxine hydrochloride. Antagonistic Lilliputians. Infinitesimal zithers.

Hm! Not bad.

Oh, hi, honey. Did you get to the bank before it closed? Oh, hold on, let me turn off the mike. Wouldn't want our conversation to wind up in my column!

O.K., back again. The software I'm using is Dragon NaturallySpeaking 9.0 (www.nuance.com), the latest version of the best-selling speech-recognition software for Windows. This software, which made its debut Tuesday, is remarkable for two reasons.

Reason 1: You don't have to train this software. That's when you have to read aloud a canned piece of prose that it displays on the screen—a standard ritual that has begun the speech-recognition adventure for thousands of people.

I can remember, in the early days, having to read 45 minutes' worth of these scripts for the software's benefit. But each successive version of NaturallySpeaking has required less training time; in Version 8, five minutes was all it took.

And now they've topped that: NatSpeak 9 requires no training at all.

I gave it a test. After a fresh installation of the software, I opened a random page in a book and read a 1,000-word passage—without doing any training.

The software got 11 words wrong, which means it got 98.9 percent of the passage correct. Some of those errors were forgivable, like when it heard "typology" instead of "topology."

But Nuance says that you'll get even better accuracy if you do read one of the training scripts, so I tried that, too. I trained the software by reading its "Alice in Wonderland" excerpt. This time, when I read the same 1,000 words from my book, only six errors popped up. That's 99.4 percent correct.

The best part is that these are the lowest accuracy rates you'll get, because the software gets smarter the more you use it—or, rather, the more you correct its errors.

You do this entirely by voice. You say, "correct 'typology,'" for example; beneath that word on the screen, a numbered menu of alternate transcriptions pops up. You see that alternate 1 is "topology," for example, so you say "choose 1." The software instantly corrects the word, learns from its mistake and deposits your blinking insertion point back at the point where you stopped dictating, ready for more.

Over time, therefore, the accuracy improves. When I tried the same 1,000-word excerpt after importing my time-polished voice files from Version 8, I got 99.6 percent accuracy. That's four words wrong out of a thousand—including, of course, "topology."

For this reason, it doesn't much matter whether or not you skip the initial training; the accuracy of the two approaches will eventually converge toward 100 percent.

(continued)

Like Having a Secretary in Your PC *(continued)*

NatSpeak 9 is remarkable for a second reason, too: it's a new version containing very little new.

Yes, they've eliminated the training requirement. And yes, the new NatSpeak is 20 percent more accurate than before if you do the initial training. Then again, what's a 20 percent improvement in a program that's already 99.4 percent accurate—99.5? That's maybe one less error every 1,000 words.

(Nuance has done some clever engineering to wring these additional drops of accuracy out of the program. For example, the program has always used context to determine a word's identity, taking into account the two or three words on either side of it to distinguish, say, "bear" from "bare." The company says that Version 9 scans an even greater swath of the surrounding words.)

But the rest of the changes are minor. The top-of-the-screen toolbar has shed the squared-off Windows 3.1 look in favor of a more rounded Windows Vista look. You can now use certain Bluetooth wireless headsets for dictation, although Nuance has found only two so far that put the microphone close enough to your mouth to get clear sound. A new toolbar indicator lets you know when you're in a "select and say" program like Word—that is, a program where you can highlight, manipulate and format any text you see on the screen using voice commands.

At least Nuance hasn't gone the way of so many software companies, piling on features and complexity in hopes of winning your upgrade dollars. For the second straight revision, the company has preferred to nip and tuck, making careful and selective improvements.

Now, Nuance isn't the only game in speech-recognition town. Microsoft says that Windows Vista, when it makes its debut next year, will come with built-in dictation software.

Nuance claims not to be worried, pointing out that Vista will understand only English. NatSpeak, on the other hand, is available in French, Italian, German, Spanish, Dutch, Japanese, British English and "World English," which can handle South African, Southeast Asian and Australian accents.

NatSpeak is also available in a range of versions for the American market, including medical and legal incarnations. Mere mortals will probably want to consider either the Standard version ($100) or the Preferred version ($200), each of which comes with a headset. Both offer the same accuracy.

The Preferred edition, however, offers several shiny bells and whistles. One of them is transcription from a digital pocket voice recorder. This approach doesn't provide the same accuracy as a headset, and it requires what today is considered an excruciating amount of training reading: at least 15 minutes. But it does free you from dictating at the computer.

The Preferred perk is voice macros, where you teach it to type one thing when you say another. For example, you can say "forget it" and have the software spit out, "Thank you so much for your inquiry. Unfortunately, after much consideration, we regret that we must decline your application at this time."

There's also a $900 version called Professional, which offers, among other advanced features, complete control over your PC by voice; it can even set in motion elaborate multi-step automated tasks.

NatSpeak also runs beautifully on the Macintosh. The setup is a bit involved: you need a recent Intel-based Mac, Apple's free Boot Camp utility, a copy of Windows XP, and a U.S.B. adapter on your headset. And you have to restart the Mac in Windows each time you want to use NatSpeak. But if you can look past all that fine print, NatSpeak on Macintosh is extremely fast and accurate.

If that sounds like too much effort, there is a Macintosh-only alternative: iListen ($130 with headset). Version 1.7, newly adapted for Intel Macs, offers better accuracy and a shorter training time than previous versions, though nothing like the sophistication or accuracy of NatSpeak. After 30 minutes of training, the program made 42 mistakes in my 1,000-word book excerpt, which the company says is better than average.

As for NaturallySpeaking: if you're already using Version 8, it's probably not worth upgrading to Version 9. Most people will find the changes to be too few and too subtle.

But if you're among the thousands who have abandoned dictation software in the past, it's a different story. Version 9 is a stronger argument than ever that for anyone who can't or doesn't like to type, dictation software is ready for prime time; the state of this art has attained nearly "Star Trek" polish.

Excuse me—what, honey?

O.K., I'm just finishing up here; I'll be right down. Let me just turn my mike off.

SOURCES

Ahuja, Anjana. "Doctor, I've Got this Little Lump on My Arm . . . Relax, that Tells Me Everything." timesonline.co.uk, July 24, 2006. http://www.timesonline.co.uk/article/0,,20909-2282789,00.html (accessed December 22, 2007).

Anderson, Sandra. *Computer Literacy for Health Care Professionals.* Albany, NY: Delmar, 1992.

Austen, Ian. "A Scanner Skips the ID Card and Zeroes In on the Eyes." nyt.com, May 15, 2003. http://www.nytimes.com/2003/05/15/technology/circuits/15howw.html (accessed December 22, 2007).

Baase, Sara. *A Gift of Fire: Social, Legal, and Ethical Issues in Computing.* Upper Saddle River, NJ: Prentice Hall, 1996.

Beekman, George. *Computer Confluence: Exploring Tomorrow's Technology.* 5th ed. Upper Saddle River, NJ: Prentice Hall, 2002.

Bureau of Labor Statistics. *Occupational Outlook Handbook (OOH), 2006–07 Edition.* http://www.bls.gov/oco/ (accessed December 22, 2007).

Divis, Dee Ann. "Bill Would Push Driver's License with Chip." *Washington Times,* May 1, 2002.

Eisenberg, Anne. "When the Athlete's Heart Falters, a Monitor Dials for Help." nyt.com, January 9, 2003. http://query.nytimes.com/gst/fullpage.html?res=9B03E0DE113EF93AA35752C0A9659C8B63 (accessed December 22, 2007).

Evans, Alan, Kendall Martin, and Mary Ann Poatsy. *Technology in Action.* Upper Saddle River, NJ: Prentice Hall, 2006.

Feder, Barnaby. "Face-Recognition Technology Improves." nyt.com, March 14, 2003. http://www.itl.nist.gov/iad/News/TimesFaceArticle031403.htm (accessed August 17, 2006).

Fein, Esther B. "For Many Physicians, E-Mail Is the High-Tech House Call." nyt.com, November 20, 1997, A1, B8.

Harmon, Amy. "U.S., in Shift, Drops Its Effort to Manage Internet Addresses." nyt.com, June 6, 1998, A1, D2.

Lohr, Steve. "Microsoft to Offer Software for Health Care Industry." nyt.com, July 27, 2006. http://www.nytimes.com/2006/07/27/technology/27soft.html (accessed December 22, 2007).

Loudon, Manette. "The FDA Exposed: An Interview With Dr. David Graham, the Vioxx Whistleblower." NewsTarget.com, August 30, 2005. http://www.newstarget.com/011401.html (accessed December 22, 2007).

Markoff, John. "High-Speed Wireless Internet Is Planned." nyt.com, December 6, 2002. http://query.nytimes.com/gst/fullpage.html?res=9807EEDB133BF935A35751C1A9649C8B63 (accessed December 22, 2007).

Oakman, Robert L. *The Computer Triangle.* 2nd ed. New York: Wiley, 1997.

Peifer, John. "Mobile Wireless Technologies for Rehabilitation and Independence," *Journal of Rehabilitation Research & Development* 42, no. 2 (March/April 2005): vii–x.

Peterson, Melody. "A Respiratory Illness: Cashing in; The Internet Is Awash in Ads for Products Promising Cures or Protection." nyt.com, April 14, 2003. http://query.nytimes.com/gst/fullpage.html?res=950DE5DA133BF937A25757C0A9659C8B63 (accessed December 22, 2007).

Pogue, David. "Like Having a Secretary in Your PC." nyt.com, July 20, 2006. http://www.nytimes.com/2006/07/20/technology/20pogue.html (accessed December 22, 2007).

Race, Tim. "What Do They Mean by Digital, Anyhow?" *New York Times*, March 19, 1998, G11.

Senn, James A. *Information Technology in Business: Principles, Practices, and Opportunities.* 2nd ed. Upper Saddle River, NJ: Prentice Hall, 1998.

Stewart, Angela. "Health Departments Will Link Up to Share Data." *Star-Ledger*, July 18, 1998.

Stewart, Angela. "A Shot-in-the-Arm Microchip Could Save Your Life." nj.com, August 7, 2006. http://www.nj.com/news/ledger/jersey/index.ssf?/news/ledger/stories/microchip_0807.html (accessed December 22, 2007).

"What Is Bluetooth?" Palowireless. http://www.palowireless.com/infotooth/whatis.asp (accessed August 17, 2006).

RELATED WEB SITES

The following Web sites provide research information on medical matters. We cannot, however, vouch for the accuracy of the information.

Healthfinder.gov (http://www.healthfinder.gov), for a government listing of nonprofit and government organizations that provide you with health-related information.

HealthTouch Online (http://www.healthtouch.com), for information on medications.

MedicineOnLine (http://www.meds.com), for information on pharmaceutical and medical device companies.

OncoLink (http://www.oncolink.upenn.edu), for information on cancer.

PubMed (http://www.ncbi.nlm.nih.gov/PubMed), for access to reliable medical information databases.

U.S. National Library of Medicine (http://www.nlm.nih.gov/). Services include Health Information, MEDLINE/PubMed, MEDLINEplus, NLM Gateway, Library Services, Catalog, Databases, Historical Materials, MeSH, Publications. Description: The world's largest medical library.

CHAPTER 2

Medical Informatics: The Health Information Technology Decade

CHAPTER OUTLINE

LEARNING OBJECTIVES

After reading this chapter, the student will be able to

- Define medical informatics.
- Define the decade of Health Information Technology (HIT).
- Define the electronic medical record (EMR) and electronic health record (EHR) and discuss the differences between the two.
- Define interoperability.
- Define regional health information organizations (RHIOs) and discuss their role in interoperability.
- Discuss the EMR developed by the U.S. Indian Health Service.
- Describe computer information systems used in health care settings.
  - Hospital information systems (HIS)
  - Financial information systems (FIS)
  - Clinical information systems (CIS)
  - Pharmacy information systems (PIS)
  - Nursing information systems (NIS)
  - Laboratory information systems (LIS)
  - Radiology information systems (RIS)
  - Picture archiving and communication systems (PACS)
- Discuss the issues raised by several studies of the computerization of health records.
- Discuss the introduction of and resistance to computer systems in health care environments.

KEY TERMS

biometrics
clinical information systems (CIS)
computer information systems
encryption
electronic health record (EHR)
electronic medical record (EMR)
electronic prescribing
e-prescribing
financial information systems (FIS)
hospital information systems (HIS)
iHealth Record
International Classification of Disease (ICD) codes
interoperability
laboratory information systems (LIS)
medical informatics
national health information network (NHIN)
nursing information systems (NIS)
picture archiving and communication systems (PACS)
pharmacy information systems (PIS)
radiology information systems (RIS)
regional health information organizations (RHIOs)

DISCUSSION QUESTIONS

1. Define medical informatics.
   Medical informatics seeks to improve the way medical information is managed and orga-nized by using computer technology. The common emphasis in all definitions is on the use of technology to organize information in health care. That information includes patient records, diagnostics, expert or decision-support systems, and therapies. The stress is not on the actual application of computers in health care, but the theoretical basis. Medical informatics is an interdisciplinary science. Medical informatics focuses on improving all aspects of health care. Some of the aspects it focuses on include improving the clarity of diagnostic images, improving image-guided and minimally invasive surgery, developing simulations that allow health care workers to improve treatments without practicing on human subjects, developing low-cost diagnostic tests, treating physical handicaps, providing consumers with information, coordinating international medical reporting, developing and improving information systems used in health care settings, and developing decision-support systems.
2. List four subspecialties of medical informatics.
   - *Bioinformatics uses computers to solve biological problems.*
   - *Dental informatics combines computer technology with dentistry to create a basis for research, education, and the solution of real-world problems in dentistry.*
   - *Nursing informatics uses computers to support nurses.*
   - *Public health informatics uses computer technology to support public health practice, research, and learning.*
3. What is the Health Information Technology decade?
   The U.S. government is attempting to make the electronic health record (EHR) and e-prescribing universal by 2014. It is calling 2004–2014 the Health Information Technology (HIT) decade. It has established an Office of the National Coordinator of Health Information Technology (ONCHIT) whose mission is to "provide leadership for the development and nationwide implementation of an interoperable health information technology infrastructure to improve the quality and efficiency of health care and the ability of consumers to manage their care and safety."
4. What are the tasks proposed for 2007 by the administration in Washington?
   The specific tasks proposed for 2007 include the following: promote interoperability; find ways to improve collecting public health surveillance data; find ways for patients to keep their own medical records; define elements of electronic health records; increase electronic prescribing (e-prescribing); attempt to solve privacy and security problems.

5. Briefly define HIPAA.
The Health Insurance Portability and Accountability Act (HIPAA) was passed by the U.S. Congress and signed into law in 1996. Its goal was to make health insurance portable from one job to another and to secure the privacy of medical records. Its privacy provisions went into effect gradually in 2003 and the enforcement rule went into effect in 2006. Its primary purpose is to protect the privacy of individually identifiable health information. Basically, patients must be aware of the privacy policy of the health care provider and be notified when their information is shared (with major exceptions detailed in the Patriot and Homeland Security acts). Patients are guaranteed the right to see and request changes and corrections in their medical records. The information may be used for research, but software exists to remove all personal identifiers. Staff must be trained to respect the privacy of patients; they should not discuss patients in a public area. Measures must be taken to ensure that only authorized people in the office see the record.
6. Define the electronic medical record (EMR).
Patient information is entered into a computer into an electronic medical record (EMR). This will form the patient's medical record. Encouraged by HIPAA and the federal government, the EMR is very gradually replacing the paper record. The federal government has set a goal of 2014 for universal adoption of electronic records and e-prescribing. However, only 14 percent of group practices are currently using e-prescribing. The EMR may be stored in a hospital's private network. But it may be kept on the Internet.
7. Define the electronic health record.
The information on a patient's EMR will form the basis of the electronic health record (EHR). Included in this information are patient demographics, progress notes, problems, medications, vital signs, past medical history, immunizations, laboratory data, and radiology reports. The EHR automates and streamlines the clinician's workflow. The EHR has the ability to generate a complete record of a clinical patient encounter, as well as supporting other care-related activities directly or indirectly.
8. Discuss the differences between the EMR and the EHR.
The EMR belongs to one health care institution—a doctor's office or hospital; it must be interoperable (be able to communicate and share information with the other computers and information systems) within that institution only. Ideally, the EHR is not the property of any one institution or practitioner. Eventually, it must be interoperable nationally and internationally. It is the property of the patient who can access the record and add information. It must include information from all the health care providers and institutions that give care to the patient. It thus eases communication among many practitioners and institutions. It is a source for research in clinical areas, health services, patient outcomes, and public health. It is also an educational source.
9. Define RHIO and NHIN.
Regional cooperation is being fostered through the establishment of regional health information organizations (RHIOs) in which data could be shared within a region. The national health information network (NHIN) is the infrastructure that would allow communication between RHIOs. Finally, a nationally interoperable system would be established, where any patient record would be available anywhere on the national network.
10. Define computer information systems in health care.
Computerized information systems are used in some hospitals and other health care facilities to help manage and organize relevant patient, financial, pharmacy, laboratory, and radiological information. To receive the full benefits of computer technology, each of these separate information systems needs to be linked under the hospital information system.
11. Does computerization improve health care?
A recent study published in Health Affairs did find the EHR and e-prescribing improved health care by decreasing errors caused by illegible handwriting and improving preventive medicine by generating reminders. Another study, completed in 2006, found that alerts led to a "22% relative decrease in prescribing of nonpreferred medications." However, the authors point to the fact that not enough providers are using the EHR to see the full benefit

of computerization, and an editorial in Health Affairs asserted that more testing is needed before "embarking on a widespread program."

With all the positive reports on the effects of IT in health care, there are many dissenting voices. In 2005, research published in JAMA and reported in the New York Times warned of some unintended and negative consequences; although decreasing some medication errors, computerized order entry systems can introduce other kinds of errors. Among the causes cited are "information on patients' medications was scattered in different places in the computer system. To find a single patient's medications, the researchers found, a doctor might have to browse through up to 20 screens of information." Computer crashes can also cause errors. Another study published in JAMA examined one hundred decision-support systems. It found "most of the glowing assessments of those clinical decision-support systems came from technologists who often had a hand in designing the systems."

12. How would you introduce a computer system into a hospital? Refer to the selected reading by Freudenheim and use the information in the text to design and implement a computerized system.
 The studies that do exist suggest that the most successful systems are created with the participation of those who will use them. Systems imposed from above are not as readily accepted. Any system that is perceived to add work or change workflow is resisted. One Canadian study of three hospitals (published in CMAJ) found that the response to physician resistance to the introduction of computer systems was a crucial variable. If the response addressed the real issues that physicians were concerned with, resistance dropped. However, a lack of response or antagonistic response increased resistance to the point of having to discontinue the use of the new information systems (in two of the three hospitals studied). A commentary on this article points out that in all three cases the introduction of the new computerized system "meant that clinicians would need to take more time to care for a patient during a particular encounter." The commentary further points out that those systems that do and are perceived to reduce workload (e.g., PACS) are readily accepted.
13. Describe the Indian Health Service Electronic Health Record.
 The Indian Health Service of the Department of Health and Human Services of the federal government has developed an electronic health record with a graphical user interface which interacts with the Resource and Patient Management System (RPMS) database of health care applications. Each patient's record is made up of several screens or pages of information including a notifications page that displays information for the provider such as new laboratory reports; a problem list page that lists a patient's problems with International Classification of Disease (ICD) codes and is easy to add to, delete from, and modify. The health care provider can use the problem list to generate a purpose of visit (POV), by picking a problem from a variety of POV lists and the patient's problem list. An adverse reactions page lists all the adverse reactions a patient has had to medications. A page of medications interacts with the pharmacy information system. The system also includes a page to list reminders and a page for crisis alerts. The laboratory orders page lists all a patient's laboratory orders and the status of each order. The laboratory results page lists laboratory results and also allows the user to graph results. The appointments and visits page lists all of a patient's appointments and visits to the health care provider. Each patient has a page of vital measurements listing such things as the patient's temperature and blood pressure. The system provides a reports section in which the provider can create any needed report. The notes page allows the provider to both review old notes and create new ones. Medications, laboratory tests, and images can be ordered from one screen (the enter orders screen). Superbills of any kind can also be generated. This EHR is customizable; it can be set to open to any screen of choice.

IN THE NEWS

Doctors Join to Promote Electronic Record Keeping

by Milt Freudenheim

He is a self-described techie, but that did not help Dr. Eugene P. Heslin harness the wonders of electronic medical records. The technology seemed too complicated and expensive for a small medical group like his six-doctor family practice in rural upstate New York.

"The large groups can afford the software," said Dr. Heslin, a family physician in Saugerties. "For the onesies and twosies, small groups like ours, there is no profit margin."

Now, though, in a collaboration with 500 like-minded doctors, as well as hospitals, insurers and employers in two Hudson Valley counties, Dr. Heslin and his partners are clearing barriers that have made modern information technology inaccessible to the hundreds of thousands of small doctors' offices around the nation.

The Hudson Valley effort is being watched as a potential model by federal and state government and industry officials, who say that up to 60 percent of Americans receive their primary care at small-scale physicians' offices. Unless those small medical practices can adopt the most modern and efficient information technology, millions of Americans may never know the benefits of the most advanced and safest care.

Electronic records, particularly ones that can be shared online by different doctors and hospitals, can improve the quality and safety of patient care by reducing errors that kill tens of thousands of patients each year. That is why, with considerable cheerleading but only modest financial help from Congress and the Bush administration, big organizations like Kaiser Permanente, the Mayo Clinic and many medical centers across the country are spending billions to convert to electronic records.

And last week, in the aftermath of Hurricane Katrina, government and private health care officials were rushing to build an electronic database of prescription drug records for hundreds of thousands of people who lost their records in the storm. Health and Human Services Secretary Mike Leavitt said the chaos wreaked by Katrina "powerfully demonstrated the need for electronic health records."

Also helping propel the electronic revolution are private insurers, Medicare and some employers, which are paying incentives to medical providers that can achieve better efficiency and patient care through improved information management.

But smaller medical practices have typically been ineligible for such bonuses because the doctors lack the computerized records that help them qualify. The hurdles typically include up-front costs as high as $30,000 for each doctor, and the need for support and training.

As a result, fewer than 5 percent of physicians nationally are using a computerized system as part of patient care, said Dr. Thomas J. Handler, a research director at the Gartner market research group. For most doctors who work in groups of five or fewer, the portion is probably 3 percent or less, he said.

To overcome such obstacles, Dr. Heslin and his regional colleagues, who call their cooperative effort the Taconic Health Information Network and Community, are pooling their resources and knowledge.

A Web-based, central database approach means that doctors need little more than a few standard PC's, a high-speed Internet connection and the willingness to pay a monthly subscription fee of $500 to $600, eliminating the initial outlay of tens of thousands of dollars.

(continued)

Doctors Join to Promote Electronic Record Keeping *(continued)*

The Taconic group, operating in Dutchess and Ulster Counties, received a seed grant of $100,000 from the eHealth Initiative, a national nonprofit organization that is intent on bringing the medical profession into the modern digital era. The organization's affiliated foundation cited the Taconic group in its annual progress report late last month. The Taconic network has also received $1.5 million from the federal Agency for Healthcare Research and Quality, to pay for an evaluation of the system by an independent researcher.

Dr. David J. Brailer, the Bush administration's health information technology coordinator, said that programs like the Taconic network "are obviously out in front of the rest.

"My mantra is to ask, How can we make electronic medical records cheaper and more valuable to the doctor?" Dr. Brailer said. "These are grass-roots efforts that are filling a hole that the federal and state governments cannot respond to."

Under the Taconic system, which is being introduced in phases, doctors can log onto a secure Web site to get prompt laboratory and X-ray and other imaging results for their patients from four local hospitals and two big lab companies. Later this year, the doctors will be able to send prescriptions electronically to participating local drugstores or online pharmacies. The biggest part of the push is to start next year: the introduction of electronic health records accessible online to the patient's doctor and, with the patient's permission, to any other medical provider on the network.

Mark Foster, a pediatrician in Wappingers Falls, in Dutchess County, has already seen the benefit of his electronic lab-results link. When a boy came in recently with a painful swollen knee, Dr. Foster suspected Lyme disease, which is endemic in the county.

"We tested him, and the next morning I looked online and called his mother and got him on antibiotics," Dr. Foster said. "Within 48 hours, his fever was gone. He's absolutely normal now."

Under the former system of communicating by fax with the laboratory and sorting through the piles of paper that arrive daily, he said, "the kid could have been suffering for two more days."

The Taconic network, along with two other medical alliances—one in Indianapolis, the other in Whatcom County, in Washington State—are "well ahead of the pack," said Janet Marchibroda, the chief executive of the eHealth Initiative.

The Taconic group is negotiating discounts with software and hardware vendors, according to Dr. A. John Blair III, a laparoscopic surgeon who is the organization's chief executive. Dr. Blair is paid by a separate regional doctors' organization that currently donates his time to the Taconic network. The day-to-day work of building and running the system, dealing with vendors and providing technical support to the doctors is performed by a rapidly growing paid staff, now numbering 15 and based in Wappingers Falls.

The key to the system is its secure shared database. "Instead of having dozens of systems in doctors' offices, it is hosted on one facility," Dr. Blair said.

All a participating doctor needs is at least one computer terminal with high-speed access to the Internet, he said, and a router computer for security protection and antivirus software. Some doctors have flat screens in each examining room. Some have wireless tablets or laptops they take from room to room. Most have separate terminals for themselves and their nurses and administrative staffs.

The Taconic network supplies the training for doctors and their staffs and maintains local support centers to troubleshoot the inevitable challenges posed by new software.

"That's what they need, that's why I like this model," said Dr. Handler at the Gartner research group. Without such technical support for small medical practices, "it's hard for them to get over the hurdles," he said.

Much of the Taconic doctors' costs for the system can be offset by payments from insurers and employers like I.B.M. and Verizon that offer bonuses to doctors in their networks who meet quality standards.

I.B.M., which has 60,000 employees in the mid-Hudson Valley region, is enthusiastic about the Taconic group's approach. "You can cut down dramatically on medical errors; you are less likely to be accidentally given a drug you are allergic to," said Dr. Paul Grundy, a medical director at I.B.M. The company will pay doctors who use the electronic prescription system an additional $6 a year for each employee they treat.

MVP Health Care is an insurer in upstate New York that has 100,000 members who receive care from the Taconic physicians. It will pay an additional $18 a year per member to doctors who meet patient satisfaction and service standards, prescribe generic drugs and log onto the Taconic system regularly, said Dr. Jerry Salkowe, an MVP vice president.

Verizon and other big local employers, like the Price Chopper and Hannaford Brothers supermarkets, are talking to MVP and the Taconic network about additional bonuses through the Bridges to Excellence program, a national employer-sponsored experiment in paying doctors for meeting quality goals.

Francois de Brantes, a General Electric health care official who is president of the e-Health Initiative Foundation, says early studies show that computerization can yield some savings for physicians, mainly in productivity, by freeing them to see more patients. "But the majority of savings go to someone else than the physician," he said. The issue is "how to redistribute a portion of those savings back to the physicians."

Bridges to Excellence pays doctors bonuses of $50 a year per insured patient—money that can add up to tens of thousands of dollars for some large groups. The Taconic group intends to make smaller doctors eligible for such bonuses.

"Many health plans are prepared to pay for performance," said Dr. Blair. "The rub is that you have to have the technology in place to garner those incentives. You need to automate the reporting capability."

SOURCES

Ackerman, Kate. "EHR Alerts Reduce Prescription Oversights." ihealthbeat.org, June 2, 2006. http://www.ihealthbeat.org/articles/2006/6/2/EHR-Alerts-Reduce-Prescription-Oversights.aspx?a=1 (accessed December 22, 2007).

Clinical Information System. 2006. http://www.biohealthmatics.com (accessed April 21, 2006).

Danielson, Erica. "A Qualitative Assessment of Changes in Nurses' Workflow in Response to the Implementation of an Electronic Charting Information System." A thesis presented to the Division of Medical Informatics and Outcomes Research and the Oregon Health & Science University School of Medicine in partial fulfillment of the requirements of the degree of Master of Science. June 2002.

Davis, Daniel C., and William G. Chismar. 'Tutorial Medical Informatics.' http://www.hicss.hawaii.edu/hicss_32/tutdesc.htm (accessed August 18, 2006).

"eHealth Spotlight: Medem Launches iHealth Record." 2005. http://www.msdc.org/newsEvents/newslineMAY2005/newsline_2005_may_IT_medem_launches_ihealth_record.shtml (accessed December 22, 2007).

"ELINCS: Developing a National Lab Data Standard for EHRs." February 2006. http://www.chcf.org/topics/chronicdisease/index.cfm?itemID=108868 (accessed December 22, 2007).

Financial Information System. 2006. http://www.biohealthmatics.com (accessed April 21, 2006).

Garets, Dave, and Mike Davis. "Electronic Medical Records vs. Electronic Health Records: Yes, There Is a Difference." A HIMSS Analytics White Paper, January 26, 2006. http://www.himssanalytics.org/docs/WP_EMR_EHR.pdf (accessed December 22, 2007).

Gennari, John. "Biomedical Informatics Is the Science Underlying the Acquisition, Maintenance, Retrieval, and Application of Biomedical Knowledge and Information to Improve Patient Care, Medical Education, and Health Sciences Research." July 22, 2002. http://faculty.washington.edu/gennari/MedicalInformaticsDef.html (accessed August 18, 2006).

Harman, Laurinda. "HIPAA: A Few Years Later." Online Journal of Issues in Nursing, July 21 2005. http://www.medscape.com/viewarticle/506841 (accessed December 22, 2007).

Healthcare Information Management Systems Society (HIMSS), "EHR: Electronic Health Record." http://himss.org/asp/topics_ehr.asp (accessed February 6, 2008).

"Health Industry Insights Survey Reveals Consumers Are Unaware of Government's Health Records Initiative." www.crm2day, February 15, 2006. http://www.crm2day.com/news/crm/117351.php (accessed December 22, 2007).

Hebda, Toni, Patricia Czar, and Cynthia Mascara. *Handbook of Informatics for Nurses and Healt Care Professionals*. 3rd ed. Upper Saddle River, NJ: Prentice Hall, 2005.

"HHS Awards Contracts to Advance Nationwide Interoperable Health Information Technology." October 6, 2005. http://www.hhs.gov/news/2005pres/20051006a.html (accessed June 29, 2006).

"HIS-EHR Walk Through." http://www.ihs.gov/CIO/EHR/pdf/ehr-walkthru-1.pdf (accessed June 26, 2006).

Hospital Information Systems. 2006. http://www.biohealthmatics.com (accessed April 21, 2006).

Hurdle, John F. "Can the Electronic Medical Record Improve Geriatric Care?" *Geriatric Times,* March/April 2004. http://www.cmellc.com/geriatrictimes/g040425.html (accessed December 22, 2007).

Kramer, Kevin M. "HIPAA 2006: HHS' HIPAA Enforcement Rule Is Now Effective." April 21 2006. http://www.gibbonslaw.com/news_publications/articles.php?action=display_publication&publication_id=2033 (accessed December 22, 2007).

Krisberg, Kim. "Improved Medical Technology Could Affect Health, Lower Cost." *The Nation's Health,* 1 November, 2005. http://www.medscape.com/viewarticle/515529 (accessed April 19, 2006).

Laboratory Information System. 2006. http://www.biohealthmatics.com (accessed April 21, 2006).

Lapointe, Liette, and Suzanne Rivard. "Getting Physicians to Accept New Information Technology: Insights from Case Studies." cmaj.com, May 23, 2006. http://www.cmaj.ca/cgi/content/full/174/11/1573 (accessed December 22, 2007).

Lohr, Steve. "Doctors' Journal Says Computing Is No Panacea." *New York Times,* March 9, 2005.

"Nursing Informatics." 2006. http://www.allnursingschools.com/faqs/informatics.php (accessed July 23, 2006).

Nursing Information System. 2006. http://www.biohealthmatics.com (accessed April 21, 2006).

Office of the National Coordinator for Health Information Technology (ONC). "Mission." August 19, 2005. http://www.hhs.gov/healthit/mission.html (accessed June 30, 2006).

PACS (Picture Archiving and Communication System). 2006. http://www.biohealthmatics.com (accessed April 21, 2006).

Pharmacy Information System. 2006. http://www.biohealthmatics.com (accessed April 21, 2006).

Public Health Informatics. April 22, 2002. http://www.nlm.nih.gov/archive//20061214/pubs/cbm/phi2001.html (accessed December 22, 2007).

Radiology Information System. 2006. http://www.biohealthmatics.com (accessed April 21, 2006).

Resource and Patient Management System. "Nurses Getting Started Guide User Manual Version 1.0." June 2005. http://www.rpms.ihs.gov/TechSupp.asp (accessed December 22, 2007).

Sarasohn-Kahn, Jane, and Matthew Holt. "The Prescription Infrastructure: Are We Ready for ePrescribing?" iHealth and Technology, California HealthCare Foundation, chcf.org,

January 2006. http://www.chcf.org/documents/ihealth/ThePrescriptionInfrastructureReadyForERx.pdf (accessed December 22, 2007).

Schiesel, Seth. "In the E. R., Learning to Love the PC." *New York Times,* October 21, 2004.

Sharpe, Virginia A. "Perspective: Privacy and Security for Electronic Health Records." medscape.com, December 19, 2005. http://www.medscape.com/viewarticle/517403 (accessed April 19, 2006).

U.S. Department of HHS Indian Health Service. "EHR Current Status." April 12, 2006. http://www.ihs.gov/CIO/EHR/index.cfm?module=currentstatus (accessed December 22, 2007).

U.S. Department of HHS Indian Health Service. "RPMS EHR Home Page." http://www.ihs.gov/CIO/EHR/index.cfm (accessed December 22, 2007).

U.S. Department of HHS Indian Health Service. "RPMS EHR Patient Information Management System." April 12, 2006. http://www.ihs.gov/CIO/EHR/index.cfm?module=pims (accessed December 22, 2007).

U.S. Department of HHS, Office of the National Coordinator for Health Information Technology (ONC). "Goals of Strategic Framework." 2004. http://www.hhs.gov/healthit/goals.html (accessed June 27, 2006).

U.S. Department of HHS, Office of the National Coordinator for Health Information Technology (ONC). "Value of HIT." HHS.gov, May 23, 2005. http://www.os.dhhs.gov/healthit/valueHIT.html (accessed January 5, 2008).

Waegmann, C. Peter. "Status Report 2002: Electronic Health Records." http://www.medrecinst.com/uploadedFiles/MRILibrary/StatusReport.pdf (accessed May 20, 2006).

Weier, Scott. "Subcommittee Recommends $98M for ONCHIT in 2007." iHealthbeat, June 15, 2006. http://www.ihealthbeat.org/articles/2006/6/15/Subcommittee-Recommends-98M-for-ONCHIT-in-2007.aspx (accessed December 22, 2007).

Zitner, David. "Physicians Will Happily Adopt Information Technology." cmaj.com, May 23, 2006. http://www.cmaj.ca/cgi/content/full/174/11/1583 (accessed December 22, 2007).

CHAPTER 3

An Introduction to the Administrative Applications of Computers: Accounting

CHAPTER OUTLINE

LEARNING OBJECTIVES

Upon completion of this chapter, the reader will be able to

- Define clinical, special-purpose, and administrative applications of computer technology in health care and its delivery.
- Define telemedicine.
- Discuss the computerization of accounting tasks in the medical office.
  - Define bucket billing.
  - Discuss coding systems, insurance, and the various accounting reports used in the medical office.

KEY TERMS

accounts receivable (A/R)
adjustments
administrative applications
assignment
authorization
balance billing
bucket billing
capitated plan
case
Centers for Medicare and Medicaid Services (CMS)
CHAMPUS
CHAMPVA
charges
claim
clearinghouse
clinical application
CMS-1500
co-payment
CPT
database
database management software (DBMS)
deductible
DRG (diagnosis-related group)
electronic health record (EHR)
electronic remittance advice (ERA)
EMC (electronic media claim)
encounter form
explanation of benefits (EOB)
fee-for-service plans
field

file
guarantor
HCFA-1500
Health Care Financing Administration (HCFA)
health maintenance organizations (HMOs)
ICD-9-CM (*International Classification of Disease*)
indemnity plan
key field
LOINC
managed care
MEDCIN
Medicaid
medical informatics
Medicare
MediSoft
patient aging report
patient day sheet
payment day sheet
payments
practice analysis report
preferred provider organization (PPO)
procedure day sheet
record
relational database
schedule of benefits
SNOMED
special-purpose application
superbill
table
telemedicine
transactions
TRICARE
worker's compensation

DISCUSSION QUESTIONS

1. Define bucket billing.
   Bucket billing is used by medical offices to accommodate two or three insurers, who must b billed in a timely fashion before the patient is billed.
2. Define relational database.
   A relational database is an organized collection of related data, in which informatio input in one part of the program can be linked to information in another part of th program.
3. Define database file, table, record, and field.
   A database file holds all related information on an entity, for example, a medical practic Within each file, there can be several tables. Each table holds related information; fo example, one table might hold information on a practice's doctors; another holds informa tion on its patients; another on its insurance carriers. A table is made up of relate records; each record holds all the information on one item in a table, for example, on patient. Each patient has a record in the practice's patient table. All the information o one patient makes up that patient's record. Each record is made up of related fields. On field holds one piece of information.
4. Define key field.
   The key field uniquely identifies a record. The information in that field cannot be dupli cated. Social Security number, chart number, and patient number are all common key fields
5. How are tables linked in a relational database?
   Tables are related through a common field. Two or more tables in a relational databas may be linked by patient number.
6. Define DRG.
   A standard grouping system is DRG (diagnosis-related group). Today, hospital reimburse ment by private and government insurers is determined by diagnosis. Each patient i given a DRG classification, and a formula based on this classification determines reim bursement. If hospital care and cost exceed the prospective cost determination, the hospita absorbs the financial loss.
7. Define CPT and ICD.
   *Services including tests, laboratory work, examinations, and treatments are coded using CPTs (*Current Procedural Terminology, *Fourth Edition). ICD-9-CM provides three- four-, or five-digit codes for thousands of diseases. The ICD is the* International Classifi cation of Diseases, *Ninth Edition.*
8. Define MEDCIN.
   MEDCIN provides 250,000 codes for such things as symptoms, history, physical exami nations, tests, diagnosis, and treatment. MEDCIN codes can be integrated with other cod ing systems.

9. Define LOINC.
   LOINC (logical observation identifiers, names, and codes) standardizes laboratory and clinical codes.
10. Define NDC.
    The national drug codes (NDC), which were developed by the Food and Drug Administration (FDA), identify drugs.
11. Define superbill.
    A superbill or encounter form is a list of diagnoses and procedures common to the practice.
12. Define charges, payments, and adjustments.
    Charges, payments, and adjustments are called transactions. A charge is simply the amount a patient is billed for the provider's service. A payment is made by a patient or an insurance carrier to the practice. An adjustment is a positive or negative change to a patient account.
13. Define guarantor.
    A guarantor is the person responsible for payment; it may be the patient or a third party.
14. Define Preferred Provider Organizations (PPOs).
    A patient with preferred provider organization (PPO) insurance can seek care within an approved network of health care providers who have agreed with the insurance company to lower their charges and accept assignment (the amount the insurance company pays). The patient may pay a co-payment, the part of the charge for which the patient is responsible. The patient may choose, however, to go out-of-network and pay the provider's customary charges. The insurance company may then reimburse the patient a small amount.
15. Define Medicaid.
    Medicaid is a "jointly funded, federal-state health insurance for certain low-income and needy people. It covers approximately 36 million individuals including children, the aged, blind, and/or disabled, and people who are eligible to receive federally assisted income maintenance payments." Medicaid resembles managed care, in that the patient is restricted to a network of providers, must get a pre-authorization for procedures, and needs referrals to any specialist.
16. Define Medicare.
    Medicare (a federal program administered by Centers for Medicare and Medicaid Services [CMS]) serves people aged 65 years and over and disabled people with chronic renal disorders. Medicare allows patients to choose their physicians; referrals are not needed. Some Medicare patients choose to belong to health maintenance organizations (HMOs). Many people supplement Medicare with private fee-for-service plans in which they are not restricted to a network of providers; they do not need referrals to specialists. The patient is required to pay a cost-sharing amount; the provider bills the insurance for the remainder.
17. Define claim.
    A claim is a request to an insurance company for payment for services.
18. Define patient day sheet.
    A patient day sheet lists the day's patients, chart numbers, and transactions. It is used for daily reconciliation.
19. Define payment day sheet.
    A payment day sheet is a grouped report organized by providers. Each patient is listed under his or her provider. It shows the amounts received from each patient to each provider.
20. Define procedure day sheet.
    A procedure day sheet is a grouped report organized by procedure. Patients who underwent a particular procedure such as a blood sugar laboratory test are listed under that procedure. This report is used to see what procedures a health care worker is performing. It also can be used to find the most profitable procedures.
21. Define practice analysis report.
    A practice analysis report is generated on a monthly basis and is a summary total of all procedures, charges, and transactions.

22. Define patient aging report.
    A patient aging report is used to show a patient's outstanding payments. Current an past due balances are listed on this report based on the number of days late. For exampl an account can be past due 30–60 days, 60–90 days, and over 90 days.
23. Define clearinghouse.
    A clearinghouse is a business that collects insurance claims from providers and sends the to the correct insurance carrier. Used by practices that submit electronic claims.
24. Define EOB.
    An insurance company's response to a paper claim includes an explanation of benefi (EOB) which explains why certain services were covered and others not.
25. Define ERA.
    An electronic remittance advice (ERA) accompanies the response to an electronic medi claim (EMC).

IN THE NEWS

Google and Microsoft Look to Change Health Care

by Steve Lohr

In politics, every serious candidate for the White House has a health care plan. So too in business, where the two leading candidates for Web supremacy, Google and Microsoft, are working up their plans to improve the nation's health care.

By combining better Internet search tools, the vast resources of the Web and online personal health records, both companies are betting they can enable people to make smarter choices about their health habits and medical care.

"What's behind this is the mass consumerization of health information," said Dr. David J. Brailer, the former health information technology coordinator in the Bush administration, who now heads a firm that invests in health ventures.

It is too soon to know whether either Google or Microsoft will make real headway. Health care, experts note, is a field where policy, regulation and entrenched interests tend to slow the pace of change, and technology companies have a history of losing patience.

And for most people, typing an ailment into a Web search engine is very different from entrusting a corporate titan with personal information about their health.

Google and Microsoft recognize the obstacles, and they concede that changing health care will take time. But the companies see the potential in attracting a large audience for health-related advertising and services. And both companies bring formidable advantages to the consumer market for such technology.

Microsoft's software animates more than 90 percent of all personal computers, while Google is the default starting point for most health searches. And people are increasingly turning to their computers and the Web for health information and advice. A Harris poll, published last month, found that 52 percent of adults sometimes or frequently go to the Web for health information, up from 29 percent in 2001.

If the efforts of the two big companies gain momentum over time, that promises to accelerate a shift in power to consumers in health care, just as Internet technology has done in other industries.

Today, about 20 percent of the nation's patient population have computerized records—rather than paper ones—and the Bush administration has pushed the health care industry to speed up the switch to electronic formats. But these records still tend to be controlled by doctors, hospitals or insurers. A patient moves to another state, for example, but the record usually stays.

The Google and Microsoft initiatives would give much more control to individuals, a trend many health experts see as inevitable. "Patients will ultimately be the stewards of their own information," said John D. Halamka, a doctor and the chief information officer of the Harvard Medical School.

Already the Web is allowing people to take a more activist approach to health. According to the Harris survey, 58 percent of people who look online for health information discussed what they found with their doctors in the last year.

It is common these days, Dr. Halamka said, for a patient to come in carrying a pile of Web page printouts. "The doctor is becoming a knowledge navigator," he said. "In the future, health care will be a much more collaborative process between patients and doctors."

Microsoft and Google are hoping this will lead people to seek more control over their own health records, using tools the companies will provide. Neither company will discuss their plans in detail. But Microsoft's consumer-oriented effort is scheduled to be announced this fall, while Google's has been delayed and will probably not be introduced until next year, according to people who have been briefed on the companies' plans.

A prototype of Google Health, which the company has shown to health professionals and advisers, makes the consumer focus clear. The welcome page reads, "At Google, we feel patients should be in charge of their health information, and they should be able to grant their health care providers, family members, or whomever they choose, access to this information. Google Health was developed to meet this need."

A presentation of screen images from the prototype—which two people who received it showed to a reporter—then has 17 other Web pages including a "health profile" for medications, conditions and allergies; a personalized "health guide" for suggested treatments, drug interactions and diet and exercise regimens; pages for receiving reminder messages to get prescription refills or visit a doctor; and directories of nearby doctors.

Google executives would not comment on the prototype, other than to say the company plans to experiment and see what people want. "We'll make mistakes and it will be a long-range march," said Adam Bosworth, a vice president of engineering and leader of the health team. "But it's also true that some of what we're doing is expensive, and for Google it's not."

At Microsoft, the long-term goal is similarly ambitious. "It will take grand scale to solve these problems like the data storage, software and networking needed to handle vast amounts of personal health and medical information," said Steve Shihadeh, general manager of Microsoft's health solutions group. "So there are not many companies that can do this."

This year, Microsoft bought a start-up, Medstory, whose search software is tailored for health information, and last year bought a company that makes software for retrieving and displaying patient information in hospitals. Microsoft software is already used in hospitals, clinical laboratories and doctors' offices, and, Mr. Shihadeh noted, the three most popular health record systems in doctors' offices are built with Microsoft software and programming tools.

Microsoft will not disclose its product plans, but according to people working with the company the consumer effort will include online offerings as well as software to find, retrieve and store personal health information on personal computers, cellphones and other kinds of digital devices—perhaps even a wristwatch with wireless Internet links some day.

Mr. Shihadeh declined to discuss specifics, but said, "We're building a broad consumer health platform, and we view this challenge as far bigger than a personal health record, which is just scratching the surface."

(continued)

Google and Microsoft Look to Change Health Care *(continued)*

Yet personal health records promise to be a thorny challenge for practical and privacy reasons. To be most useful, a consumer-controlled record would include medical and treatment records from doctors, hospitals, insurers and laboratories. Under federal law, people can request and receive their personal health data within 90 days. But the process is complicated, and the replies typically come on paper, as photocopies or faxes.

The efficient way would be for that data to be sent over the Internet into a person's digital health record. But that would require partnerships and trust between health care providers and insurers and the digital record-keepers.

Privacy concerns are another big obstacle, as both companies acknowledge. Most likely, they say, trust will build slowly, and the online records will include as much or as little personal information as users are comfortable divulging.

A person might start, for example, by typing in age, gender and a condition, like diabetes, as a way to find more personalized health information. If a person creates a personal health record and later has second thoughts, a simple mouse click should erase it. The promise, the companies say, will be complete consumer control.

There are plenty of competitors these days in online health records and information from start-ups like Revolution Health, headed by AOL's founder, Stephen M. Case, and thriving profit-makers led by WebMD.

Potential rivals are not underestimating the two technology giants. But the smaller companies have the advantage of being focused entirely on health, and some have been around for years. WebMD, for example, traces its lineage to Healtheon, a fallen star of the dot-com era, founded by the Netscape billionaire Jim Clark.

Google and Microsoft are great companies, said Wayne T. Gattinella, WebMD's chief executive, but "that doesn't mean they will be expert in a specific area like health."

Specialized health search engines—notably Healthline—are gaining ground and adding partners. AOL recently began using Healthline for searches on its health pages, even though Google is a close partner.

Still, 58 percent of people seeking health information online begin with a general search engine, according to a recent Jupiter Research report, and Google dominates the field. "Google is the entry point for most health search, and that is a huge advantage," said Monique Levy, a Jupiter analyst.

Indeed, it is the market reach and deep pockets that Google and Microsoft can bring to consumer health information that intrigues medical experts, and has lured recruits. Dr. Roni Zeiger, a graduate of Stanford's School of Medicine, a medical informatics researcher and a former primary care doctor, joined Google last year. The 36-year-old, who still sees patients some evenings and weekends at a nearby clinic, said, "At Google, I can use my expertise and knowledge to potentially help millions of people each day."

Planned Medicaid Cuts Cause Rift with States

by Robert Pear

WASHINGTON, Aug. 12—The White House is clashing with governors of both parties over a plan to cut Medicaid payments to hospitals and nursing homes that care for millions of low-income people.

The White House says the changes are needed to ensure the "fiscal integrity" of Medicaid and to curb "excessive payments" to health care providers.

But the plan faces growing opposition. The National Governors Association said it "would impose a huge financial burden on states," already struggling with explosive growth in health costs.

More than 330 members of Congress, including 103 Republicans, have objected to the plan. A letter signed by 82 House Republicans says it "would seriously disrupt financing of Medicaid programs around the country." A bipartisan group of 50 senators recently urged President Bush to scrap the proposed rules, which were set forth in his 2007 budget and could be issued before the end of this year.

Medicaid finances health care for more than 50 million low-income people, with money provided by the federal government and the states.

Under the White House plan, the federal government would reduce Medicaid payments to many public hospitals and nursing homes by redefining allowable costs. It would also limit the states' ability to finance their share of Medicaid by imposing taxes on health care providers. About two-thirds of the states have such taxes.

The federal government pays at least 50 percent of Medicaid costs in each state and more than 70 percent in the poorest states. Bush administration officials say states have used creative bookkeeping and accounting gimmicks to obtain large amounts of federal Medicaid money without paying their share. Moreover, they contend, some states have improperly recycled federal money to claim additional federal Medicaid money.

"States have managed to draw down more federal Medicaid dollars with fewer state dollars," said Dennis G. Smith, director of the federal Center for Medicaid and State Operations.

State and local officials, members of Congress, hospitals, nursing homes and advocates for poor people make several arguments. First, they say, Mr. Bush is doing by regulation what he unsuccessfully asked Congress to do by legislation in the last two years. Second, they say, prior administrations and the Bush administration itself approved many of the state taxes that would be deemed improper under the new rules.

Gov. Arnold Schwarzenegger of California, a Republican, said, "The administration is attempting to reverse decades of federal Medicaid policy through the regulatory process," less than a year after "Congress rejected these misguided cuts."

In Missouri, Gov. Matt Blunt, a Republican, said the change "could mean a loss of more than $84.9 million" for his state. That, he said, would "jeopardize the continuity of care for Medicaid recipients" and set back efforts to improve care in nursing homes.

Gov. M. Jodi Rell of Connecticut, a Republican, protested the White House plan in a letter to Mr. Bush. She said the effects would be "disastrous" in states like Connecticut, which relies on fees collected from nursing homes to help pay its share of Medicaid costs.

(continued)

Planned Medicaid Cuts Cause Rift with States *(continued)*

Democratic governors, including Janet Napolitano of Arizona, Edward G. Rendell of Pennsylvania and Kathleen Sebelius of Kansas, also denounced the White House plan. Ms. Sebelius said the cuts would make it much more difficult for health care providers like the University of Kansas Hospital to serve Medicaid recipients and people without insurance.

The cuts contemplated by the White House would not reduce the cost of care. But state officials said the changes would put pressure on states to reduce Medicaid benefits, restrict eligibility or lower payments to health care providers.

Medicaid is one of the largest, fastest-growing items in state budgets. To pay their share of the costs, states often rely on general revenue from sales and income taxes. But many also levy special taxes on hospitals, nursing homes and other health care providers. In many cases, providers willingly pay such taxes because the revenue shores up Medicaid and can be used by states to obtain federal matching payments.

Under current rules, a state can impose a tax equal to 6 percent of the revenue of a hospital or nursing home. The administration wants to lower the allowable tax rate to 3 percent. The federal government would reduce its Medicaid payment to any state that levied taxes above that.

Michael O. Leavitt, the secretary of health and human services, said this change would "remove incentives for states to shift the responsibility to fund their share of the Medicaid program to health care providers." Hospitals and nursing homes, he said, should welcome the change because it would reduce their taxes.

But Thomas P. Nickels, senior vice president of the American Hospital Association, and Bruce A. Yarwood, president of the American Health Care Association, a trade group for nursing homes, said the plan was simply a way to cut Medicaid.

"If provider taxes are cut, the Medicaid program will be reduced, and that will harm beneficiaries," Mr. Nickels said. "We do not see a political will, at the federal or state level, to supplant provider taxes with other types of revenue."

In February, Mr. Bush signed a bill that gave states power to revamp Medicaid by altering eligibility and benefits. That measure is expected to cut the growth of federal Medicaid spending by $4.9 billion over five years. The White House estimates that the new rules will save the federal government even more: $12.2 billion over five years.

The administration said it needed to impose stricter limits on Medicaid payments to public hospitals and nursing homes because such payments far exceeded "the actual cost of services" in many states.

The changes may seem technical. But Marvin R. O'Quinn, president of Jackson Health System in Miami, said they would directly and adversely affect patients.

Dr. Bruce A. Chernof, director of the Los Angeles County Department of Health Services, said the cuts would "reduce access to services in a county where 33 percent of residents are uninsured." The county's five public hospitals operate trauma centers and burn treatment units for all patients, not just Medicaid recipients, he said.

The effects are magnified by the way Medicaid is financed. For each dollar that a state loses in provider tax revenue, the federal government will reduce its contributions—by $1 in California and Connecticut, and by $3 in a poor state like Mississippi.

The White House said Mr. Bush would also adopt stricter policies on Medicaid payments for rehabilitation and school-based health services.

SOURCES

Anderson, Sandra. *Computer Literacy for Health Care Professionals.* New York: Delmar Publishers Inc., 1992.

Baase, Sara. *A Gift of Fire: Social, Legal, and Ethical Issues in Computing.* Upper Saddle River, NJ: Prentice Hall, 1996.

Ball, Marion J., and Kathryn J. Hannah. *Using Computers in Nursing.* Norwalk, CT: Appelton-Century-Crofts, 1984.

Burke, Lillian, and Barbara Weill. *MediSoft Made Easy: A Step-by-Step Approach.* Upper Saddle River, NJ: Prentice Hall, 2004.

CMS. September 2002. http://cms.hhs.gov/medicaid/default.asp (accessed April 4, 2003).

Computers in the Medical Office: Using Medisoft for Windows. New York: McGraw-Hill, 1995.

Davis, Daniel C., and William G. Chismar. "Tutorial Medical Informatics." http://www.hicss.hawaii.edu/hicss_32/tutdesc.htm (accessed August 18, 2006).

Felton, Bruce. "EARNING IT; Technologies that Enable the Disabled." nyt.com, September 14, 1997. http://query.nytimes.com/gst/fullpage.html?res=9A0CE3D81139F937A2575AC0A961958260 (accessed January 5, 2008).

Holland, Gina. "Court Backs Regulation of HMOs." *The Star-Ledger,* April 3, 2003, 43.

Ito, Lloyd. "Medical Insurance." August 3, 1999. http://phys-advisor.com/Insure.htm (accessed November 18, 2006).

MedcomSoft Record 2006 Standards. 2006. http://www.medcomsoft.com (accessed July 5, 2006).

MediSoft Training Manual. Mesa, AR: NDC Health.

Newby, Cynthia. *Computers in the Medical Office Using Medisoft.* New York: Glencoe, McGraw-Hill, 1995.

CHAPTER 4

Telemedicine

CHAPTER OUTLINE

LEARNING OBJECTIVES

Upon completion of this chapter, the student will be able to

- Define telemedicine.
- Discuss store-and-forward technology and interactive videoconferencing.
- Define the various subspecialties of teleradiology, telepathology, teledermatology, telecardiology, teleneurology, telestroke, telepsychiatry, and telehome care.
- Discuss the use of telemedicine in prisons.
- Discuss the changing role of the telenurse.
- Discuss the legal, licensing, insurance, and privacy issues involved in telemedicine.

KEY WORDS

arrhythmia monitoring
Baby CareLink
Bluetooth
interactive videoconferencing
remote monitoring devices
SATELLIFE
store-and-forward technology
teleconferencing
teledermatology
telehealth
telehome care
telemedicine

teleneurology
telenurse
telepathology
telepsychiatry
teleradiology
telespirometry
telestroke

DISCUSSION QUESTIONS

1. Define telemedicine and discuss some of its positive effects.
   Telemedicine uses computers and telecommunications equipment to deliver medical care a a distance. Several technologies are used: from plain old telephone service to Integrate Services Digital Network (ISDN) lines, to digital subscriber line (DSL), to dedicated T lines, to satellite, to broadband cable, to the Internet. The medical information transmi ted can be in any form including voice, data, still images, and motion video. Telemedicin delivers the whole range of medical care from diagnosis to patient monitoring to treatmen It gives patients remote access to experts who in turn have access to patient information.
2. List ten subspecialties of telemedicine.
   Telemedicine encompasses many subspecialties of medicine including radiology, patholog oncology, ophthalmology, cardiology, stroke, dermatology, psychiatry, telehome care, an teletriage.
3. Define store-and-forward technology. Where is it appropriate to use?
   Store-and-forward technology involves sharing information in a time- and place-independen way over the Internet. The information is stored, digitized, and then sent. If a medical spe cialty is image based, store-and-forward technology may be appropriate. The information ma include digital images and clinical information.
4. Define teleconferencing. Give one example of its use.
   Interactive videoconferencing or teleconferencing allows doctors to consult with each othe and with patients in real time, at a distance. A patient may be in his or her primary physi cian's office with a camera and a telecommunications link to a specialist's office. All ca see and hear each other in real time. It might require only a videophone and a connectio to the Internet. However, the most sophisticated systems involve microphones, scanner cameras, medical instruments, and dedicated telephone lines. One form of video telecon ferencing is the remote house call, involving only one medical practitioner and a patient i another location.
5. Describe telepathology.
   Telepathology is the transmission of microscopic images over telecommunications lines. Th pathologist sees images on a monitor instead of under a microscope. Telepathology require a microscope, camera, and monitor, as well as a connection to a telemedicine system Telepathology can use real-time videoconferencing for consultation during an operation But in daily practice, store-and-forward technology is common. Pathology is based on th study of images; diagnosis is based on the study of images on slides from a microscope look ing for diagnostic features. If a second opinion is needed from a distant expert, telepathol ogy may be used. The images are taken from the slides by camera. Still images usually are a a higher resolution than those sent in real time. The images and other clinical data are use for a complete case description and then sent, in many cases, over the Internet.
6. Describe teledermatology. How would you judge its effectiveness? Write you answer referring to studies mentioned in the text.
   Teledermatology uses both videoconferencing and store-and-forward technology. Bot methods appear effective. The advantage of the videoconference is that it closely resemble the traditional visit to the doctor, but is more expensive. Studies have shown that diagnosi made via videoconferencing agree with face-to-face dermatology visits 59–88 percent A small study comparing store-and-forward teledermatology with face-to-face dermatolog found 61–91 percent agreement. Certain skin conditions were found to be more difficult t diagnose via teledermatology. Diagnostic confidence was lower and the rate of biopsie higher. The advantage of store-and-forward technology is the high quality of the images an the low cost. To date, there have been no definitive outcomes studies. Some small studie

have found that although there are limitations with store-and-forward technology (image quality and lack of patient interaction), teledermatology reduced unnecessary visits to dermatologists by more than 50 percent. A small pilot study (2003) found that teledermatology was useful at assessing skin conditions.

7. Briefly discuss the history of listening to the heart at a distance.
   The earliest attempt at listening to the heart at a (small) distance—through a rolled paper occurred in 1816. Since the invention of the telephone, doctors have attempted to send heart and lung sounds over long distances. But the quality of the sound was not good enough. During the 1960s, it became possible to transmit heart sounds more accurately, and faxes could be used to send electrocardiograms (ECGs). By the 1990s, echocardiograms could be telecommunicated. Second opinions via telecardiology are one of the most common requests in telemedicine.
8. Discuss why the time-saving aspects of telemedicine are crucial in dealing with stroke victims.
   Saving time is essential in treating strokes. If the stroke is caused by a clot [determined by a computed tomography (CT) scan], the victim may be helped by the administration of a clot-busting drug called tPA (tissue plasminogen activator) if it is given within a few hours. However, if the stroke is caused by excessive bleeding, tPA can kill the patient. Immediate and accurate diagnosis is crucial. However, many small hospitals do not have experts. One study showed that 70 percent of stroke patients did not receive tPA either because they arrived at the hospital too late or because the hospitals could not provide the correct therapy. Telestroke programs connect small hospitals with urban medical centers; stroke experts at the large hospitals can diagnose via telemedicine.
9. Discuss advantages and disadvantages of telepsychiatry.
   Telepsychiatry involves the delivery of therapy using teleconferencing. It usually makes use of some sort of hardware that can transmit and receive both voice and picture. Experts warn that therapy at a distance is not a substitute for the human contact involved in face-to-face counseling. However, sometimes it is the only choice, for example, in rural areas where there are very few therapists and patients would have to travel long distances to see them. Studies of psychiatric consults between primary care providers and psychiatrists in New Hampshire came to the same conclusion—that videoconferencing and face-to-face consults were similar. A study of telemedicine for diagnosing patients with obsessive-compulsive disorder found it as successful as face-to-face therapy. A small study compared videoconferencing and face-to-face cognitive behavioral therapy in treating childhood depression and found them equally effective. Some studies have found patients more comfortable talking to a distant psychiatrist. Others found that using a telenurse and a traditional psychiatrist improved depression more than only a psychiatrist, although there was no improvement in the numbers of clients taking their medication properly. Telepsychiatry was also found to be successful in delivering therapy to the family of a girl suffering from anorexia. However, there are some negative aspects to telepsychiatry: the technology limits the therapist's perception of nonverbal clues and the equipment can be distracting; the therapist has to be sensitive to distortions in eye contact and the fact that a patient can appear to have stopped speaking when in fact he or she has not.
10. Define smart stretcher.
    A smart stretcher includes a respirator, heart machine, intravenous drugs, and monitors that transmit all the data they gather immediately to the hospital. Using the smart stretcher means that no time needs to be wasted transporting the patient. Monitoring and treatment can begin immediately.
11. Briefly describe telehome care.
    Telehome care involves the monitoring of vital signs from a distance via telecommunications equipment and the replacement of home nursing visits with videoconferences. It is usually used to manage chronic conditions such as congestive heart failure and diabetes, but it should be noted that it is beginning to be used for remote monitoring by intensive care unit (ICU) doctors at home. Telehome care involves a link between the patient's home and a hospital or central office that collects the data.

12. Discuss teleneurology.
Neurology was slower to use telemedicine when compared to other specialties. Now, however, e-mail and videoconferencing are replacing the letter and telephone call. One of the first subspecialties to use telemedicine in neurology is in stroke diagnosis.
Telestroke (in diagnosis) has already been discussed. Telemedicine was also found to be effective in a stroke rehabilitation program. It improved both balance and functioning. Using an e-mail triage system for new referrals halved the number of people attending clinics. Teleneurology helps to cope with some common problems of people with epilepsy. Many live in areas with no or little access to neurologists. Restrictions on driving for people with epilepsy can limit care. So teleneurology, which brings the care to the patient, is crucial.
13. Discuss the use of telemedicine in prison settings.
Telemedicine is now widely used in state prisons in Arizona, Iowa, Maryland, Texas, Massachusetts, Virginia, Pennsylvania, and New York and in the federal prison system. The stated reasons for introducing telemedicine are cost-containment, security, and enhanced medical care for inmates. Telemedicine is used to provide specialist care, not primary care, which is delivered onsite. A review of the literature on Texas indicates that both patients and providers are satisfied with the care and that the vast majority of systems experienced reductions in travel and security costs. One preliminary study found that 95 percent of the telemedical consults have saved a trip to a clinic. A teleconsult clinic for human immunodeficiency virus (HIV)-positive inmates was established in Texas in 1999; it was found to cut costs, but has no effect on outcomes. There seems to be a consensus that telemedicine in prisons saves money and increases security by decreasing off-site visits. Survey data also indicate that both prisoners and prison administrators are satisfied with telemedicine. It may be that more prisoners seek treatment because they do not have to travel; in states like Texas, a visit to a clinic can mean four days of travel shackled in a truck.
14. Define and discuss the Baby CareLink program.
Baby CareLink is a highly successful program. Its purpose was to compare high-risk, premature infants receiving traditional care with an experimental group, which in addition to traditional care received a telemedicine link to the hospital while the babies were hospitalized and for six months after. The families could see and hear their babies in the nursery, although they were at home. They could log on to a secure Web page with up-to-date information about their babies. Once home, the families had access to the nursery and experts and could ask any question they pleased. The doctor or nurse could see the baby and reassure the parent. One purpose of Baby CareLink was to see whether parents felt more comfortable and knowledgeable about their babies' care, so that the hospital stay would be shorter. The experimental group did have shorter hospital stays. In a later case study of Baby CareLink in Chicago, it was found that the average length of stay for the experimental group was 2.73 days shorter, only 18 percent were readmitted (less than the expected 40 percent), medical staff were happy with the program, and parents were more comfortable with their infants. The Baby CareLink pilot program was so successful that Baby CareLink is now used in many hospitals throughout the United States.
15. How is telenursing contributing to a change in the role of the nurse?
Telenursing puts nurses in a more autonomous position. Telenursing involves teletriage and the telecommunication of health-related data, the remote house call, and the monitoring of chronic disease. Teletriage starts with a call from a worried patient or parent with a question to the nurse. Software helps the nurse ask a series of questions to aid in diagnosis and make a recommendation to the patient. Telenursing increases access to medical advice to patients by making it available in their homes. Nurses may be in more autonomous positions in telemedicine programs. In England, there is a twenty-four-hour telephone line staffed by nurses. The nurses use diagnostic software and are linked to databases, hospitals, primary care providers, and ambulances. The nurses staffing these lines need to know how to use the software and how to get the correct information; the nurse also needs knowledge of local health care services. In the United States, the Veterans Affairs telephone care program is staffed by registered nurses (RNs) only.

16. What technical, legal, and insurance issues need to be addressed for telemedicine to fulfill its promise?
    Certain aspects of telemedicine require high-speed, broadband media, because the files transmitted may be so huge (greater than 1 gigabyte). These lines are not in place in many areas. Legal issues include state licensing of medical personnel. Acquiring a license is a costly and time-consuming process. Practicing without a license is a crime. Licensing laws are different in each state. Some states allow consultations across state lines. Only twelve states have agreements that make it easier for nurses to practice across state lines. Currently, there is minimal insurance coverage for telemedicine, although this is changing slowly.
17. Discuss telemedicine and privacy.
    Telemedicine raises many privacy issues; medical information routinely crosses state lines, some of it via e-mail, which is not private. There are typically nonmedical personnel involved including technicians and camera operators. According to the Final Health Insurance Portability and Accountability Act (HIPAA) Privacy Rules, several privacy issues are relevant: Under HIPAA, "Federal laws preempt state laws that are in conflict with regulatory requirements or those that provide less stringent privacy protections. But those states that have more stringent privacy laws would preempt Federal law." This leads to a "patchwork" of different standards. In a telemedical consultation, many people (both medical and nonmedical) may be present—but not apparent to the patient. Telemedicine requires greater concern with patient privacy and more complicated consent from patients.

IN THE NEWS

TV Screen, Not Couch, Is Required for This Session

by Kirk Johnson

FLAGSTAFF, Ariz.—Dr. Sara Gibson looked into the television screen and got right down to it.

"What's keeping you alive at this point?" she asked her patient, a middle-aged woman who asked to be identified only as D. D grimaced, looked down, then to the side and finally into Dr. Gibson's face, which filled the screen before her in a tiny clinic three hours east of here in the Arizona desert.

"Nothing," said D, who Dr. Gibson says suffers from bipolar disorder and post-traumatic stress from the sexual abuse she suffered as a child.

It is Wednesday in the hinterlands of rural Arizona, and the psychiatrist is in. Sort of.

Actually, Dr. Gibson was here in Flagstaff in a closet-size office of a nonprofit medical group, with a pale blue sheet behind her as a backdrop and a cup of tea at her side. She is one of a growing number of psychiatrists practicing through the airwaves and wires of telemedicine, as remote doctoring is known.

Psychiatry, especially in rural swaths of the nation that also often have deep social problems like poverty and drug abuse, is emerging as one of the most promising expressions of telemedicine. At least 18 states, up from only a handful a few years ago, now pay for some telemedicine care under their Medicaid programs, and at least eight specifically include psychiatry, according to the National Association of State Medicaid Directors. Six states, including California, require private insurers to reimburse patients for telepsychiatry, according to the National Conference of State Legislatures.

Growing prison populations have a lot to do with the trend. Since reimbursement for prison care is easy and safety issues for doctors are significant, many

(continued)

TV Screen, Not Couch, Is Required for This Session *(continued)*

telemedicine programs, notably an ambitious one in Texas, started there. Now, the falling price of technology is making care available to far-flung rural residents like D.

Dr. Gibson rides a disembodied circuit through this terrain. On Wednesdays, she sees patients in the tiny community of Springerville near the New Mexico border through a firewalled T1 data line, and on Thursdays in St. Johns. Each side of the exchange has its own television-mounted camera, angled so that doctor and patient can maintain the illusion of looking into each other's eyes in real time.

And so, through illusion and delusion, depression, anxiety, paranoia—and here and there a laugh or two—a day in the life of a rural telepsychiatrist and her patients unfolded.

"Is there self-harm going on, too?" Dr. Gibson pressed D, typing notes into the computer and glancing back at the screen. D paused, then quietly said, "Yeah."

Dr. Gibson, 44, was a pioneer in the field. She has been seeing patients only this way for 10 years and is still one of a handful of doctors in the country who practice telepsychiatry exclusively. Her territory is Apache County, which is about the size of Massachusetts and Connecticut combined, but which lacks even a single psychiatrist on the ground for its 69,000 residents despite widespread problems of poverty, drug use, child abuse and a suicide rate that is twice the national average.

The American Psychiatric Association says on its Web site that it supports telemedicine, "to the extent that its use is in the best interest of the patient," and practitioners meet the rules about ethics and confidentiality. But in places like Apache County, where the alternative is no treatment at all, most mental health workers say that every new wire and screen is to be deeply cheered.

"Basically, doctors can do, surprisingly, almost everything," said Don McBeath, the director of telemedicine and rural health at the Texas Tech University Health Sciences Center in Lubbock. "The difference is they can't touch you or smell you."

Dr. Gibson said the lack of smelling and touching, at least when it comes to psychiatry, has proved to be a good thing. Being physically in the presence of another human being, she said, can be overwhelming, with an avalanche of sensory data that can distract patient and doctor alike without either being aware of it.

"Initially we all said, 'Well, of course it would be better to be there in person,'" she said. "But some people with trauma, or who have been abused, are actually more comfortable. I'm less intimidating at a distance."

Some of the doctor's patients, who agreed to allow a reporter and photographer to observe their therapy sessions over two recent days—one day in Flagstaff with Dr. Gibson, the second day in a field clinic in St. Johns, population 3,000—said they were in fact perfectly happy with the doctor's being hundreds of miles away, though some were quick to add that no offense was intended.

"Some people don't want to have to deal with a real person," said one patient, a 63-year-old woman who has dementia and bipolar disorder.

One thing Dr. Gibson has learned over the years is that she should not wear stripes or zigzag patterns, which can look strange on television, especially to already disturbed people. For patients with paranoia, she regularly pans the camera around her little room to prove that no one else is lurking and listening. (A white-noise machine purrs outside Dr. Gibson's office door, muting the exchanges within, and no session is ever recorded.)

She worries, sometimes, about the children she sees, almost all of whom immediately and enthusiastically embrace the idea of a talking to the nice, chatty woman on the television. "Do they understand that the TV doesn't always talk to them?" Dr. Gibson said.

Another patient, Mike Kueneman, who allowed his full name to be used, has seen Dr. Gibson for about five years, through the periods with the voices in his head and what he calls the "psychotic episode" that landed him in jail this year on burglary charges. Mr. Kueneman said he felt more comfortable with Dr. Gibson, even though they have never met in person, than he does with most of the people he knows.

Like most of Dr. Gibson's patients, he pays little or nothing to see her. State programs for low-income and mentally ill people pay for the $120 psychiatric evaluations and $40 follow-up visits—and for the medicines she prescribes, which can cost thousands of dollars.

"It's hard for me to trust any other doctor," said Mr. Kueneman, who attended a telesession in the St. Johns clinic in leg shackles and handcuffs, accompanied by an Apache County sheriff's deputy.

Some things did not happen as expected. Dr. Gibson predicted, for example, that at least one patient would incorporate the teleconferencing technology into his or her delusions and come to believe that telemedicine could be used to read people's thoughts or get inside their heads.

To the contrary, in matters of the psyche—two people in two rooms looking at each other across a cool electronic medium—it is still all about human connection.

"I just feel like she's here," said a 24-year-old mother of three who asked to be referred to as C. C was struggling with depression, anxiety and fantasies of suicide. "I sometimes forget we're not in the same room."

Dr. Gibson spoke up from her room in Flagstaff: "That's funny, I would say that I feel the same way."

Dr. Gibson and C have known each other across the telewaves since C became a single mother on her own at age 17.

The emotions ran deep as they spoke and C described the dark thoughts that sometimes come at night. Gripped by insomnia, convinced that someone else is in the trailer she lives in, her mind races, she said, and the fantasy rolls out of how she might take her youngest child with her and disappear, driving off into the night.

"I don't want you killing yourself," Dr. Gibson said with a matter-of-fact tone. "So that means talking."

Apache County had a genuine, in-the-flesh psychiatrist once, Dr. Julia Martin, who practiced there for about 10 years until her retirement in 1996.

Dr. Martin was trained as a pediatrician and went back to school for psychiatry in her 50's. For more than a decade, she was it, the county's solo psychiatrist and also the only one serving the nearby Fort Apache Indian Reservation.

"You did get to know your patients pretty well—sometimes better than you'd like," Dr. Martin, 74, said in a telephone interview from her home in a remote corner of the county. Sometimes people would show up in the middle of the night, she said, desperate to see her. Other times, they delivered brownies.

What Dr. Gibson's patients imagine of her life and what she is like when she is not on camera is unknown. She sometimes mentions her children to them, and her passions for music and singing. She speculated that telemedicine has probably in some ways amplified and enlarged her image in the minds of some patients—that if she is on television she must be really important, larger than life.

She has been to Apache County once, for a "meet the psychiatrist" event in St. Johns years ago. Many of the patients who showed up remarked, she said, about how much shorter she was than they had expected.

SOURCES

American Heart Association. "Stroke Treatment and Ongoing Prevention Act: Fact Sheet." Americanheart.org, after December 2003 (accessed August 19, 2006).

"American Indian Diabetic Teleophthalmology Grant Program." http://tie.telemed.org/funding/default.asp?return=record&type=program&genus=State&id=22 (accessed August 22, 2006).

Austen, Ian. "For the Doctor's Touch, Help in the Hand." nyt.com, August 22, 2002. http://query.nytimes.com/gst/fullpage.html?res=9A0CE2DD163CF931A1575BC0A9649C8B6 (accessed December 28, 2007).

Baby CareLink in the News. "Clinician Support Technology Announces Major Enhancements in 2003 Release of Baby CareLink." April 1, 2003. http://www.babycarelink.com/news (accessed August 22, 2006).

Baby CareLink In the News. "Clinician Support Technology Helps Colorado Develop New Infant Care Program for Hospitals." 2002. http://www.babycarelink.com/news (accessed August 22, 2006).

Baby CareLink In the News. "Iowa Hospitals to Use CST's Baby CareLink to Improve Care of Premature Infants." December 3, 2002. http://www.babycarelink.com/news (accessed August 22, 2006).

Baby CareLink In the News. "Medicaid Case Study: Mount Sinai Hospital in Chicago." 2002. http://www.babycarelink.com/news (accessed August 22, 2006).

Baby CareLink In the News. "More than a Baby Monitor." CBS News, 2002. http://www.babycarelink.com/news (accessed August 22, 2006).

Bates, James, Barbara R. Demuth, Christine M. Trimbath, Bonnie Pepon, Sueong K. Mun, and Betty Levine. "Telemedicine Versus Traditional Therapy in the Management of Diabetes." PPT presentation, April 2003. http://www.americantelemed.org/news/selected2003.htm#diabetes (accessed December 24, 2007).

Brown, Nancy, and Robert Roberts. "Telemedicine Information Exchange News." March 13, 2003. http://tie.telemed.org/news/partnerships.asp (accessed December 28, 2007).

Burg, Gunter. "Store-and-Forward Teledermatology." August 25, 2005. http://www.emedicine.com/derm/topic560.htm (accessed August 22, 2006).

Cantrell, Mark. "Nurses Keep Watch for Miles Away of at the Bedside." January 10, 2005. http://community.nursingspectrum.com (accessed March 15, 2006).

Chin, Tyler. "Remote Control: The Growth of Home Monitoring." amednews.com, November 18, 2002. http://www.ama-assn.org/amednews/2002/11/18/bisa1118.htm (accessed December 24, 2007).

Choi, Candace. "Screen Presents a Picture of Health." *Star Ledger,* March 15, 2006, 25.

"Clarity Medical Systems Announces Major Move into Adult Eye Care Market: Company to Introduce New Technology Aimed at Revamping How Eye Exams Are Performed." June 23, 2006. http://www.claritymsi.com/news/060623.html (accessed December 24, 2007).

"The Comprehensive Telehealth Act of 1997." Arent Fox, 1997, 1–2. http://www.thecre.com/fedlaw/legal17/105.htm (accessed December 28, 2007).

"Computers Broaden Capabilities in Medicine." *Doctor's Guide Medical and Other News,* June 18, 1997, 1. http://www.pslgroup.com/dg/2CB4A.htm (accessed August 22, 2006).

"Computers in Medicine Online." January 4, 2006. http://www.brickellresearch.com/news.shtml (accessed January 28, 2006).

"Department of Corrections Brief History." http://www.vadoc.state.va.us/about/history.shtm (accessed December 24, 2007).

Doolittle, G. C., A. Allen, C. Wittman, E. Carlson, and P. Whitten. "Oncology Care for Rural Kansans via Telemedicine: The Establishment of a Teleoncology Practice (Meeting Abstract)." asco.org, 1996. http://www.asco.org/portal/site/ASCO/template.ERROR/;jsessionid=H1NrHhq19VtMhGpGZZF7qCs2GZP7rT2VfZyfhQY7QWz9Bc0xTpyq!-1886814676 (accessed January 18, 2008).

Doolittle, G. C., A. R. Williams, and D. J. Cook. "An Estimation of Costs of a Pediatric Telemedicine Practice in Public Schools." *Medical Care* 41, no. 1 (2003): 100–9. http://www.ncbi.nlm.nih.gov/sites/entrez?db=pubmed&uid=12544547&cmd=showdetailview (accessed December 24, 2007).

"E-Messaging Enhances Patient Satisfaction, Research Shows." August 15, 2005. http://www.health-itworld.com/newsletters/index_08172005.html (accessed January 18, 2008).

Eckholm, Erik. "The New Kind of Care in a New Era of Casualties." nyt.com, January 31, 2006. http://www.nytimes.com/2006/01/31/national/31wounded.html (accessed December 28, 2007).

Engle, Will, ed. "Telemedicine and Telehealth News." August 2, 2006. http://telemed.org/news/#item1380 (accessed August 22, 2006).

"Federal Legislative Issues Update – July 2005." The Stop Stroke Act, July 27, 2005. http://www.arota.org/pdfs/July2005legupdate.pdf (accessed August 19, 2006).

"Federal Telemedicine Legislation 105th Congress." Arent Fox. http://www.thecre.com/fedlaw/legal17/105.htm (accessed December 28, 2007).

Ferris, Nancy. "The Missing Last Mile." April 17, 2006. http://www.govhealthit.com/print/3_7/news/94029-1.html (accessed December 28, 2007).

Finkelstein, Stanley M., Stuart M. Speedie, and Sandra Potthof. "Home Telehealth Improves Clinical Outcomes at Lower Cost for Home Healthcare." *Telemedicine and e-Health* 12, no. 2 (2006): 128–36.

Fischman, Josh. "Bringing Doctors to Day Care." May 27, 2002. http://www.usnews.com/usnews/newsletters/healthsmart/hs020522.htm (accessed December 28, 2007).

Galea, Marinella, Janine Tumminia, and Lisa Garback. "Telerehabilitation in Spinal Cord Injury Persons: A Novel Approach." *Telemedicine and e-Health* 12, no. 2 (2006): 160–2.

Garshnek, V., et al., "The Telemedicine Frontier: Going the Extra Mile." http://www.quasar.org/21698/knowledge/telemedicine_frontier.html (accessed August 22, 2006).

Goldfield, G. S., and A. Boachie. "Delivery of Family Therapy in the Treatment of Anorexia Nervosa Using Telehealth: A Case Report." Abstract, 2003. http://www.ncbi.nlm.nih.gov/sites/entrez?db=pubmed&uid=12699614&cmd=showdetailview (accessed December 28, 2007).

Gray, James E., Charles Safra, Roger B. Davis, Grace Pompilio-Weitzner, Jane E. Stewart, Linda Zaccagnini, and DeWayne Pursley. "Baby CareLink: Using the Internet and Telemedicine to Improve Care for High-Risk Infants." *Pediatrics* 106, no. 6 (2000): 1318–24 (accessed December 28, 2007).

"Great-West Insurer First Commercial User of CST's Baby CareLink Neonatal Care Programme." *Virtual Medical Worlds Monthly,* October 21, 2002. http://www.hoise.com/vmw/02/articles/vmw/LV-VM-11-02-21.html (accessed December 28, 2007).

Hafner, Katie. "'Dear Doctor' Meets 'Return to Sender.'" nyt.com, June 6, 2002. http://query.nytimes.com/gst/fullpage.html?res=9C0CE1DC1F3AF935A35755C0A9649C8B63 (accessed December 28, 2007).

"Harnessing the Power of ICT for health." May 2005. http://www.i4donline.net/may05/healthNet.pdf (accessed December 28, 2007).

"History of Stethoscopes and Sphygmomanometers." October 7, 2003. http://www.hhmi.org/biointeractive/museum/exhibit98/content/b6_17info.html (accessed August 19, 2006).

Hoffmann, Allan. "Is There a Doctor in the Net." *Star-Ledger,* April 6, 1998, 21, 25. "Indian Docs Read CT Scans from US." March 28, 2006. http://sify.com/finance/fullstory.php?id=141171542 (accessed March 30, 2006).

Iwamoto, J., Y. Yonezawa, H. Maki, H. Ogawa, I. Ninomiya, K. Sada, S. Hamada, A. W. Hahn, and W. M. Caldwell. "A Mobile Phone-Based ECG Monitoring System." Abstract, 2006. http://www.ncbi.nlm.nih.gov/pubmed/16817611?ordinalpos=2&itool=EntrezSystem2.PEntrez.Pubmed.Pubmed_ResultsPanel.Pubmed_RVDocSum (accessed December 28, 2007).

Jeffrey, Susan. "Telemedicine System May Increase tPA Use in Stroke." July 17, 2007. http://www.medscape.com/viewarticle/559914 (accessed December 28, 2007).

Jette, Julie. "A Life-Saving Link: Stroke Patients Can Connect with Mass General." May 16, 2002. http://www.massgeneral.org/stopstroke/newsStory051602.aspx (accessed January 18, 2008).

Johnson, B., L. Wheeler, J. Deuser, and K. H. Sousa. "Outcomes of the Kaiser Permanente Tele-Home Health Research Project." Abstract, January 2000. http://archfami.ama-assn.org/cgi/content/full/9/1/40 (accessed January 25, 2008).

Johnson, Kirk. "TV Screen, Not Couch, Is Required for This Session." nyt.com, June 8, 2006 (accessed December 28, 2007).

Joseph, Amelia M. "Care Coordination and Telehealth Technology in Promoting Self-Management Among Chronically Ill Patients." *Telemedicine and e-Health* 12, no. 2 (2006): 156–9.

Kim, Hyungjin, Julie C. Lowery, Jennifer B. Hamill, and Edwin G. Wilkins. "Patient Attitude Toward a Web-Based System for Monitoring Wounds." *Telemedicine Journal and e-Health* 10, no. 2 (2004): S-26–S-34. http://www.liebertonline.com/doi/abs/10.1089/tmj.2004.10.S-26 (accessed December 28, 2007).

Kloss Thompson, Kathy. "Telemedicine and the Congestive Heart Failure Patient." PowerPoint Presentation, 2003. http://www.atmeda.org/news/2003_presentations/Mlbl.klossthompson.htm (accessed August 22, 2006).

Kowalczyk, Liz. "Going the Distance in Stroke Treatment." *Boston Globe,* April 3, 2006. http://www.boston.com/yourlife/health/diseases/articles/2006/04/03/going_the_distance_in_stroke_treatment/ (accessed December 28, 2007).

Lane, Kenneth. "Telemedicine News." *Telemedicine and e-Health* 12, no. 2 (2006): 81–84.

"Latest News in Minimally Invasive Medicine." Society of Interventional Radiology, March 23 2006. http://www.newswise.com/articles/view/518995/ (accessed December 28, 2007).

Lesher, Jack L., Jr., L. S. Davis, F. W. Gourdin, D. English, and W. O. Thompson. "Telemedicine Evaluation of Cutaneous Diseases: A Blinded Comparative Study." *The Journal of the American Academy of Dermatology* 38, no. 1 (1998). http://www.ncbi.nlm.nih.gov/sites/entrez?db=pubmed&uid=9448201&cmd=showdetailview (accessed December 28, 2007).

Lewis, Carol. "Emerging Trends in Medical Device Technology: Home Is Where the Heart Monitor Is." FDA Consumer, May–June 2001. http://www.fda.gov/Fdac/features/2001/301_home.html (accessed December 28, 2007).

"Literature Review on Aspects of Nursing Education: The Types of Skills and Knowledge Required to Meet the Changing Needs of the Labour Force Involved in Nursing." December 14, 2001. http://www.dest.gov.au/archive/highered/nursing/pubs/aspects_nursing/1.htm (accessed August 22, 2006).

Maddox, Peggy Jo. "Ethics and the Brave New World of E-Health." November 21, 2002. http://www.nursingworld.org/MainMenuCategories/ANAMarketplace/ANAPeriodicals/OJIN/Columns/Ethics/Ethicsandehealth.aspx (accessed December 28, 2007).

Maiolo, C., E. I. Mohamed, C. M. Fiorani, and A. De Lorenzo. "Home Telemonitoring for Patients with Severe Respiratory Illness: the Italian Experience." *Journal of Telemedicine and Telecare* 9, no. 2 (2003): 67–71. http://www.ncbi.nlm.nih.gov/sites/entrez?db=pubmed&uid=12699574&cmd=showdetailview (accessed December 28, 2007).

Mea, Vincenzo Della. "Store-and-Forward Telepathology." 1999. http://www.dimi.uniud.it/~dellamea/workshop.html (accessed August 22, 2006).

Milior, S. "A Wearable Health Care System Based on Knitted Sensors." Abstract, September 2005. http://www.ncbi.nlm.nih.gov/sites/entrez?orig_db=PubMed&db=PubMed&cmd=Search&TransSchema=title&term=A%20Wearable%20Health%20Care%20System%20Based%20on%20Knitted%20Sensors (accessed December 28, 2007).

"Monitoring Devices Help Reduce Rehospitalizations." ihealthbeat.org, June 26, 2006. http://www.ihealthbeat.org/articles/2006/6/26/Monitoring-Devices-Help-Reduce-Rehospitalizations.aspx?topicID=53 (accessed December 28, 2007).

Montana Office of Rural Health. "Rural Community-Based Home Health Care and Support Services – a White Paper." Abstract, August 2001. http://ruralwomenshealth.psu.edu/resources.html (accessed January 18, 2008).

Murphy, Kate. "Telemedicine Getting a Test in Efforts to Cut Costs of Treating Prisoners." *New York Times,* June 8, 1998, D5.

Nacci, Peter, US Department of Justice Office of Justice Programs, National Institute of Justice. "Telemedicine." March 1999. http://www.ncjrs.gov/telemedicine/toc.html (accessed August 22, 2006).

Nelson, E. L., M. Barnard, and S. Cain. "Treating Childhood Depression over Videoconferencing." *Telemedicine Journal and e-Health Spring* 9, no. 1 (2003): 49–55. http://www.ncbi.nlm.nih.gov/sites/entrez?db=pubmed&uid=12699607&cmd=showdetailview (accessed December 28, 2007).

Nesbitt, Thomas S., Stacy L. Cole, Lorraine Pellegrin, and Patricia Keast. "Rural Outreach in Home Telehealth: Assessing Challenges and Reviewing Successes." *Telemedicine and e-Health* 12, no. 2 (2006): 107–13.

Ng, C. H., and J. F. Yeo. "The Role of Internet and Personal Digital Assistant in Oral and Maxillofacial Pathology." July 2004. http://annals.edu.sg/pdf200409/V33N4p50S.pdf (accessed December 28, 2007).

"NLM National Telemedicine Initiative Summaries of Awards Announced October 1996." October 1996. http://www.nlm.nih.gov/research/initprojsum.html (accessed December 28, 2007).

Office of Telemedicine, Department of Corrections, Virginia. Virginia.edu (accessed May 17, 2003).

Ohio Department of Rehabilitation and Correction Technology, Telemedicine. January 8, 2001. drc.state.oh.us (accessed August 22, 2006).

Paar, David. "Telemedicine in Practice: Texas Department of Criminal Justice," UTMB Correctional Managed Care, May 2000. http://www.aegis.com/pubs/hepp/2000/HEPP2000-0501.html (accessed December 28, 2007).

Pak, H. S. "A Teledermatology Outcomes Study: A Prospective Randomized Evaluation." PowerPoint Presentation, April 2003. http://www.atmeda.org/news/2003_presentations/M2e2.pak.htm (accessed August 22, 2006).

Patterson, Victor, and Ena Bingham. "Telemedicine for Epilepsy: A Useful Combination." *Epilepsia* 44, no. 5 (2005): 614–15.

Patterson, Victor, and Richard Wooten. "How Can Teleneurology Improve Patient Care?" medscape.com, July 17, 2006. http://www.medscape.com/viewarticle/540191 (accessed August 4, 2006).

Patterson, V., J. Humphreys, and R. Chua. "Teleneurology by Email." *Journal of Telemedicine and Telecare* 9, no. 2 (2003): S42–3. http://www.ncbi.nlm.nih.gov/sites/entrez?cmd=Retrieve&db=PubMed&list_uids=14728758&dopt=AbstractPlus (accessed December 28, 2007).

Pyke, Bob. "Research, Training, & Practical Applications: A Look at Developing Programs at the University of Texas Medical Branch at Galveston." Interview with Vincent E. Friedewald, 2003. http://www.telehealth.net/interviews/friedewald.html (accessed August 22, 2006).

Raimer, Ben G., Patti Patterson, and Oscar Boultinghouse. "Correctional Health Care in the Texas Department of Criminal Justice." August 16, 2006. http://www.utmb.edu/cmc/Publications/articles_press/CorrectionalHealthCare.asp (accessed August 22, 2006).

Ramo, Joshua Cooper. "Doc in a Box." *Time,* Fall 1996, 55–57.

"Remote Healthcare Monitoring Not So Distant." March 21, 2005. http://www.medicalnewstoday.com/articles/21599.php (accessed December 28, 2007).

"Rochester Expands Use of Telemedicine in Day Care Centers." May 5, 2005. http://www.ihealthbeat.org/index.cfm?Action=dspItem&itemID=110905 (accessed August 22, 2006).

Rohland, Barbara M., Shadi S. Saleh, James E. Rohrer, and Paul A. Romitti. "Acceptability of Telepsychiatry to a Rural Population." May 2000. http://psychservices.psychiatryonline.org/cgi/content/full/51/5/672 (accessed August 22, 2006).

Schoffer, Kerrie L., Victor Patterson, Stephen J. Read, et al., "Guidelines for Filming Digital Camera Video Clips for the Assessment of Gait and Movement Disorders by Teleneurology." *Journal of Telemedicine and Telecare* 11, no. 7 (October 2005): 368–71(4), http://www.ingentaconnect.com/content/rsm/jtt/2005/00000011/00000007/art00008 (accessed February 7, 2008).

"Secretary Shalala Announces National Telemedicine Initiative." 1996. http://www.nih.gov/news/pr/oct96/nlm-08.htm (accessed August 22, 2006).

Shepard, Scott. "Telemedicine Brings Memphis Healing to Third-World Patients." January 17, 2003. http://memphis.bizjournals.com/memphis/stories/2003/01/20/story4.html (accessed December 28, 2007).

"'Smart' Fabrics to Keep Patients Healthy." March 16, 2005, http://www.medicalnewstoday.com/articles/21338.php (accessed December 28, 2007).

Spotswood, Stephen. "Blast Injury Programs at VA Targets Source." usmedicine.com, January 2006. http://usmedicine.com/article.cfm?articleID=1238&issueID=83 (accessed December 28, 2007).

Struber, Janet C. "An Introduction to Telemedicine and Email Consultations." July 2004. http://ijahsp.nova.edu/articles/Vol2number3/telemedicine_Struber.htm (accessed August 22, 2006).

Suzuki, Ryoji, Sakuto Otake, Takeshi Izutsu, Masaki Yoshida, and Tsutomu Iwaya. "Monitoring Daily Living Activities of Elderly People in a Nursing Home Using an Infrared Motion-Detection System." *Telemedicine and e-Health* 12, no. 2 (2006).

Telecardiology. *Telemedicine Today.* 2002. www2.telemedtoday.com (accessed August 22, 2006).

"Telehealth Update: Final HIPAA Privacy Rules." February 20, 2001. http://www.hrsa.gov/telehealth/pubs/hippa.htm (accessed December 28, 2007).
"Telemedicine for Psychiatry." medgadget.com, June 9, 2006. http://medgadget.com/archives/2006/06/telemedicine_fo_1.html (accessed December 28, 2007).
"Telemedicine Helps Victims of Stroke." August 9, 2005. http://www.networkworld.com/news/2005/052305-stroke.html (accessed December 28, 2007).
"Telemedicine Programs Database." 2003. http://telemed.org/programs/ (accessed August 22, 2006).
"Telemedicine Report to Congress." January 31, 1997. http://www.ntia.doc.gov/reports/telemed/intro.htm (accessed October 9, 2003).
"Telepathology Page." http://www.hoslink.com/telepathology.htm (accessed August 22, 2006)
Tufts University Department of Medicine. "Massachusetts Telehealth Access Program." 2001 http://www.ntia.doc.gov/otiahome/top/research/exemplary/tufts.htm (accessed August 22, 2006).
Turisco, Fran, Tania Shahid, and Lauri Paoli. "Technology Use in Rural Health Care: California Survey Results." chcf.org, April 2003. http://www.chcf.org/documents/hospitals/RuralHealthCareSurvey.pdf (accessed December 24, 2007).
Turner, Jeanine. "Telepsychiatry as a Case Study of Presence: Do You Know What You Are Missing?" *JCMC* 6, no. 4 (2001). http://jcmc.indiana.edu/vol6/issue4/turner.html (accessed December 24, 2007).
Tye, Larry. "A High-Tech Link to Boston Aids Vineyard Stroke Victims." July 10, 2001. http:/ www.massgeneral.org/stopstroke/newsStory071001.aspx (accessed December 24, 2007)
"Using Telemedicine to Save Babies' Vision." businesswire.com, April 11, 2006. http://www.genengnews.com/news/bnitem.aspx?name=356247 (accessed December 24, 2007).
VA Technology Assessment Program Short Report. "Physiologic Telemonitoring in CHF." January 2001. http://www.va.gov/vatap/telemonitorchf.pdf (accessed December 24, 2007).
Wachter, Glenn W. "HIPAA's Privacy Rule Summarized: What Does It Mean For Telemedicine?" February 23, 2001. http://tie.telemed.org/articles/article.asp?path=legal&article hipaaSummary_gw_tie01.xml (accessed August 22, 2006).
Wachter, Glenn W. "Telemedicine Legislative Issue Summary: Interstate Licensure for Telenursing." tie.telemed.org, May 2002. http://tie.telemed.org/articles/article.asp?path=legal&article=telenursingLicensure_gw_tie02.xml (accessed December 24, 2007).
Wright, Sarah. "Media Lab Hosts Workshop on Body Sensors." mit.edu, April 12, 2006. http://web.mit.edu/newsoffice/2006/media-sensors.html (accessed December 24, 2007)

RELATED WEB SITES

The American Telemedicine Association (http://www.atmeda.org) is a non-profit association "promoting greater access to medical care via telecommunications technology." It provides almost unlimited information on the latest developments in telemedicine.

Arent Fox (http://www.arentfox.com) is an excellent source of information on legislative matters relating to telemedicine.

The Center for Telemedicine Law (http://www.ctl.org), a nonprofit organization, "distribute information and serves as a resource on legal issues related to telemedicine."

The National Library of Medicine (http://www.nlm.nih.gov) can provide you with access to a great deal of information including bibliographies.

Telemedicine and Telehealth Networks: The Newsmagazine of Distance Healthcare (http://www.telemedmag.com) is a journal covering the field. Online access to past issues is free.

The University of Iowa's Telemedicine Resource Center (http://telemed.medadmin.uiowa.edu/TRCDocs/trc.html) coordinates the National Laboratory for the Study of Rural Telemedicine.

CHAPTER 5

Information Technology in Public Health

CHAPTER OUTLINE

LEARNING OBJECTIVES

After reading this chapter, you will be able to

- Define the field of public health and public health informatics.
- Discuss the impact of inequality on health.
- Discuss the use of computers in the study of disease.
- Define epidemics and pandemics, and the role of computers and statistics in their study.
- Define computer modeling of disease.
- Define global warming and its effects.
- Discuss Hurricane Katrina (2005) as a public health issue.

KEY TERMS

acquired immune deficiency syndrome (AIDS)
bird flu
Ebola virus
epidemic
epidemiology
global warming
human immunodeficiency virus (HIV)
mad cow disease
Models of Infectious Disease Agent Study (MIDAS)
National Electronic Disease Surveillance System (NEDSS)
pandemic
polio
public health
public health informatics
severe acute respiratory syndrome (SARS)
SATTELIFE
simulations
syndromic surveillance
vaccination
vector-borne disease
West Nile virus
what-if scenarios
World Health Organization (WHO)
WHONET

DISCUSSION QUESTIONS

1. Define public health.
   Public health measures protect the health of the whole community, usually by understanding the epidemiology of a disease—its patterns, where and how it emerges and spreads—and attacking it at its weak points. This can lead to prevention by means of public health measures like better sanitation, or providing cleaner water and air and guaranteeing the safety of the food supply. It can also lead to the development and widespread distribution of information and vaccinations.
2. Define epidemiology.
   Epidemiology refers to "the study of diseases in populations by collecting and analyzing statistical data."
3. What roles can computers play in the field of public health?
   The collection of data on infectious diseases and their spatial and temporal patterns is crucial to public health. National Institutes of Health researchers attempted to do this with pocket PCs and global positioning system (GPS).

   Information technology (IT) can play a significant role in helping the infection control practitioner (ICP), by monitoring disease outbreaks and spread; collecting the statistics that are necessary to even define the existence of an epidemic (an excess of cases over the expected cases).

   Computers can create what-if scenarios or simulations of what would happen to an infectious disease if something else happened (e.g., if air travel increased or decreased, or the temperature rose or fell, if there was an adequate supply of antiviral drugs, if a vaccine existed or did not exist). Computer simulations or models may help the public health officials prepare for outbreaks in states, nations, and globally.
4. Discuss the relationship between social inequality and health.
   Social inequality as well as absolute poverty is one important determinant of health. That is, a poor country with a more equal distribution of wealth and income may have a healthier population than a rich country with an unequal distribution of wealth. For example, the United States, which is first in health spending, has a health system judged thirty-seventh in the world by the World Health Organization (WHO). On statistics including longevity and infant mortality, we are not among the top twenty nations in the world. To effectively address questions of the health of a local community, a nation, or the international community, therefore, one has to minimize or at least decrease social inequality, for example, provide universal health care, day care, subsidies to bring people above the poverty line, and use the tax system to reduce inequality. The fact that health depends more on social class and relative inequality than on the availability of medical treatment was recognized in 1975 by Theodore Cooper, then U.S. Assistant Secretary for Health. It has been hypothesized that the constant stress on of poor people in a highly stratified society may account for higher rates of illness and death.

5. Discuss the uses of simulations in public health.
Computational models are the programs that create the simulations. All of these what-ifs are plugged into a model. Models can be built to answer all sorts of different questions about epidemics. Anyone in the community can catch or spread disease through contact with other people. Scientists are using a model to see how a person gets infected and then how he or she spreads the disease. They can change variables to yield different results and answer different questions. Two of these variables are the size of the community and the virulence of the infection. Using very powerful computers the models may produce millions of possible outcomes, none of which may develop. Computer simulations or models may help the public health officials prepare for outbreaks in states, nations, and globally. Currently MIDAS is modeling flu, and asking can we contain it at the source. In the model, they test such measures such as vaccination, the distribution of antiviral medications, the closing of schools, the quarantining of neighborhoods or of infected people. Public health officials are also studying what could happen if the flu spreads, for example, in the United States, given the amount that people travel.
6. Define epidemic.
An epidemic is "an excess in the number of cases of a given health problem. . . . [T]o determine what constitutes an excess implies knowing what is normal or to be expected." Thus, the very definition of epidemic is based on statistics.
7. Define pandemic.
A pandemic is a global disease outbreak to which everyone is susceptible.
8. Define syndromic surveillance.
Syndromic surveillance uses "health-related data that precede diagnosis and signal a sufficient probability of a case or an outbreak." Syndromic surveillance can be used, for example, in shelters where there are no medical personnel; people can look out for signs and symptoms (for instance, diarrhea) and report them.
9. What is national electronic disease surveillance system (NEDSS)?
The national electronic disease surveillance system (NEDSS) (a part of the Public Health Information Network) will promote "integrated surveillance systems that can transfer . . . public health, laboratory and clinical data . . . over the Internet." This will be a national electronic surveillance system, which will allow epidemics to be identified quickly. Eventually it would automatically collect data in real time.
10. On May 23, 2005, the World Health Organization (WHO) approved new rules to control the international spread of disease. Briefly discuss these rules.
The rules went into effect in 2007. They "require member countries to . . . develop . . . capabilities to identify and respond to public health emergencies of international concern and to take routine preventive measures at ports, airports, and border stations." It provides a list of reportable diseases including smallpox, SARS, and polio. Its objectives are to establish global disease surveillance systems and to overcome technical, political, resource, and legal obstacles.
11. Discuss the MIDAS project.
In 2004, the United States funded a plan for researchers to use computers to model diseases called Models of Infectious Disease Agent Study (MIDAS). The goal of the project is to develop statistical tools to identify and monitor infectious disease. It will (if successful) use electronic health information. The investigators will combine a variety of electronic health information to detect the outbreak of infectious disease, devise models of communities, and simulate the effects of outbreaks. They will also evaluate preventive measures and containment strategies. Once models of disease and their spread are created, they will enable public health officials to make more meaningful use of health statistics. Newly gathered statistics will simply be plugged in to the model.
12. What is global warming?
Our planet is warming, and we are helping to make it happen by adding more heat-trapping gases, primarily carbon dioxide (CO_2), to the atmosphere. The burning of fossil fuel (oil, coal, and natural gas) alone accounts for about 75 percent of annual CO_2 emissions from human activities. Deforestation, the cutting and burning of forests that trap and store carbon, accounts for about another 20 percent.

13. What are some of the effects of global warming?
More intense heat waves lead to more heat-related deaths. Asthma and eczema in childre have been linked to global warming. Intensity of storms and the flooding of major rive are increasing. A study by the National Academy of Science in 2004 predicted a doublin of heat waves. More intense storms also cause increasing run-off that may pollute wat supplies. California depends on the Sierra Nevada snow pack for water. Global warmin could cut the snow pack by 29 percent in the next one hundred years. Droughts mc increase. When sea levels rise, coastal areas may disappear. Global warming has also co tributed to forest fires in California. In the developing world, global warming is having devastating effect. Drought has destroyed crops.
14. Discuss Hurricane Katrina as a natural and human-made disaster.
Hurricane Katrina hit the Gulf Coast on August 29, 2005; the next day some of the leve protecting the city failed, and the city was flooded. The storm damage can be classified both a natural disaster (a category five hurricane: winds above 175 miles per hour) and human-made disaster. (According to one scientist who studied hurricanes, "We've ha plenty of knowledge to know this was a disaster waiting to happen.") Katrina flooded Ne Orleans both because it was a "monster hurricane" and because the levees failed; th should not have been surprising. Computer models of hurricanes had predicted this. Wi this knowledge in hand, an adequate public health plan could have been in place befo the storm: evacuation plans; the designation of shelters provided with adequate foo clean water, medications, and vaccinations; plans to get all the people to those shelter and plans to clean up and rebuild the city. Apparently, adequate plans were not in plac More than a year after the hurricane ninety-nine thousand people are living in Federc Emergency Management Agency (FEMA) trailers.
15. Describe some of the new diseases that public health officials have to conten with.
AIDS: Acquired immune deficiency syndrome (AIDS) attacks the immune system leadin to susceptibility to opportunistic infection. After years of study, it was found that peop were infected through body fluids, not casual contact. Human Immunodeficiency vir (HIV), the virus that causes AIDS, was identified in 1984. However, more than twent five years after the first cases were identified, although there are effective treatments lengthen life, there is no cure for or vaccination against AIDS.

SARS: Severe acute respiratory syndrome (SARS) first appeared in 2002, in Chin The epidemic, caused by a corona virus, appeared at a time in human history when eas international travel could spread disease as well as information about the disease. SAR demonstrated that epidemics need to be fought within the nation as well as internationall The epidemic was contained through public health (not medical) measures including ide tifying patients and people with whom they had contact, quarantine, canceling any larg public gathering, issuing travel advisories, and checking travelers at borders using therm scanners to detect fevers. People were advised to wash their hands, and maintain good pe sonal hygiene. Expedient reporting resulted in the isolation of patients more quickly.

Bird Flu: The first human cases of avian flu were confirmed in 1997. The viru called H5N1 or A(H5N1) that causes the disease currently presents itself in the anim population. The virus would have to mutate to spread to humans. The known cases cam from birds; human-to-human transmission of this disease is rare or nonexistent (yet).

West Nile virus: West Nile virus first appeared in the 1930s. It is a form of encephal tis or brain inflammation. It cycles between mosquitoes and birds. Infected birds will infe mosquitoes. Mosquitoes can spread the disease to humans. It can be diagnosed by MRI There is no treatment or vaccine.

Mad cow disease: Mad cow disease or "Bovine spongiform encephalopathy (BSE) is progressive neurological disorder of cattle that results from infection. . . ." Cows contra this by eating infected food. The transmission agent is called a prion. There have been 16 confirmed human cases caused by the consumption of infected meat. All of the cases we fatal. The human form of mad cow disease is called Creutzfeldt-Jakob disease (CJD). It is fatal progressive neurodegenerative disorder.

Ebola virus: Ebola virus was first identified in Zaire in 1976. The same disease appeared in Sudan. It has been seen in the United States in monkeys, but no human cases are known to have occurred here. Very little is known about the disease. It appears only sporadically. And it is contracted by direct contact with body fluids, skin, or mucus. It can also be spread through contaminated needles in hospitals. It spreads easily among people in close contact, such as family members and health care workers. Among human beings, the mortality rate is 50–90 percent. It is very difficult to diagnose Ebola early. Usually the symptoms include "fever, headache, joint and muscle aches, sore throat, and weakness, followed by diarrhea, vomiting and stomach pain." Other symptoms—"rash, red eyes, hiccups and internal and external bleeding"—may also occur. According to the CDC, scientists need to develop additional diagnostic tools because a person with Ebola has to be isolated immediately.

IN THE NEWS

City Tackles Meningitis in Brooklyn

by Richard Pérez-Peña

City health officials yesterday announced a novel assault on a large meningitis outbreak in Brooklyn, seeking to vaccinate thousands of drug users and others in and around Bedford-Stuyvesant against the bacterium that has sickened 23 people and killed eight of them.

That group of cases, over the past seven months, "is one of the largest outbreaks of meningitis described in the U.S. literature in the last couple of decades," said Health Commissioner Thomas R. Frieden. And the department's response, a mass vaccination for meningococcal meningitis, made possible by a new, more effective vaccine, appears to be the first in the city's history, he said.

The Department of Health and Mental Hygiene put out a call yesterday urging people to step forward and be vaccinated if they have used crack, heroin or methadone in the past three months and either live in or have used drugs in the Brooklyn neighborhoods within the ZIP codes 11206, 11216, 11221 and 11233. Anyone who lives with those drug users is also encouraged to get the vaccine.

Dr. Frieden said the department's twin challenges would be to reach the drug users who may be at risk, and to prevent panic among the much larger number of people who are deemed not at risk. "Meningitis evokes such fear in people," he said, but the city will not give the vaccine—of which there is a national shortage—to people who do not need it.

Dr. Frieden said he could not say how many drug users there might be in the target area of four ZIP codes, which was home to 263,000 people when the census was taken in 2000. "What we do hope is we'll be able to vaccinate at least several thousand people," he said. People seeking inoculations can contact drug treatment programs, homeless shelters, needle exchanges, doctors' offices and clinics.

All 23 cases in and around Bedford-Stuyvesant were caused by the same strain of meningococcus bacteria, according to the health department, meaning that the cases are probably connected. Most of the cases involved drug users, but officials do not believe drug use played a role in transmission, just that the patients spent time in physical contact, perhaps in cramped quarters, with each other or with people who were infected but did not develop meningitis.

Vaccination protects people against infection, but it is not clear whether it would offer any benefit to a person already carrying the bacterium.

Meningitis is an infection of the linings of the brain and spinal cord. It can be caused by several different bacteria or viruses, but the bacterial forms are much more dangerous.

(continued)

City Tackles Meningitis in Brooklyn *(continued)*

The vast majority of people who are infected with meningococcus do not develop meningitis; instead, they fight off the infection within a week or two and develop immunity to that particular strain.

But each year, 1,400 to 2,800 people nationwide do get sick from meningococcus, including 30 to 40 cases in New York City, according to the federal Centers for Disease Control and Prevention. Among all cases, 11 percent to 19 percent suffer permanent harm like brain damage, deafness or loss of a limb, and 10 percent to 14 percent die, the C.D.C. says. Most victims recover fully with antibiotic treatment, especially when the disease is caught early.

The bacteria generally spread through droplets in the breath—especially in coughs and sneezes—or through contact with saliva or mucus. The bacteria are much less contagious than some other germs, like cold and flu viruses, that are transmitted the same way. Usually, meningococcus passes only between people who spend a lot of time in close contact, like students in a dorm or soldiers in barracks.

The most recent cases in Brooklyn struck earlier this month, and drew widespread attention because there were three victims at once, two of whom were related. They lived in the same apartment complex in Bedford-Stuyvesant, knew each other well, and had attended a party together in that complex a few days earlier. One patient, a woman in her 40's, died.

Symptoms of meningococcal meningitis typically include fever, intense headaches, vomiting, a stiff neck and sometimes rashes. The standard response by public health officials, employed already in the Brooklyn outbreak, is to give antibiotics as soon as possible to all people who have had close contact with the patient.

"In the public health world, a case of meningococcal meningitis is way up there in terms of things that need an immediate response," Dr. Frieden said.

In the program announced yesterday, the city plans to use a new vaccine, MCV4, sold under the brand name Menactra, which can ward off most strains of meningococcus. The vaccine was approved for use in the United States last year and is widely expected to supplant a meningococcus vaccine that is decades old and considered less effective.

The C.D.C.'s Advisory Committee on Immunization Practices has recommended giving MCV4 to all children over the age of 11, but that remains a distant prospect, in part because it is in short supply.

Another vaccine, against a different bacteria that can also cause meningitis, pneumococcus, has been in widespread use for more than a decade, and is among the inoculations routinely given to small children. But it does not work against meningococcus.

Hurricane and Floods Overwhelmed Hospitals

by Sewell Chan and Gardiner Harris

BATON ROUGE, La., Sept. 13—Confusion and desperation permeated the New Orleans hospital system as floodwaters rose, emergency generators failed and dozens of patients died in the three chaotic days after the levees broke, doctors and other witnesses said on Tuesday.

While all of the city's major hospitals had detailed evacuation and emergency plans, officials said, none were prepared for a catastrophic flood. And each responded differently when disaster struck.

At Memorial Medical Center, where 45 bodies were discovered this week, staff members said they could do little more than try to comfort dying patients.

Frightened and exhausted nurses and doctors squeezed hand-held ventilators for patients who could not breathe. The cook reduced the daily meal ration from three to two to one. Doctors ranked patients for evacuation by helicopter, taping a number to each patient, with 3 for the sickest and 1 for the least critical.

Charity and University, two public hospitals that are part of the Louisiana State University system, did not have the money to hire helicopter companies to evacuate patients, said Don Smithburg, the system's chief executive. As a result, they were among the last to be evacuated.

The two hospitals relied almost entirely on the military and federal authorities. Charity and University managed to evacuate their 28 babies—18 of them in intensive care—only by early Friday morning, nearly two days after the other hospitals. Twenty bodies were left behind at the two hospitals; 12 of the patients had died before the storm.

At Memorial, a private 317-bed hospital opened in 1926, "there were patients who were lying on the floor," said Dr. John J. Walsh Jr., a surgeon who stayed until the early hours of Friday, Sept. 2, when helicopters finally evacuated the last patients.

Dr. Walsh compared the scene to the railyard hospital for wounded soldiers in "Gone With the Wind," saying: "The nurses were basically standing, and giving them food or water. There were some medications we could give, but nothing like modern medicine. We were back to the 1800's."

The hospital's owner, the Tenet Healthcare Corporation, the country's second-largest hospital chain, said on Tuesday that of the 45 dead, 25 were patients in an 82-bed acute-care ward run by LifeCare Holdings, of Plano, Tex., that was full at the time of the storm. Officials at LifeCare did not respond to three telephone messages.

A Tenet spokesman, Harry Anderson, acknowledged that the failure of ventilators, dialysis machines and heart-rate monitors contributed to the deaths of patients. The hospital's generators shut down "as part of a general failure of the entire electrical system," not because of low fuel, he said. Of the 45 bodies, 8 to 11 had died before the storm.

Dr. Louis Cataldie, the state's emergency medical director, said he did not fault the management for the deaths. "I don't think it's any reflection on that hospital," he said. "They did all the right things. They ultimately got their own helicopters to come in."

The suffering at the hospital played out over four anguished days. On Sunday, Aug. 28, as city officials ordered an evacuation of the city, hundreds of residents began streaming into Memorial, in the city's Uptown section. About 260 patients were there, not including the LifeCare ward. In the early hours of Monday, hospital employees awoke with relief. The wind had shattered windows and the glass walkways connecting the buildings and parking garages, and water had pooled

(continued)

Hurricane and Floods Overwhelmed Hospitals *(continued)*

around the complex, but there was little structural damage. Around 4:30 a.m., the main power lines to the hospital were disrupted and the backup generators kicked on. By dusk on Monday, most of the people who had taken refuge in the hospital had left. But hundreds of people stayed behind. All of them assumed they would be able to leave within a day or so.

On Tuesday morning, the hospital's chief executive, L. René Goux, called an emergency meeting. The administrators decided to evacuate the hospital and not to admit more evacuees from the neighborhood.

The telephones had died, and Mr. Goux began sending frantic e-mail messages to Tenet's headquarters in Dallas, requesting assistance. Company officials began calling the Coast Guard, the National Guard and even H. Ross Perot, the investor and former presidential candidate, who is a friend of Tenet's chief executive, Trevor Fetter.

Meanwhile, workers at Memorial managed to clear up an abandoned landing pad, on top of the Magnolia Street parking garage, for use as a heliport. They strung together extension cords from the generator to the landing pad and shined lights to guide the pilots. Getting patients to the helipad was not easy. They were passed through a three-by-three-foot hole on the second floor, which led from a maintenance room into the parking garage. From there, vehicles drove the patients up the ramp. Then they had to be unloaded and carried up three flights of steps to the landing pad.

Nothing was clear. At least two helicopters tried to land on the helipad and deliver evacuees to the hospital, which was trying to clear everyone out. Some pilots only wanted to take pregnant women, or babies.

Meanwhile, private boats started ferrying away the 1,800 residents who had taken shelter at Memorial. They were taken to dry land on St. Charles Avenue. From there, they left on foot or in buses.

Around 1:30 a.m. on Wednesday, the generators started to fail. Lights flickered and died.

Dr. Timothy Allen, an anesthesiologist, was astonished. "We were told and we believed that our generators would last six days, and of course they died after two and one-half days, whether because they shorted out or were flooded," he said.

On Wednesday evening, the boats stopped—before everyone could be evacuated. About 115 patients were left. "We were waiting, lined up," said Mary Jo D'Amico, a longtime nurse at Memorial who evacuated on the night of Sept. 1. "We figured that once a boat came, we'd be ready to go. When nightfall came on Wednesday and we still didn't have all our patients out and the boats had stopped, we just brought them in, fed them, gave them more fluids and put them on cots so they could rest." And helicopters never arrived that night.

William P. Quigley, a law professor at Loyola University who was at Memorial until that afternoon with his wife, Debbie, an oncology nurse, said: "They didn't have enough food. One night, I remember one of the doctors saying, 'If you've eaten food today, we can't feed you tonight.' Then they passed out little tin cans of Vienna sausage."

By Thursday morning, doctors were in crisis mode. "We said we had to find a way to get these people out faster," Dr. Allen said. "We could just sense what was coming. It was so hot. We were down to one meal a day. There was no running water or sewage." At 9 a.m., six helicopters chartered by Tenet finally started arriving, carrying away wave after wave of patients and evacuees. The last living patient left that evening. For others, help had come too late.

"As people died, they were wrapped into blankets," said Dr. Glenn A. Casey, the chief anesthesiologist and one of three doctors who left on the final flight. "We didn't have body bags to put them in."

John J. Finn, president of the Metropolitan Hospital Council of New Orleans, said the chiefs of the city's 20 hospitals had realized late last year in a planning exercise that they should come up with a plan to cope with a devastating hurricane. "We were going to fix those things in our planning," he said. "We just ran out of time."

SOURCES

"10 Million People at Risk from Pollution." nyt.com, October 18, 2006 (accessed October 18, 2006).

Abrams, Sarah. "The Gathering Storm." Harvard.edu/review, 1997. http://www.hsph.harvard.edu/review/the_gathering.shtml (accessed January 18, 2008).

Altman, Lawrence K. "Report Shows AIDS Epidemic Slowdown in 2005." nyt.com, May 31, 2006. http://www.nytimes.com/2006/05/31/world/31aids.html (accessed December 26, 2007).

"Background on Public Health Surveillance." http://www.cdc.gov/nedss/About/purpose.htm (accessed April 21, 2006).

Baker, Michael G., and David P. Fidler. "Global Public Health Surveillance Under New International Health Regulations." cdc.gov, July 10, 2006. http://cdc.gov/ncidod/eid/vol12no07/05-1497.htm (accessed December 26, 2007).

Barringer, Felicity. "Officials Reach California Deal to Cut Emissions." nyt.com, August 31, 2006. http://www.nytimes.com/2006/08/31/washington/31warming.html (accessed December 26, 2007).

Barry, John M. *The Great Influenza.* New York: Penguin, 2005.

Bell, David. "Public Health Interventions and SARS Spread, 2003." medscape.com, November 2004. http://www.medscape.com/viewarticle/490561 (accessed December 26, 2007).

"Bird Flu Measures Benefit Public Health: WHO." lomasin.com, 2006. http://www.lomasin.com/20060403/Bird-Flu-Measures-Benefit-Public-Health-WHO,9155/ (accessed December 26, 2007).

Bortman, Marcelo. "Establishing Endemic Levels or Ranges With Computer Spreadsheets." *Pan American Journal of Public Health* 5, no. 1 (January 1999): 1–8(8), Pan American Health Organization (PAHO), http://www.ingentaconnect.com/content/paho/pajph/1999/00000005/00000001/art00001 (accessed January 26, 2008).

Caldwell, Diane. "City Unveils a Plan to Identify, and Contain, a Flu Outbreak." nyt.com, July 11, 2006. http://www.nytimes.com/2006/07/11/nyregion/11flu.html?fta=y (accessed December 26, 2007).

Campbell, Carl Ann. "Medicare Ends Coverage of Hospital Errors." *The Sunday Star-Ledger,* August 12, 2007, 1, 11.

"Carbon Monoxide Poisoning After Hurricane Katrina—Alabama, Louisiana, and Mississippi, August—September 2005." *MMWR Weekly,* October 7, 2005. http://www.cdc.gov/mmwR/preview/mmwrhtml/mm5439a7.htm (accessed December 26, 2007).

CBS news. "Better Tracking in Mad Cow Wake?" cbsnews.com, December 31, 2003. http://www.cbsnews.com/stories/2003/12/31/tech/main590915.shtml (accessed December 26, 2007).

CDC. "Key Facts About Avian Influenza (Bird Flu) and Avian Influenza A (H5N1) Virus." cdc.gov, June 30, 2006. http://www.cdc.gov/flu/avian/gen-info/facts.htm (accessed December 26, 2007).

CDC. "Prion Diseases." cdc.gov, January 26, 2006. http://0-www.cdc.gov.pugwash.lib.warwick.ac.uk/ncidod/dvrd/prions/ (accessed December 26, 2007).

CDC. "West Nile Virus." cdc.gov, October 6, 2005. http://www.cdc.gov/ncidod/dvbid/westnile/index.htm (accessed July 31, 2006).

"Climate Change." 2006. http://worldwildlife.org/climate/ (accessed December 26, 2007).
"Computers Combat Disease: New Modeling Grants Target Epidemics, Bioterror." NIH.gov, May 4, 2004. http://www.nih.gov/news/pr/may2004/nigms-04.htm (accessed December 26, 2007).
Corley, Cheryl. "Emotional Scars Still Haunt Katrina Survivors." npr.org, June 14, 2006. http://www.npr.org/templates/story/story.php?storyId=5485268 (accessed December 26, 2007).
DePalma, Anthony. "New York's Water Supply May Need Filtering." nyt.com, July 20, 2006. http://www.nytimes.com/2006/07/20/nyregion/20water.html (accessed December 26, 2007).
Elliott, Phil. newsvote.bbc.co.uk, July 4, 2005 (accessed March 17, 2006).
"Experts Link Asthma to Global Warming." healthandenergy.com, June 22, 2004. http://healthandenergy.com/asthma_&_global_warming.htm (accessed December 26, 2007).
Faiola, Anthony. "Japan Says Man Died of Mad Cow Disease." washingtonpost.com, February 5, 2005. http://www.washingtonpost.com/wp-dyn/articles/A64818-2005Feb4.html (accessed December 26, 2007).
Fee, Elizabeth, and Daniel M. Fox, eds. *AIDS: The Making of a Chronic Disease.* Berkeley: University of California Press, 1991.
"G8 Commitments to Infectious Disease Can Improve Global Health Security." medicalnewstoday.com, July 18, 2006. http://www.medicalnewstoday.com/articles/47491.php (accessed December 26, 2007).
Gertner, Jon. "Incendiary Device." *New York Times,* June 12, 2005.
"Global Warming Linked to Increase in Western U.S. Wildfires." ens-newswire.com, July 12, 2006. http://www.ens-newswire.com/ens/jul2006/2006-07-12-04.asp (accessed December 26, 2007).
"Glossary of Mesothelioma Related Terminology." MesotheliomaOnline.com, 2005. http://www.mesotheliomaonline.com/resources/glossary.php (accessed July 24, 2006).
Grady, Denise. "Maker Calls New Bird Flu Vaccine More Effective." nyt.com, July 27, 2006. http://www.nytimes.com/2006/07/27/health/27vaccine.html?_r=1&ref=health&oref=slogin (accessed December 26, 2007).
"Graphs and Models of SARS Epidemic." sarswatch.org, 2003 (accessed March 29, 2006).
Greenough, P. Gregg, and Thomas D. Kirsch. "Public Health Response—Assessing Needs." *The New England Journal of Medicine* 353, no. 15 (2005): 1544–6. http://content.nejm.org/cgi/content/full/353/15/1544 (accessed December 26, 2007).
Heymann, D. L. "SARS and Emerging Infectious Diseases: A Challenge to Place Global Solidarity Above National Sovereignty." medscape.com, 2006 (accessed July 31, 2006).
Ho, Andy. "Why Epidemics Still Surprise Us." nyt.com, April 1, 2003. http://query.nytimes.com/gst/fullpage.html?res=9A03E0D91339F932A35757C0A9659C8B63 (accessed December 26, 2007).
"Integration of Telehealth Activities and Electronic Patient Records Systems Imperative for Telemedicine Market Growth." biohealthmatics.com, July 6, 2005. http://news.biohealthmatics.com/PressReleases/2005/07/06/000000002350.aspx (accessed December 26, 2007).
Kates, Jennifer. "HIV Testing in the United States." Kaiser Family Foundation, September 2006. http://www.kff.org/hivaids/upload/6094-05.pdf (accessed December 26, 2007).
Kates, Jennifer. "The HIV/AIDS Epidemic in the United States." Kaiser Family Foundation, July 2007. http://www.kff.org/hivaids/upload/3029-071.pdf (accessed December 26, 2007).
Kennedy, Michael T. *A Brief History of Disease, Science & Medicine.* Portland, OR: Asklepiad Press, 2004.
"Kenya: First Case of Polio in Decades." nyt.com, October 18, 2006. http://query.nytimes.com/gst/fullpage.html?res=9B03E0DE1F30F93BA25753C1A9609C8B63&fta=y (accessed December 26, 2007).
Lardner, James, and David A. Smith, eds. *Inequality Matters.* New York: The New Press, 2005.
Lobitz, Brad. "NIH Researchers Track Disease with Pocket PCs." pocketpcmag.com, July 2004. http://www.pocketpcmag.com/_archives/Jul04/NIHResearch.aspx (accessed December 26, 2007).
Markel, Howard. *When Germs Travel.* New York: Vintage, 2005.
"Mathematics and Statistics Combat Epidemics and Bioterror." terradaily.com, February 2, 2006. http://www.terradaily.com/reports/Mathematics_And_Statistics_Combat_Epidemics_And_Bioterror.html (accessed December 26, 2007).

Mawson, Nicola. "Supercomputers Accelerate the Search for HIV/AIDS Cure." meraka.org.za, January 23, 2006. http://www.meraka.org.za/news/Supercomputers_hiv_cure.htm (accessed December 26, 2007).
Mayo Clinic. "Threat of Avian Influenza Pandemic Grows, but People Can Take Precautions." sciencedaily.com, December 6, 2005. http://www.sciencedaily.com/releases/2005/12/051206084029.htm (accessed December 26, 2007).
McNeil, Donald G., Jr. "U.S. Reduces Testing for Mad Cow Disease, Citing Few Infections." nyt.com, July 21, 2006. http://query.nytimes.com/gst/fullpage.html?res=9C0DE6D8173FF932A15754C0A9609C8B63&sec=health&spon= (accessed December 26, 2007).
"The Morning Edition." National Public Radio, November 23, 2006.
National Public Radio. "New Orleans: Are the Levees Ready?" npr.org, May 26, 2006. http://www.npr.org/templates/story/story.php?storyId=5434630 (accessed December 26, 2007).
"Nicotine Levels Rose 10 Percent in Last Six Years, Report Says." nyt.com, August 31, 2006 (accessed August 31, 2006).
Office of the National Coordinator for Health Information Technology (ONC). "Goals of Strategic Framework." hhs.gov, December 10, 2004. http://www.hhs.gov/healthit/goals.html (accessed December 26, 2007).
"An Overview of the NEDSS Initiative." http://www.cdc.gov/nedss/About/overview.html (accessed December 26, 2007).
Pérez-Peña, Richard. "City Tackles Meningitis in Brooklyn." nyt.com, June 29, 2006 (accessed August 10, 2006).
Reaney, Patricia. "Bird Flu Measures Benefit Public Health: WHO." lomasin.com, 2006. http://www.lomasin.com/20060403/Bird-Flu-Measures-Benefit-Public-Health-WHO,9155/ (accessed December 26, 2007).
"Researchers Model Avian Flu Outbreak, Impact of Interventions." sciencedaily.com, August 3, 2005. http://www.sciencedaily.com/releases/2005/08/050803172829.htm (accessed December 26, 2007).
Rogers, Naomi. *Dirt and Disease.* New Brunswick, NJ: Rutgers University Press, 1996.
Rosenthal, Elisabeth. "Some Countries Lack Resources to Fully Track Bird Flu Cases." nyt.com, June 1, 2006 (accessed July 27, 2006).
Saavedra, Tony. "County System Would Track Disease." www.ocregister.com, December 20, 2005. http://www.ocregister.com/ocregister/news/local/article_904817.php (accessed December 26, 2007).
Schraag, Jennifer. "How Informatics Helps the ICP." infectioncontroltoday.com, January 1, 2006. http://www.infectioncontroltoday.com/articles/611feat4.html (accessed December 26, 2007).
Sideman, Andrew. "Handheld Computers Used to Address Critical Health Needs in Rural Africa and Asia." medicalnewstoday.com, August 21, 2005. http://www.medicalnewstoday.com/articles/29443.php (accessed December 26, 2007).
Simmons, Ann M. "New Orleans Endures the 'New Normal.' " calendarlive.com, July 15, 2006. http://pqasb.pqarchiver.com/latimes/access/1077350371.html?dids=1077350371:1077350371&FMT=ABS (accessed December 26, 2007).
Spiegel, Alix. "Suicide Attempts Increase in Katrina's Aftermath." npr.org, November 16, 2005. http://www.npr.org/templates/story/story.php?storyId=5014682 (accessed December 26, 2007).
Statement of the National Association of County & City Health Officials. "Health Disparities in the Gulf Coast Before and After Katrina: The Public Health Response." September 23, 2005. http://www.umaryland.edu/healthsecurity/mtf_conference/Documents/Additional%20Reading/Session%203/Health%20Disparities%20in%20the%20Gulf%20Coast%20Before%20and%20After%20Katrina.pdf (accessed December 26, 2007).
"The Surveillance and Monitoring Component of the Public Health Information Network." CDC.gov (accessed April 21, 2006).
"Syndromic Surveillance: An Applied Approach to Outbreak Detection." cdc.gov, January 13, 2006. http://www.cdc.gov/EPO/dphsi/syndromic.htm (accessed December 26, 2007).
Travis, John. "Hurricane Katrina: Scientists' Fears Come True as Hurricane Floods New Orleans." *Science* 309, no. 5741 (2005): 1656–9. http://www.sciencemag.org/cgi/content/full/309/5741/1656 (accessed December 26, 2007).
"UCI Joins International Effort to Model Influenza Outbreaks." uci.edu, February 1, 2006. http.//today.uci.edu/news/release_detail.asp?key=1427 (accessed March 27, 2006).

Wake, Cameron. "Indicators of Climate Change in the Northeast over the Past 100 Years." http://www.climateandfarming.org/pdfs/FactSheets/I.2Indicators.pdf (accessed July 17, 2006).

Waknine, Yael. "Highlights from MMWR: Minimizing Polio Spread in Polio-Free Countries and More." medscape.com, February 17, 2006. http://www.medscape.com/viewarticle/523891 (accessed December 26, 2007).

"WHO Updates Rules to Prevent the Spread of Disease." May 24, 2005. http://www.cidrap.umn.edu/cidrap/content/bt/bioprep/news/may2405regs.html (accessed December 26, 2007).

Wynn, Gerard. "Global Warming Major Threat to Humanity: Kenya." abcnews.go.com, 2006 (accessed November 14, 2006).

Zuger, Abigail. "AIDS, at 25, Offers No Easy Answers." nyt.com, June 6, 2006. http://www.nytimes.com/2006/06/06/health/06aids.html (accessed December 26, 2007).

Zuger, Abigail. "What Did We Learn From AIDS?" nyt.com, November 11, 2003. http://query.nytimes.com/gst/fullpage.html?res=9800E1D71139F932A25752C1A9659C8B63 (accessed December 26, 2007).

RELATED WEB SITES

http://www.cleanair-coolplanet.org/information/pdf/indicators.pdf
http://environment.newscientist.com/channel/earth/climate-change/
www.PandemicFlu.gov
www.AvianFlu.gov

CHAPTER 6

Information Technology in Radiology

CHAPTER OUTLINE

LEARNING OBJECTIVES

After reading this chapter, you will be able to

- Describe the contributions of digital technology to imaging techniques.
- List the uses of traditional X-rays and the advantages of digital X-rays.
- Define the uses of ultrasound.
- Discuss the newer digital imaging techniques of computerized tomography (CT) scans, magnetic resonance imaging (MRIs), functional MRIs, and positron emission tomography (PET) scans, and single-photon emission computed tomography (SPECT) scans, their uses, advantages, and disadvantages.
- Define picture archiving and communications systems (PACS).
- Describe interventional radiology techniques of bloodless surgery.

KEY TERMS

computerized tomography (CT)
cyber knife
digital imaging and communications in medicine (DICOM)
diffusion tensor imaging (DTI)
dual X-ray absorptiometry (DEXA) scan
focused ultrasound surgery
functional MRIs (fMRIs)
gamma knife
gamma knife surgery
Innova
interventional radiology
LUMA Cervical Imaging System
magnetic resonance imaging (MRI)

picture archiving and communications system (PACS)
positron emission tomography (PET)
scientific visualization
single-photon emission computed tomography (SPECT)
SoftScanR
stereotactic radiosurger
ultrafast CT
ultrasound
X-ray

DISCUSSION QUESTIONS

1. Briefly describe a traditional X-ray.
   A traditional X-ray uses high-energy electromagnetic waves to produce a two-dimension picture on film. If the X-ray encounters bone, which it cannot penetrate, this appears whi on the film. Whatever organ the X-ray passes through appears black on the film. Some so tissue appears gray. Contrast agents can improve the clarity of the images, but X-rays c not produce good images of all organs and cannot see behind bones at all.
2. Discuss some advantages of digital over traditional X-rays.
   Digital images have several advantages over images on film. Digital X-rays do not have be developed, but are immediately available and can be viewed directly on a comput screen, making them accessible to more than one person at a time, that is, to anyone on computer network. They are more flexible: areas can be enhanced, emphasized and hig lighted, and made larger or smaller. The quality of a copy of a digital X-ray is as good the quality of the original. They can be immediately transmitted over telephone lines for second opinion.
3. Briefly describe ultrasound.
   Ultrasound (although pre-dating computers) now makes use of computers to crea dynamic images. Unlike X-rays, ultrasound uses no radiation. It uses very high frequen sound waves and the echoes they produce when they hit an object. This information is use by a computer to generate an image, producing a two-dimensional moving picture on screen.
4. Describe a CT scan.
   Computerized tomography (CT) scan uses X-rays and digital technology to produce cross-sectional image of the body. CT scans use radiation passing a series of X-ra through the patient's body at different angles. The computer then creates cross-section images from these X-rays. Soft tissue can be distinguished because it absorbs the X-ray di ferently. A CT scan produces a more useful image than a traditional X-ray.
5. What are some differences between a CT scan and an MRI?
   Magnetic resonance imaging (MRI) machines use computer technology to produce imag of soft tissue within the body that cannot be pictured by traditional X-rays. Unlike C scans, MRIs can produce images of the insides of bones. CT scans use radiation. MR use magnetic fields and radiowaves.
6. MRIs are more useful in certain areas than CT scans. Discuss these areas.
   MRI can produce accurate and detailed pictures of the structures of the body and th brain, and can distinguish between normal and abnormal tissue. MRI is more accura than other imaging methods for detecting cancer that has spread to the bone, althoug PET/CT scans find cancer of the lungs more accuratel. MRIs may be used for diagnos and for the treatment of certain conditions that used to require surgery: For exampl using MRI, radiologists can now clean or close off arteries without surgery. MRIs do n use radiation and are non-invasive. MRIs are used to image brain tumors and in he diagnose disorders of the nervous system such as multiple sclerosis (MS). MRIs also dete stroke at an earlier stage than other tests. MRIs can help find brain abnormalities i patients suffering from dementia. It is particularly useful with brain disorders because can distinguish among different types of nerve tissue.
7. Discuss the uses of functional MRIs.
   functional MRIs (fMRIs) measure small metabolic changes in an active part of the brai fMRIs identify brain activity by changes in blood oxygen. fMRIs can be used to identi

brain area by function in the operating room and help the surgeon avoid damaging areas such as those that are associated with speech. Strokes, brain tumors, or injuries can change the areas of the brain where functions such as speech, sensation, and memory occur. fMRIs can help locate these areas and can then be used to help develop treatment plans. They can also help in the treatment of brain tumors, and assess the effects of stroke, injury, or other disease on brain function.

8. Define PET scan.
   Positron emission tomography (PET) scans use radioisotope technology to create a picture of the body in action. PET scans use computers to construct images from the emission of positive electrons (positrons) by radioactive substances administered to the patient. PET scans—unlike traditional X-rays and CT scans—produce images of how the body works, not just how it looks.
9. What are some of the uses of PET scans?
   PET scans create representations of the functioning of the body and the mind. They are used to study Alzheimer's, Parkinson's, epilepsy, learning disabilities, moral reasoning, bipolar disorder, and cancer. PET scans are also used to diagnose arterial obstructions.
10. How is PET useful in studying brain functioning?
    PET scans can show the functioning of the brain by measuring cerebral blood flow. PET scans produce a picture of activity, of function. A person is administered a small amount of radioactive glucose. The area of the brain, which is active, uses the glucose more quickly, and this is reflected in the image that the computer constructs. Neuroimaging techniques using PET can present a picture of brain activity associated with cognitive processes like memory and the use of language. PET scans are used to study the chemical and physiological processes that take place in the brain when a person speaks correctly or stutters. PET can show the specific brain activity associated with schizophrenia, manic depression, post-traumatic stress disorder, and obsessive-compulsive disorder. They have shown the precise area of the brain that malfunctions in certain mental illnesses and the effects of drugs, such as Prozac, and traditional talking therapy on nerve cells.
11. Describe a bone density (DEXA) scan.
    A bone-density scan or dual X-ray absorptiometry scan is a special kind of low radiation X-ray that shows changes in the rays' intensity after passing through bone. Doctors can see small changes in bone density from the amount of change in the X-ray.
12. Briefly define and discuss PACS.
    Picture archiving and communications systems (PACS) is "a system that transmits, stores, retrieves, and displays digital images . . . and communicates the information over a network." PACS is a server. [The standard communication protocols of imaging devices are called digital imaging and communications in medicine (DICOM).] The use of PACS to transmit and store digital images offers new speed in transmission of digital images. The "copy" is available as soon as the original. There is no need to move patients to a facility that has the better imaging equipment. PACS moves the images, and makes the images available to any authorized physician.
13. Describe stereotactic radiosurgery.
    Stereotactic radiosurgery (gamma knife surgery) is a noninvasive technique that is currently used to treat brain tumors in a one-day session. The use of the gamma knife for brain surgery has grown exponentially over the last few years. It is appropriate for brain tumors because the head can completely immobilized. Radiosurgery can be performed by a modified linear accelerator, which rotates around the patient's head and delivers blasts of radiation to the tumor or by a gamma knife.
14. List some advantages and disadvantages of gamma knife surgery.
    Some of the advantages of gamma knife surgery involve its relatively low cost, the lack of pain to the patient, the elimination of the risks of hemorrhage and infection, and short hospital stay. Patients are able to resume daily activities immediately. However, as the procedure grows in popularity, some doctors are questioning its safety and efficacy. What will the effects of high doses of radiation be in the long run? Although it is recognized as effective in treating some brain tumors, they question its widespread use.

15. What is focused ultrasound surgery?
    Focused ultrasound surgery does not involve cutting, but the use of sound waves. Studi involve the use of ultrasound to stop massive bleeding and to treat cancer. By focusing high-powered ultrasonic beam, roughly ten thousand times the power used for prenatal pi tures, they can raise the temperature of cancerous tissue at the focal point to nearly boilin Within seconds, the tissue dies.

IN THE NEWS

Treating Troubling Fibroids Without Surgery

by Lawrence K. Altman

Condoleezza Rice, the national security adviser, shares at least one thing with millions of other American women: she had fibroids, benign tumors in the uterus that required treatment.

Ms. Rice, the nominee for secretary of state, entered the hospital for an overnight stay last week to undergo a procedure—uterine artery embolization—that is rapidly becoming an alternative to major surgery for troublesome fibroids.

For most women, fibroids, consisting of muscle and fibrous tissue, are no bother. But for millions of others, fibroids can be so large (in some cases, the size of a melon) or so numerous that they cause discomfort, severe bleeding, anemia, urinary frequency and other symptoms.

What causes fibroids is unknown, although estrogen is known to promote their growth. More than one woman in five age 40 and older has the tumors, with higher rates among black women.

For decades, major surgery—a hysterectomy to remove the uterus or a myomectomy to remove selected fibroids while leaving the uterus in place—was the main therapy for women whose symptoms were not controlled by oral contraceptives or other hormonal therapies. About 30 percent of the 600,000 hysterectomies performed in the United States each year are for fibroids.

With the introduction of technologies like ultrasound, C.T. scans, magnetic resonance imaging and new drugs, however, doctors have in recent years developed a number of alternative therapies.

This year in the United States, about 13,000 women are expected, like Ms. Rice, to choose the embolization technique, which is less invasive than surgery. French doctors first reported the embolization procedure in 1995. Since then, the number of the procedures has grown, in part because of direct-to-consumer advertising by interventional radiologists, who perform them.

Embolization involves injecting pellets the size of grains of sand, made from plastic or gels, into uterine arteries to stop blood flow and shrink the tumors by starvation. The procedure is so named because the pellets are emboli, objects that lodge and stop blood flow. M.R.I. scans are often used to screen out fibroid patients who are not candidates for the embolization procedure.

In performing the procedure, interventional radiologists insert a thin tube into an artery in the groin and thread it up to the main uterine artery in the pelvis. A dye is injected that outlines the smaller arterial branches on an X-ray, producing a map that guides injection of pellets through the tube into the arteries that nourish the fibroids.

"Of the patients we see, at least a third have fibroids the size of an orange or larger," and the size does not influence the outcome of the procedure, said Dr. John H. Rundback, an interventional radiologist at Columbia University.

The procedure, which may be painful, usually lasts 60 to 90 minutes. Most patients also experience intense pain for several hours afterward and stay overnight in the hospital. For some patients, the pain persists for several days, or even two weeks. Surgery for fibroids requires a longer hospital stay.

Additional complications from the embolization procedure can include abscesses and other infections; heavy uterine bleeding; early menopause from the pellets damaging the ovaries; or destruction of the uterus, requiring emergency surgery.

Although the procedure is safe, "there are still significant uncertainties about the procedure, especially in terms of future fertility and long-term outcomes," said Dr. Evan R. Myers, chief of the division of clinical and epidemiologic research in Duke University's department of obstetrics and gynecology.

Judging the safety and effectiveness of embolization compared with to other therapies is hard because randomized controlled studies are lacking and because earlier studies did not report how different symptoms responded to different treatments, Dr. Myers said.

"It is amazing that for a condition as common as fibroids, that has such significant impact on reproductive-age women, there is not a lot of high-quality scientific evidence for many of the things that are done for fibroids," Dr. Myers said.

"There still is no gold standard randomized trial comparing embolization to the other interventions," he added. This is largely because patients and physicians have such strong preferences for one method or another that it is hard to recruit enough patients for clinical trials comparing the embolization procedure to hysterectomy, myomectomy, hormonal and other therapies.

Dr. Myers directs a registry that the Society of Interventional Radiology has created to monitor the outcome of 3,000 women who have undergone the embolization procedure. He said that the effectiveness and complication rates for embolization seem comparable to surgery. But there is insufficient information to draw conclusions about the procedure's safety for women who desire to become pregnant, according to Dr. Myers, the interventional society and the American College of Obstetricians and Gynecologists.

In very rare cases—less than 1 percent—fibroids are cancerous. The cancers usually develop among postmenopausal women and the embolization procedure is not recommended for that group. Biopsies are not routinely performed on fibroid patients before embolization, and even if they were done, biopsies would not be able to detect cancerous fibroids deep in the uterine muscle. So statistically, as more women undergo embolization procedures, the cancers are unlikely to be detected in the very few patients who have them.

"That small risk has to go into the counseling before the embolization procedure," said Dr. Howard T. Sharp, chief of the general division of obstetrics and gynecology at the University of Utah.

Dr. Sharp said he believed that there were probably more cases of cancer than the single report in the medical literature, because doctors often "don't report the bad outcomes."

While some researchers are trying to study the embolization procedure further, others, like Dr. Elizabeth Stewart of the Brigham and Women's Hospital in Boston, are testing another fibroid treatment, the ExAblate 2000 System, that won approval from the Food and Drug Administration last month.

The system, made by InSightec Ltd. of Israel, uses ultrasound to destroy the fibroids with heat and M.R.I. to map the uterine anatomy and monitor the degree of fibroid destruction from a repeated application of multiple ultrasound waves on the tumor. The device centers the ultrasound waves similarly to the way a magnifying glass focuses light.

The patient remains in an M.R.I. machine for about three hours and then can go home. Initial studies found that serious side effects occurred in 2 percent

(continued)

Treating Troubling Fibroids Without Surgery *(continued)*

of cases, compared with 13 percent among women who underwent a hysterectomy, Dr. Stewart said. Additional studies are being conducted at a small number of hospitals. The procedure is intended for women who have completed childbearing or who do not intend to become pregnant.

Political Clout in the Age of Outsourcing

by David Leonhardt

A FEW years ago, stories about a scary new kind of outsourcing began making the rounds. Apparently, hospitals were starting to send their radiology work to India, where doctors who make far less than American radiologists do were reading X-rays, M.R.I.'s and CT scans.

It quickly became a signature example of how globalization was moving up the food chain, threatening not just factory and call center workers but the so-called knowledge workers who were supposed to be immune. If radiologists and their $350,000 average salaries weren't safe from the jobs exodus, who was?

On ABC, George Will said the outsourcing of radiology could make health care affordable again, to which Senator Charles E. Schumer of New York retorted that thousands of American radiologists would lose their jobs. On NPR, an economist said the pay of radiologists was already suffering. At the White House, an adviser to President Bush suggested that fewer medical students would enter the field in the future.

"We're losing radiologists," Representative Sherrod Brown, an Ohio Democrat, said on CNN while Lou Dobbs listened approvingly. "We're losing all kinds of white-collar jobs, all kinds of jobs in addition to manufacturing jobs, which we're losing by the droves in my state."

But up in Boston, Frank Levy, an economist at the Massachusetts Institute of Technology, realized that he still had not heard or read much about actual Indian radiologists. Like the once elusive Snuffleupagus of Sesame Street, they were much discussed but rarely seen. So Mr. Levy began looking. He teamed up with two other M.I.T. researchers, Ari Goelman and Kyoung-Hee Yu, and they dug into the global radiology business.

In the end, they were able to find exactly one company in India that was reading images from American patients. It employs three radiologists. There may be other such radiologists scattered around India, but Mr. Levy says, "I think 20 is an overestimate."

Some exodus.

URBAN myths feed off real fears, and this myth caught on because Americans don't know quite what to think about globalization. There is no doubt that trade makes countries richer, but it also creates victims. And since the country is doing almost nothing right now to ease the burden of those victims—the people whose jobs really have gone to India or another country—it is easy to become scared.

Radiologists seem like just the sort of workers who should be scared. Computer networks can now send an electronic image to India faster than a messenger can take it from one hospital floor to another. Often, those images are taken during emergencies at night, when radiologists here are sleeping and radiologists in India are not.

There also happens to be a shortage of radiologists in the United States. Sophisticated new M.R.I. and CT machines can detect tiny tumors that once would have gone unnoticed, and doctors are ordering a lot more scans as a result.

When I talked this week to E. Stephen Amis Jr., the head of the radiology department at Montefiore Medical Center in the Bronx, he had just finished looking at some of the 700 images that had been produced by a single abdominal CT exam. "We were just taking pictures of big, thick slabs of the body 20 years ago," Dr. Amis said. "Now we're taking thinner and thinner slices."

Economically, in other words, radiology has a lot in common with industries that are outsourcing jobs. It has high labor costs, it's growing rapidly and it's portable.

Politically, though, radiology could not be more different. Unlike software engineers, textile workers or credit card customer service employees, doctors have enough political power to erect trade barriers, and they have built some very effective ones.

To practice medicine in this country, doctors are generally required to have done their training here. Otherwise, it is extremely difficult to be certified by a board of other doctors or be licensed by a state government. The three radiologists Mr. Levy found in Bangalore did their residencies at Baylor, Yale and the University of Massachusetts before returning home to India.

"No profession I know of has as much power to self-regulate as doctors do," Mr. Levy said.

So even if the world's most talented radiologist happened to have trained in India, there would be no test he could take to prove his mettle here. It's as if the law required cars sold here to have been made by the graduates of an American high school.

Much as the United Automobile Workers might love such a law, Americans would never tolerate it, because it would drive up the price of cars and keep us from enjoying innovations that happened to come from overseas. But isn't that precisely what health care protectionism does? It keeps out competition.

For now, the practical effect on radiology is small. At its highest levels, the United States health care system may be the best the world has ever known. India doesn't even have many radiologists today, let alone a large number who measure up to American standards.

But that's going to change. Eventually, Indian doctors will be able to do the preliminary diagnoses that are a big part of radiology. Something similar will happen in accounting, architecture, education, engineering and the law, as Mr. Levy and his colleagues suggest in the coming Milken Institute Review.

These fields tend to be regulated already, giving them noble excuses—like certification, client privacy and legal accountability—to put up trade barriers. But the real reason will usually be a simple desire to protect jobs and salaries.

When factory workers have asked for that kind of protection, the country has told them no. So why does the answer change when the request comes from a wealthier, more influential group of workers?

SOURCES

"Analogic Corporation Receives 510(k) FDA Clearance for Wide-Beam Fetal Ultrasound Transducer." finance.breitbart.com, March 29, 2006 (accessed July 13, 2006).

"Analogic OK'd on Fetal Ultrasound Device." upi.com, March 29, 2006. http://www.upi.com/Health_Business/Analysis/2006/03/29/analogic_okd_on_fetal_ultrasound_device/2684/ (accessed December 26, 2007).

"ART Initiates Clinical Trials of the SoftScan 'R' System at the University of California-San Diego as Part of Its North American Pivotal Study." cnnmatthews.com, March 29, 2006 (accessed March 30, 2006).

Beardsey, Tim. "Putting Alzheimer's to the Tests." *Scientific American,* February 1995, 12–13.

Blakeslee, Sandra. "Watching How the Brain Works as It Weighs a Moral Dilemma." September 25, 2001. https://notes.utk.edu/bio/greenberg.nsf/0/ed7ab7daf 43c355b85256ad3004ba9e0?OpenDocument (accessed August 23, 2006).

Cluett, Jonathan. "Do I Need a Bone Density Test?" http://orthopedics.about.com/cs/ osteoporosis/a/bonedensitytest.htm (accessed August 23, 2006).

Cluett, Jonathan. "What Is a Bone Scan?" http://orthopedics.about.com (accessed August 23, 2006).

"Computed Tomography Images Help Radiologists Diagnose SARS." DGNews, May 14, 200 http://main.pslgroup.com/news/content.nsf/MedicalNews/8525697700573E188525 D26004E0806?OpenDocument&id= (accessed December 26, 2007).

"Computerized Scanner Double-Checks Suspicious Mammograms." August 1999. http:// www.patientnews.net/articles/julyaugust/suspiciousmammograms.html (accessed August 23, 2006).

"Diffusion Tensor Imaging." http://www.sci.utah.edu/research/diff-tensor-imaging.html (accessed December 26, 2007).

Dye, Mark. "PET and SPECT: Happy Together." June, 2005. http://www.medicalimagingmag.com issues/articles/2005-06_01.asp (accessed December 26, 2007).

Eisenberg, Anne. "What's Next; a Budding Tumor Unmasked by the Vessels That Feed It." nyt.com, July 24, 2003. http://query.nytimes.com/gst/fullpage.html?res= 9E0CE1D 7153FF937A15754C0A9659C8B63 (accessed December 26, 2007).

Eisenberg, Anne. "What's Next; Lasers Set Cells Aglow for a Biopsy Without the Knife." nyt.com, June 26, 2003. http://query.nytimes.com/gst/fullpage.html?res= 9C05E5DA163AF935A15755C0A9659C8B63 (accessed December 26, 2007).

"Esophageal Cancer." 2006. http://www.cancer.org/downloads/PRO/EsophagealCancer. pdf (accessed December 26, 2007).

"FDA Clears GE Healthcare's New Innova Digital Flat Panel Biplane Imaging System." March 14, 2006. http://home.businesswire.com (accessed March 18, 2006).

FDA Talk Paper. "FDA Approves First Digital Mammography System." January 31, 2000. http:/ www.fda.gov/bbs/topics/ANSWERS/ANS01000.html (accessed December 26, 2007).

Foreman, Judy. "Brain Scanning and OCD." June 3, 2003. http://www.myhealthsense.com/ F030603_Brain.html (accessed December 26, 2007).

Fox, Peter T., Roger J. Ingham, Janis C. Ingham, Traci B. Hirsch, J. Hunter Downs, Charles Martin, Paul Jerabek, Thomas Glass, and Jack L. Lancaster. "A PET Study of the Neural Systems of Stuttering." *Nature* 382, no. 6587 (1996): 158–62.

Friedman, Richard A. "Like Drugs, Talk Therapy Can Change Brain Chemistry." August 27, 2002. http://www.forensic-psych.com/articles/artNYTTalkTherapy8.27.02.html (accessed December 26, 2007).

"Full Body Scan for Breast Cancer." September 7, 2000. http://www.abc.net.au/science/ news/stories/s358885.htm (accessed August 23, 2006).

"Functional MR Imaging (fMRI) - Brain." 2006. http://www.radiologyinfo.org/en/info.cfm pg=fmribrain&bhcp=1 (accessed August 23, 2006).

"Gamma Knife® Surgery." 2006. http://www.irsa.org/gamma_knife.html (accessed August 23, 2006).

Giesel, F. L., H. Bischoff, H. von Tengg-Kobligk, M. A. Weber, C. M. Zechmann, H. U. Kauczor, and M. V. Knopp. "Dynamic Contrast-Enhanced MRI of Malignant Pleural Mesothelioma: A Feasibility Study of Noninvasive Assessment, Therapeutic Follow-up, and Possible Predictor of Improved Outcome." June 2006. http://www. mesotheliomamedical.com/modules.php?name=News&file=print&sid=1677 (accessed August 23, 2006).

Giger, Maryellen, and Charles A. Pelizzari. "Advances in Tumor Imaging." *Scientific American* September 1996, 110–12.

"Going Beyond CT Angiography—SPECT/CT Heart Study Is SNM's Image of the Year." radiologytoday.com, July 3, 2006 (accessed July 7, 2006).

Goode, Erica. "Experts See Mind's Voices in New Light." nyt.com, May 6, 2003. http://query nytimes.com/gst/fullpage.html?res=9C05EEDC103CF935A35756C0A9659C8B63 (accessed December 26, 2007).

Goode, Erica. "Studying Modern-Day Pavlov's Dogs, of the Human Variety." August 26, 2003. http://www.hnl.bcm.tmc.edu/articles/Studying%20Modern-Day%20Pavlov's%20Dogs,%20of%20the%20Human%20Variety.htm (accessed August 23, 2006).

Gould, Paula, and John C. Hayes. "Informatics Integration Drives Intraoperative Planning." CARS/EuroPACS 2005 Conference Reporter. October 5, 2005. http://www.diagnosticimaging.com/pacsweb/features/showArticle.jhtml?articleID=171202282 (accessed December 26, 2007).

Heiken, Jay P., Christine M. Peterson, and Christine O. Menias. "Virtual Colonoscopy for Colorectal Cancer Screening: Current Status." July 9, 2006. http://2006.confex.com/uicc/uicc/techprogram/P10382.HTM (accessed August 23, 2006).

Hooper, Judith. "Targeting the Brain." *Time,* Special Issue Fall 1996, 46–50.

"Hospital Implements Latest Advances in Radiology System." March 22, 2006. http://www.newportnewstimes.com (accessed March 30, 2006).

"Imaging Technique Helps Predict Breast Cancer Spread Before Surgery." August 23, 2006. http://main.pslgroup.com/news/content.nsf/medicalnews/852571020057CCF6852571D3004958BB?OpenDocument&id=&count=10 (accessed August 23, 2006).

"The Impact of Osteoporosis on Men's and Women's Health." August 18, 2006. http://www.muscles-and-bones.com/osteoporosis/index.php (accessed August 23, 2006).

Johnston, P. J., W. Stojanov, H. Devir, and U. Schall. "Functional MRI of Facial Emotion Recognition Deficits in Schizophrenia and Their Electrophysiological Correlates." February 2005. http://www.ncbi.nlm.nih.gov/entrez/query.fcgi?cmd=Retrieve&db=PubMed&list_uids=16176365&dopt=Abstract (accessed August 23, 2006).

Kevles, Bettyanne. "Body Imaging." *Newsweek,* Winter 1997–98, 74–76.

Kevles, Bettyanne Holzmann. *Naked to the Bone: Medical Imaging in the Twentieth Century.* New Brunswick, NJ: Rutgers University Press, 1997.

Khafagi, Frederick A., and S. Patrick Butler. "Nuclear Medicine." *The Medical Journal of Australia* 176, no. 1 (2002): 27. http://www.mja.com.au/public/issues/176_01_070102/kha10734_fm.html (accessed August 23, 2006).

"Latest News in Minimally Invasive Medicine." newswise.com, March 23, 2006. http://www.newswise.com/articles/view/518995/ (accessed December 26, 2007).

Marano, Lou. "Ethics and Mapping the Brain." June 4, 2003. http://www.hawaiireporter.com/story.aspx?03357186-c0f2-4a84-9eb4-0457be143480 (accessed August 23, 2006).

Marriott, Michel. "A Palm-Size Ultrasound Scans Safely in a Flash." nyt.com, October 10, 2002. http://query.nytimes.com/gst/fullpage.html?res=9906E1D91F3BF933A25753C1A9649C8B63 (accessed December 26, 2007).

Motluk, Alison. "Cutting Out Stuttering." *New Scientist,* February 1, 1997, 32–35.

Mount Sinai. "What Is a PET Study of the Heart?" 2003. http://www.mountsinai.org/hospitals/msh/pet/pet_whatis_c.htm (accessed August 23, 2006).

"MRI of the Head." 2003. http://www.radiologyinfo.org/en/info.cfm?pg=headmr (accessed August 23, 2006).

"MTCC to Host 5000 Interventional Radiologists in Professional Society's International Meeting." March 30, 2006. http://www.newswire.ca (accessed March 30, 2006).

Murray, Michael. "At MGH, the Stakes Don't Get Any Higher." March 29, 2006. www.miningjournal.net (accessed March 30, 2006).

"New Device Clearance: Given® Diagnostic Imaging System – K010312." August 1, 2001. http://www.fda.gov/cdrh/mda/docs/k010312.html (accessed August 23, 2006).

"Nuclear Medicine." 2000. http://www.mountsinai.org/msh/msh_frame.jsp?url= clinical_services/msh_nucmed.htm (accessed August 23, 2006).

"Osteoporosis: A Guide to Prevention and Treatment." Health.harvard.edu, 2006. http://www.health.harvard.edu/special_health_reports/Osteoporosis.htm (accessed December 26, 2007).

Parlikar, Urmilla R. "Heart Imaging Procedure Helps Physicians Evaluate Patients Suspected of Having a Heart Attack." http://www.swedish.org/17697.cfm (accessed December 26, 2007).

"PET Accurately Identifies Esophageal Cancer Patients' Positive Responses to Chemotherapy," *ScienceDaily* June. 4, 2007. http://www.sciencedaily.com/releases/2007/06/070603215320.htm (accessed January 5, 2008).

"PET Scan." May 2006. http://www.betterhealth.vic.gov.au/BHCV2/bhcarticles.nsf/pages/PET_scan?Open (accessed August 23, 2006).

"PET Scans Promising for Assessing Treatment Response in Esophageal Cancer." 2006. http://www.harborhospital.org/sm6/websitefiles/medstarharbor37266/ccnewsbody.cfm?TierID=265&DocumentId=34881 (accessed August 23, 2006).

"Quantitative Computed Tomography." In *The Encyclopedia of Medical Imaging Volume 1.* http://www.medcyclopaedia.com/library/topics/volume_i/q/quantitative_computed tomography_qct_.aspx?s=Quantitative+Computed+Tomography&mode=1&syn=&scope= (accessed December 26, 2007).

Raichle, Marcus E. "Visualizing the Mind." *Scientific American,* April 1994, 58–64.

Rajendran, Joseph. "Positron Emission Tomography in Head and Neck Cancer." Abstract, June 6, 2003. http://www.appliedradiology.com/articles/article.asp?Id=855&SubCatID=223&CatID=48&ThreadID=&Search= (accessed August 23, 2006).

Scott, A. M. "Current Status of Positron Emission Tomography in Oncology." Abstract, January–February 2001. http://www.ncbi.nlm.nih.gov/entrez/query.fcgi?cmd=Retrieve&db=PubMed&list_uids=11478353&dopt=Abstract (accessed August 23, 2006).

Spinasanta, Susan. "Nuclear Imaging: PET and SPECT Scans." December 8, 2004. http://www.spineuniverse.com/displayarticle.php/article231.html (accessed December 26, 2007).

Stewart, Angela. "Seeing into the BRAIN." *The Star Ledger,* March 14, 2006, 33.

Susman, Ed. "Positron Emission/Computed Tomography Fusion and Magnetic Resonance Imaging Detect Different Cancerous Lesions: Presented at RSNA." *Doctor's Guide,* December 9, 2002. http://www.docguide.com/news/content.nsf/news/ 8525697700573E1885256C8A00702AD2?OpenDocument&id=48DDE4A73E09A96985256888008C249&c=Diagnostic%20Radiology&count=10 (accessed December 26, 2007).

Sylvain, Jaume, Matthieu Ferrant, Benoît Macq, Lennox Hoyte, Julia R. Fielding, Andreas Schreyer, Ron Kikinis, and Simon K. Warfield. "Tumor Detection in the Bladder Wall with a Measurement of Abnormal Thickness in CT Scans." March 2003. http://people.csail.mit.edu/sylvain/jaume-ieee-tbme03.pdf (accessed August 23, 2006).

Tarkan, Laurie. "Brain Surgery, Without Knife or Blood, Gains Favor." nyt.com, April 29, 2003. http://query.nytimes.com/gst/fullpage.html?res=9A01E2D7133 DF93AA15757C0A9659C8B63 (accessed December 26, 2007).

"Telemedicine Glossary." http://www.acponline.org/computer/telemedicine/glossary.htm (accessed December 26, 2007).

Tempany, Clare, and Barbara McNeil. "Advances in Biomedical Imaging." *JAMA* 285 (2001) 562–7.

Vaccari, Guido, and Claudio Saccavini. "Radiology Informatics and Work Flow Redesign." *PsychNology Journal* 4, no. 1 (2006): 87–101. http://www.psychnology.org/File/PNJ4(1)/PSYCHNOLOGY_JOURNAL_4_1_VACCARI.pdf (accessed December 26, 2007).

Wang, Gene-Jack, ed. "Study Reveals Biochemical Signature of Cocaine Craving in Humans. June 13, 2006. http://www.bnl.gov/bnlweb/pubaf/pr/PR_display.asp?prID=06-74 (accessed December 26, 2007).

"What Is DEXA Scanning?" http://www.gorhams.dk/html/what_is_dexa_scanning.html (accessed August 23, 2006).

Wu, D., and S. S. Gambhir. "Positron Emission Tomography in Diagnosis and Management of Invasive Breast Cancer: Current Status and Future Perspectives." Abstract, April 2003 http://www.ncbi.nlm.nih.gov/entrez/query.fcgi?cmd=Retrieve&db=PubMed&list_uids=12756080&dopt=Abstract (accessed August 23, 2006).

"X-Rays Go Digital." October 2003. http://css.sfu.ca/update/vol15/15.3-digital-x-rays (accessed August 23, 2006).

Zimmer, Carl. "What if There Is Something Going on in There?" nyt.com, September 28, 2003. http://query.nytimes.com/gst/fullpage.html?res= 9503E0D71E3AF93BA1575AC0A9659C8B63 (accessed December 26, 2007).

RELATED WEB SITES

http://www.acponline.org/computer/telemedicine/glossary.htm
http://www.acponline.org/computer/telemedicine/links.htm

CHAPTER 7

Information Technology in Surgery—the Cutting Edge

CHAPTER OUTLINE

LEARNING OBJECTIVES

After reading this chapter you will be able to

- List some of the uses of computers in surgery.
- Describe the role of computers in surgical planning.
- Define robot, endoscopic surgery, minimally invasive surgery, augmented reality, and telepresence surgery; be aware of the Socrates system which allows long distance mentoring of surgeons in real time.
- Describe NASA Extreme Environment Mission Operation (NEEMO).
- Describe the Operating Room of the Future.
- List some of the robots used in surgery including ROBODOC and AESOP, ZEUS and da Vinci.
- Describe some of the advantages and disadvantages of computer-assisted surgery.
- Describe the use of lasers in surgery.

KEY TERMS

automated endoscopic system for optimal positioning (AESOP)
Aquarius
ARTEMIS
artificial intelligence (AI)
augmented reality
computer-assisted surgery
da Vinci
distance (or telepresence surgery)
endoluminal surgery
endoscope
HERMES
image-guided surgery
KISMET
laparoscope
laser
MINERVA
minimally invasive surgery (MIS)
nanotechnology
NEEMO
radio frequency identification (RFID) tags
Raven
ROBODOC
robots
telepresence surgery (distance surgery)
Socrates
virtual environment
virtual reality (VR)
ZEUS

DISCUSSION QUESTIONS

1. Briefly discuss the use of virtual reality in surgical planning and training.
Computer-assisted surgical planning involves the use of virtual environment technolog to provide surgeons with realistic accurate models on which to teach surgery and plan an practice operations. With virtual reality (VR) technology, the computer can create an env ronment that seems real, but is not. Currently, these lifelike simulations are used in th health care field. The models created by VR technology can look, sound, and feel real. Th models can respond to pressure, by changing shape, and to being cut, by leaking. A mod such as this, which is interactive, allows surgeons not only to plan surgeries more precisel but also to practice operations without touching a patient. Some models include a predi tive element that shows the results of the doctor's actions. For example, plastic surgeons ca practice on a model of a face and see the results of their work.
2. Define minimally invasive surgery.
Minimally invasive surgery, utilizing an endoscope, performs procedures through sma incisions that involve a minimum of damage to healthy tissue. There is less bleeding an pain and a shorter recovery time. This means a shorter hospital stay and lower costs.
3. What are some advantages of using robots in the operating room?
Robots, unlike humans, can hold endoscopes and other instruments without becomin tired or shaky. Robots are also used to scale down the surgeon's motions. Some surgeon report that this makes their hands "rock steady," making surgery on small delicate are such as the eye safer.
4. Describe ROBODOC.
The earliest use of a robot in surgery was in hip replacement operations. Integrated Surgic Systems' ROBODOC (which is undergoing FDA-approved clinical trials) is a compute controlled, image-directed robot that performed its first hip replacement in 1992. It can b used only with cementless implants—which constitute about one-third of those done eac year. It has been used in thousands of hip replacement operations worldwide. Becaus ROBODOC actually cuts into a patient's femur, there have to be strict built-in safeguard The safeguards come from the program that controls the robot and physical limitations o how much ROBODOC can move.
5. Describe AESOP.
Automated endoscopic system for optimal positioning (AESOP), which was introduced i 1994 by Computer Motion Inc., is the first FDA-cleared surgical robot. Originally deve oped for the space program, AESOP is now used as an assistant in endoscopic procedure It holds and moves the endoscope under the direction of the surgeon. AESOP was first deve oped to be controlled by foot pedals. However, currently it responds to voice commands.

6. Describe ZEUS.
   ZEUS has three interactive robotic arms, one of which holds the endoscope, while the other two manipulate the surgical instruments. The surgeon, sitting at a console, controls them. The endoscope is controlled by voice commands. The surgeon manipulates instruments, which resemble surgical tools, while looking at a monitor; the surgeon's manipulations control the robotic arms, which are actually doing the surgery. ZEUS includes a feedback system so that the surgeon "feels" the tissue. The computer-controlled robotic arms also scale down the surgeon's movements, filtering out any hand tremor. This means that a one-inch movement by the surgeon becomes a one-tenth of an inch movement of the robot's surgical instrument. By eliminating the hand's vibrations, ZEUS makes delicate procedures safer.
7. Describe HERMES.
   System software is required to connect the operating room hardware into a network that a surgeon can control with voice commands. HERMES is an FDA-cleared operating system that performs these tasks, allowing the surgeon to use his or her voice to control all the electronic equipment in the operating room, coordinating the endoscope and robotic devices. It also allows the surgeon to adjust lighting with a voice command. The surgeon can use HERMES to take and print pictures and access the patient's electronic medical record including images and other information.
8. What is augmented reality surgery?
   Augmented reality surgery uses computer-generated imagery to provide the surgeon with information that would otherwise be unavailable. The computer-generated images may be either fused with the image on the monitor or projected directly onto the patient's body during the operation allowing the doctor to virtually see inside the patient. However, an image on a monitor is two-dimensional. A head-mounted display that combines the computer-generated images and the image of the patient allows the surgeon to see a three-dimensional field and see different views by simply turning her or his head instead of adjusting the endoscope, making it more like traditional open surgery.
9. How was the U.S. government involved in the early development of telepresence surgery?
   The National Aeronautics and Space Administration (NASA) first sought to develop telepresence surgery for space flight medical emergencies. Distance surgery thus has the potential of making surgical expertise available on battlefields, on space stations, and in remote rural areas. Several research groups are working on telesurgical systems. Some of this work is funded by the Advanced Research Projects Agency (ARPA) of the U.S. Department of Defense, which first conceived of robotic surgery and which still sees remote surgery as a way of saving lives on the battlefield and protecting surgeons from dangerous environments.
10. Briefly describe NEEMO.
    NASA Extreme Environment Mission Operation (NEEMO) is a series of NASA missions in which groups of scientists live in Aquarius. Aquarius is the only undersea laboratory in the world. Aquarius is now sixty-seven feet under the ocean's surface off the Florida Keys. It is thirteen feet wide and forty-five feet long with approximately four hundred square feet of space for living and laboratory activities.
    Early NEEMO missions tested living and building in an extreme environment, similar to outer space. NEEMO 7 and 9 included doctors but no surgeons. The major purpose of these projects is to enable astronauts to be operated on in space from earth using wireless technology and robotics. One of NEEMO 7's goal was to see whether doctors with no training in surgical techniques could successfully perform surgery with the help of telementoring and telerobotics.
11. Define the Operating Room of the Future.
    In the Operating Room of the Future, images from all sources will be integrated and available to surgeons and other personnel. ". . . [M]ultiple image display processors integrate OR video cameras, laparoscopic and endoscopic cameras, MRI, CT, and PET imagery, PACS images, fluoroscopic imaging, ultrasound, patient monitoring data, hemodynamic activity, and patient history on a single, centralized screen for viewing by the surgical

team." Information displayed includes a patient's vital statistics, allergies, and the wher abouts of operating room personnel. Eventually, the equipment will be identified an tracked also. The display on four screens (called the wall of knowledge) shows integrate patient information in an easy-to-understand format, in one location.

IN THE NEWS

Surgical Device Poses a Rare but Serious Peril

by Barnaby J. Feder

Kristina A. Fox entered a Portland, Ore., hospital in the fall of 1998 hoping a routine, minimally invasive form of surgery called laparoscopy would relieve a painful gynecological condition.

She went home the same day destined to become part of a simmering debate over whether medical device makers and health care providers have been overlooking—some would say ignoring—an easily preventable, but potentially devastating, laparoscopy hazard.

Severe complications are rare among the 4.4 million Americans who undergo laparoscopic surgery each year. And deaths are rarer still. But experts say that what happened to Mrs. Fox is a type of injury that occurs far more often than reported.

As in many laparoscopies, Mrs. Fox's surgeon inserted a wand-like electrical tool into her abdomen to cut tissue and seal blood vessels. A miniature video camera let him view his work, but did not show the stray electricity escaping from the wand's shaft. No one suspected when Mrs. Fox was sent home that a wayward spark might have seared a tiny hole in her colon.

Two days later, Mrs. Fox was rushed to the emergency room, perilously ill from the infectious bacteria that had leaked into her abdomen. Mrs. Fox, now 33, ended up with a malfunctioning bladder and disabling pain that despite frequent follow-up treatments—13 operations so far—prevent her from working or bearing children. She has a lawsuit pending against the device makers, the hospital and the doctor involved.

Her lawsuit argues, as do a number of medical experts, that the risk of accidents from laparoscopic surgery could be sharply reduced with the use of fault-detection devices on the market. But so far, industry sources say, fewer than 25 percent of the nation's hospitals—including more than two dozen military hospitals—have made such investments. Some doctors and nurses say that many surgeons, hospitals and major equipment vendors simply do not recognize the extent of the hazard.

"It wouldn't surprise me in the least if it caused more than 100 deaths and 10,000 injuries annually," said Dr. Alan Johns, a Fort Worth gynecologist who frequently teaches courses on the complications of laparoscopy.

No one has precise data, because the physical evidence of the initial burn is often destroyed in the effort to save patients when infections or other symptoms become apparent days or weeks later, and by then the surgical tools have been discarded or cleaned for reuse. What's more, hospitals are under no obligation to look for evidence of such burns or report the details of such cases.

Safety advocates say the risk of burns can be reduced by relatively inexpensive scanning devices that can be used before surgery to test electrical wands for insulation cracks. Moreover, the risk can be virtually eliminated by using wands with monitoring systems that shut them down instantly if power is leaking.

The shut-off technology, known as active electrode monitoring, costs less than $1,000 per instrument, about the same list price as comparable traditional devices without the safety feature. But because the traditional devices are often bundled with other equipment to reduce their actual price, the electrode monitoring gear often costs more.

Proponents of the safety technology say the repair surgeries and potential malpractice claims from a single major burn exceed the cost of the safety investments.

"The research is out there that shows you need this," said Kay Ball, past president of the Association of Perioperative Registered Nurses, a professional group for operating room nurses that has recommended adoption of safer laparoscopic technology.

One former operating room nurse, Trudy L. Hamilton, says she knows of the risks all too well. She suffered a burned bowel in 1991 as a laparoscopy patient in the Tampa, Fla., hospital where she worked. "I don't think people who say they aren't seeing this problem are lying; I think they are grossly misinformed," said Ms. Hamilton, who now lives in Dublin, Ohio, and has been treated many times for bowel obstructions since her injury.

The risk of inadvertent burns has been recognized since the invention of the first electrical surgical tools in the late 1920's. But the accident rate soared in the 1980's as laparoscopic versions of the devices became widely used in gynecology, gall bladder removal and gastric bypass surgery. By 1993, 54 percent of the laparoscopic surgeons knew colleagues who had run into such burns and 18 percent of them had encountered such "misadventures" in their own practice, according to a survey conducted at a meeting of the American College of Surgeons.

The debate these days is over whether the risks have now been reduced to the point that it is a waste of resources to install safeguard systems or replace the older technology.

The major device makers deny that safer technology is needed. Ethicon Endo-Surgery, a division of Johnson & Johnson, said it had not received any complaints from surgeons or hospitals about malfunctions in its electrical laparoscopes although it has been named a defendant in a burn lawsuit. U.S. Surgical, a Tyco subsidiary, sells wands without an automatic shut-off feature, even though a subsidiary called ValleyLabs, which makes surgical power generators, recommends on its Web site that customers seek out the technology.

Equipment companies that do acknowledge hearing of electrical mishaps like Mrs. Fox's say they occur in isolated cases where hospitals ignore specified limits on how long or frequently to use wands before replacing them. And many doctors agree.

"We don't know how prevalent the problem is, but as surgeons we haven't seen it very often," said Dr. Eric Z. Matayoshi, one of a group of surgeons who track laparoscopic technology for Kaiser Permanente, the nation's largest private health care provider.

Another major health organization, the Veterans Health Administration, said its records showed only four laparoscopic burn cases of any sort since 2000, including those caused by surgical error.

But Kaiser does have the issue on its watch list for possible future action, and some V.A. hospitals have decided on their own to invest in the active electrode monitoring technology, which is made by a small company called Encision.

Encision, based in Boulder, Colo., went public at $10.50 a share in 1996 but now trades below $3.

(continued)

Surgical Device Poses a Rare but Serious Peril *(continued)*

Although Encision has been sounding alarms about the problem for years, its tiny size—revenue of $6.71 million in the nine months that ended Dec. 31—has made it hard to be heard. The company must also battle the perception that its claims, which include injury and death rates several times higher than those estimated by more objective experts like Dr. Johns, may be self-serving.

The InsulScan, the device that scans laparoscopic wands to detect microscopic insulation cracks that can cause burns, was invented by Medicor, a start-up that went bankrupt in 2000 trying to commercialize the device. One of its distributors, privately held Mobile Instrument Service and Repair Inc., took over the business.

Sales are not disclosed but are growing slowly but steadily with backing from Medline Industries, a large medical products distributor, according to Summer L. Babyak, InsulScan's product manager. She said 1,500 hospitals, about 25 percent of the nation's total, use the devices to scan laparoscopic and other electrical surgery equipment. Sold in bulk, InsulScans cost about $50 a wand.

Sales would probably climb if more lawsuits like Mrs. Fox's were filed, but safety advocates say lawyers, like patients, health care providers and insurers, rarely hear of such burns. Mrs. Fox's lawyer, Brian R. Whitehead, who has another similar case pending, said he never thought to look for such injuries until he ran into a friend whose sales portfolio included laparoscopic devices. Over a beer, the salesman said the devices were injuring people and that there was technology available to prevent it.

"He was wondering how the companies got away with it," Mr. Whitehead said. "A week later, Kristina Fox walked into my office."

Computer-Assisted Surgery: An Update

by Michelle Meadows

- A Minimally Invasive Approach
- Patient Safety

The Food and Drug Administration first cleared the da Vinci Surgical System in 2000 for general laparoscopic surgeries such as gall bladder removal and for treatment of severe heartburn. Since then, use of the system has increased and expanded into several other surgical areas. These include removal of the prostate (radical prostatectomy); non-cardiac chest procedures involving the lungs, esophagus, and a blood vessel inside the chest cavity (internal thoracic artery); and certain procedures involving surgical incisions into the heart, such as mitral valve repair.

In April 2005, the FDA cleared the da Vinci system for gynecological laparoscopic procedures. Surgeons are now able to remove the uterus (hysterectomy) and to remove uterine fibroids (myomectomy) using the device. The system has also been cleared for use in all urologic procedures. And, in 2004, the FDA broadened the application of the da Vinci system for assisting in coronary artery bypass surgery.

"The development of this system for use in the heart is a step forward in new technology that eventually could change the practice of surgery," Acting FDA Commissioner Dr. Lester M. Crawford says.

A MINIMALLY INVASIVE APPROACH

Experts say the key benefit of computer-assisted surgery is being able to perform surgery through smaller incisions. W. Randolph Chitwood Jr., M.D., chairman of the department of cardiothoracic surgery at East Carolina University, in Greenville, N.C., says he's experienced the long healing time that comes with big incisions firsthand. For his own heart surgery in 1994, he underwent the traditional procedure for open heart surgery called a sternotomy. It involves a foot-long incision through the breast bone. "It was around that time that I became interested in minimally invasive heart surgery," says Chitwood, who has performed close to 200 mitral valve repairs using the da Vinci system.

"Making smaller incisions means the potential for less pain, less blood loss, and faster recovery for patients," Chitwood says. He is able to repair narrowing or leaking heart valves by making a few small incisions between the ribs. In 2004, the da Vinci system was used in more than 2,400 surgeries related to the heart and chest in the United States. These include mitral valve repair and coronary revascularization, a procedure that bypasses blockages in the coronary arteries so that blood flow to the heart can be restored.

While sitting at a console several feet away from the operating table, the surgeon views the inside of the patient's body by looking through lenses. A magnified 3-D vision system gives an enhanced view of the surgical field. The surgeon moves controls to manipulate the device at the operating table. The da Vinci system has up to four arms that are inserted into the patient through small incisions. One arm holds a miniature camera, and the other arms hold a variety of instruments. Chitwood says the camera serves as his "eyes." The arms have flexible wrists that give surgeons access to hard-to-reach areas. The device doesn't move on its own, but rather cuts and sews at the surgeon's direction.

"The improved vision and flexibility of the instruments allow for increased precision," says Thomas Ahlering, M.D., chief of the division of urologic oncology at the University of California, Irvine, Medical Center. Since 2002, Ahlering has used the da Vinci system to remove the prostate (prostatectomy) in men with prostate cancer. He performed about 100 radical prostatectomies with da Vinci in 2004.

"Even though it's a walnut-sized gland, the prostate is highly functional," Ahlering says. Located below a man's bladder, the prostate is surrounded by nerves and muscles that affect urinary, rectal, and sexual function. Great care and precision are required to remove the prostate without damaging these structures.

With computer-assisted surgery, Ahlering's patients have returned to work in 10 to 14 days, about half the recovery time required for conventional, open surgery, he says. Conventional surgery for removal of the prostate typically requires about a seven-inch incision in the lower abdomen.

"With the da Vinci system, the blood loss for patients is about one-fifth to one-tenth of what it would be for open surgery," Ahlering says. "Also, the urinary catheter remains in for about half as long, and patients tend to get urinary control and sexual function back more quickly." Research has shown that there is also less use of narcotic medication during the recovery period. In 2004, there were more than 8,000 radical prostatectomies performed with the da Vinci system in the United States.

(continued)

Computer-Assisted Surgery: An Update *(continued)*

PATIENT SAFETY

Ahlering says that based on his experience so far, the risks with computer-assisted surgery appear to be less than with other forms of surgery. "Risks such as bleeding and needing a transfusion or cutting into the rectum are lower with this procedure," he says.

Rarely, doctors may have to switch from the device to a traditional method of surgery. "Once a camera went out, but we had another system and were able to use that," Ahlering says. "If I didn't have another one, I would have either had to switch to open surgery or reschedule it for another day if it was early enough in the procedure."

To date, there have been no patient injuries or deaths attributed to system failures with the device, according to the da Vinci manufacturer, Intuitive Surgical Inc., of Sunnyvale, Calif. The FDA tracks adverse events related to medical devices. Chitwood says he has had one patient die during a computer-assisted procedure. "This was due to a medication reaction, not a device failure," he says.

In 2002, a Florida man died two days after blood vessels were accidentally cut during a surgery for kidney removal with da Vinci. Shortly after the death, officials at St. Joseph's Hospital in Tampa, Fla., called the incident "a tragic, isolated event."

Patients considering robotic surgery should talk with their doctors about the benefits, risks, and any factors that would exclude them as candidates. For example, previous abdominal surgery, obesity, or a prostate that's too large are among the factors that might exclude a patient from having a radical prostatectomy with da Vinci, Ahlering says. He suggests that consumers consider the experience of the surgeon and seek out medical centers that focus on computer-assisted procedures.

The da Vinci Surgical System is the only operative surgical device of its kind on the market in the United States. In 2003, Intuitive Surgical bought Computer Motion of Goleta, Calif. Computer Motion was the manufacturer of the Zeus Robotic Surgical System, which is no longer actively being marketed.

According to Intuitive Surgical, there are 286 da Vinci systems installed worldwide, including 204 in the United States, 56 in Europe, and 26 in Asia and other parts of the world.

SOURCES

Ackerman, Jeremy. "Ultrasound Visualization Research." June 15, 2000. http://www.cs.unc.edu/Research/us/ (accessed December 14, 2007).

Argenziano, Michael. "Robotically Assisted, Minimally Invasive Cardiac Surgery." 2002. http://www.nyp.org/masc/davinci.htm (accessed December 14, 2007).

"Artemis Medical Receives 510K Clearance on New Image Guided Biopsy Device." April 22, 2002. http://goliath.ecnext.com/coms2/summary_0199-1664257_ITM (August 23, 2006).

Bargar, W. L., A. Bauer, and M. Borner. "Primary and Revision Total Hip Replacement Usin the Robodoc System." September 1998. http://www.ncbi.nlm.nih.gov/entrez/query.fcgi?cmd=Retrieve&db=PubMed&list_uids=9755767&dopt=Abstract (accessed December 14, 2007).

Christensen, Bill. "NEEMO 7: NASA's Undersea Robotic Telemedicine Experiment." October 15, 2004. http://www.technovelgy.com/ct/Science-Fiction-News.asp?NewsNum=227 (accessed December 14, 2007).

Cleary, Kevin, and Charles Nguyen. "State of the Art in Surgical Robotics: Clinical Applications and Technology Challenges." http://www3.interscience.wiley.com/cgi-bin/abstract/93012897/ABSTRACT (accessed December 14, 2007).

Cropper, Carol Marie. "The Robot Is In—and Ready to Operate." *Business Week,* March 14, 2005.

Cuellar, Al. "What Is New in Total Hip and Knee Replacement Surgery." August 14, 2006. http://www.ksfortho.com/en/art/?19 (accessed August 23, 2006).

Eisenberg, Anne. "What's Next; a Sharper Picture of What Ails the Body." January 24, 2002. http://query.nytimes.com/gst/fullpage.html?res=9E04E7DE113BF937A15752C0A9649C8B63 (accessed December 14, 2007).

Eisenberg, Anne. "What's Next; Restoring the Human Touch to Remote-Controlled Surgery." May 30, 2002. http://query.nytimes.com/gst/fullpage.html?res=9506EED7113BF933A05756C0A9649C8B63 (accessed December 14, 2007).

"FDA Clearance of da Vinci Surgical System for Intracardiac Surgery Now Encompasses 'ASD' Closure." 2005. http://findarticles.com/p/articles/mi_m0EIN/is_2003_Jan_30/ai_97073329 (accessed December 21, 2007).

"FINANCE: Medical Device Company Closes $12 Million Series B Financing." January 19, 2004. http://www.newsrx.com/article.php?articleID=132367 (accessed December 14, 2007).

"Florida Man Dies After Surgery Involving Robotic Device." October 31, 2002. http://www.injuryboard.com/national-news/florida-man-dies.aspx? (accessed December 14, 2007).

Graham Rowe, Duncan. "Scrubbing Up for Robotic Surgery in Space." October 11, 2004. http://www.newscientist.com/article/dn6512-scrubbing-up-for-robotic-surgery-in-space.html (accessed December 14, 2007).

Hall, Alan. "Surgical Robots Make the Cut." June 14, 2001. http://www.businessweek.com/bwdaily/dnflash/jun2001/nf20010614_799.htm (accessed December 14, 2007).

"Heart Surgery Without the Surgeon: Researchers Test Evalve for Noninvasive Mitral Valve Repair." August 23, 2006. http://www.columbiasurgery.org/pat/cardiac/news_evalve.html (accessed December 14, 2007).

Hendrickson, Dyke. "EndoVia Sees a Better Surgical Way." *Mass High Tech: The Journal of New England Technology,* September 6, 2002. http://masshightech.bizjournals.com/masshightech/stories/2002/09/09/story14.html (accessed December 14, 2007).

Humphries, Kelly, and Delores Beasley. "NASA Prepares for Space Exploration in Undersea Lab." March 28, 2006. http://www.nasa.gov/home/hqnews/2006/mar/HQ_06109_NEEMO_9.html (accessed December 14, 2007).

"Integrated Operating Room Systems Look to Become OR of the Future." 2006. http://www.medcompare.com/spotlight.asp?spotlightid=123 (accessed December 14, 2007).

Lanfranco, Anthony R., Andres E. Castellanos, Jaydev P. Desai, and William C. Meyers. "Robotic Surgery. A Current Perspective." January 2004. http://www.pubmedcentral.nih.gov/articlerender.fcgi?artid=1356187 (accessed August 23, 2006).

"Leading Edge Display Technologies for the 'Digital Operating Room of the Future.'" rgb.com, June 23, 2006 (accessed July 7, 2006).

Livingston, Mark. "UNC Laparoscopic Visualization Research." August 11, 1998. http://www.cs.unc.edu/Research/us/laparo.html (accessed December 14, 2007).

Mack, Michael J. "Minimally Invasive and Robotic Surgery." *JAMA* 285, no. 5 (2001): 568–72.

Malik, Tariq. "NASA's NEEMO 9: Remote Surgery and Mock Moonwalks on the Sea Floor." April 19, 2006. http://www.space.com/businesstechnology/060419_neemo9_techwed.html (accessed December 14, 2007).

Martinez-Serna, T., and C. J. Filipi. "Endoluminal Surgery." *World Journal of Surgery* 23, no. 4 (1999): 368–77. http://www.ncbi.nlm.nih.gov/sites/entrez?db=pubmed& uid=10030860&cmd=showdetailview (accessed December 14, 2007).

Matthews, Melissa, Kelly Humphries, Nicole Gignac, and Fred Gorell. "Undersea Habitat Becomes Experimental Hospital for NEEMO 7." August 11, 2004. http://www.nasa.gov/centers/johnson/news/releases/2004/H04-264.html (accessed December 14, 2007).

Meadows, Michelle. "Computer-Assisted Surgery: An Update." July–August 2005. http://www.fda.gov/fdac/features/2005/405_computer.html (accessed December 14, 2007).

Meadows, Michelle. "Robots Lend a Helping Hand to Surgeons." *FDA Consumer,* May–June 2002. http://www.fda.gov/Fdac/features/2002/302_bots.html (accessed December 14, 2007).

"Medical Robotics @ UC Berkeley." January 2002. http://robotics.eecs.berkeley.edu/medical/ (accessed December 14, 2007).

"Memorial Sloan-Kettering Cancer Center Using LiveData's OR-Dashboard: 'Wall of Knowledge' Deployed to 21 New Operating Rooms." June 19, 2006. http://www.livedata.com/content/view/83/ (accessed December 14, 2007).

NASA Feature. "About Aquarius." March 28, 2006. http://www.nasa.gov/lb/mission_pages/NEEMO/facilities.html (accessed December 14, 2007).

"NASA, NEEMO History." March 21, 2006. http://www.nasa.gov/mission_pages/NEEMO/history.html (accessed December 14, 2007).

"New York Weill Cornell Performs Among First Minimally Invasive Kidney Removals in Children and Infants in New York." January 2002. http://www.nycornell.org/news/press/kidney1.html (accessed December 14, 2007).

Olsen, Stefanie. "Tomorrow's Operating Room to Harness Net, RFID." October 19, 2005. http://www.news.com/Tomorrows-operating-room-to-harness-Net%2C-RFID/2100-1008_3-5900990.html?tag=ne.gall.related (accessed December 21, 2007).

Peterson, Lynne. "Trends-in-Medicine." April 2004. http://www.crtonline.org/PDF/trends-in-medicine-4-04.pdf (accessed December 14, 2007).

Rafiq, Azhar, James A. Moore, Xiaoming Zhao, Charles R. Doarn, and Ronald C. Merrell. "Digital Video Capture and Synchronous Consultation in Open Surgery." *Annals of Surgery* 239, no. 4 (2004): 567–73. http://www.pubmedcentral.gov/articlerender.fcgi?tool=pmcentrez&rendertype=abstract&artid=1356263 (accessed August 24, 2006).

"Redefining Surgery." August 23, 2006. http://robodoc.com/ (accessed August 23, 2006).

"Remote Control Telemedicine: Sponsored by the National Institutes of Health." http://www.nitrd.gov/ngi/apps/nih/rem.html (accessed December 14, 2007).

Rentschler, Mark E., Jason Dumpert, Stephen E. Platt, Shane M. Farritor, and Dmitry Oleynikov. "Natural Orifice Surgery with an Endoluminal Mobile Robot" (presented at the 2006 SAGES Meeting). http://robots.unl.edu/Files/Papers2/Rentschler_Natural_Orifice_Robot_with_figures.pdf (accessed December 14, 2007).

"Revolutionizing Trauma Surgery." August 23, 2006. http://ortho.smith-nephew.com/uk/Standard.asp?NodeId=3399 (accessed December 14, 2007).

"Robot Reduces Spinal Injury Risk." March 12, 2000. http://news.bbc.co.uk/2/hi/health/672815.stm (accessed December 14, 2007).

"Robotic Surgical Assistant for Brain Surgery." NASA Space Telerobotic Program, May 10, 1996. http://ranier.hq.nasa.gov/telerobotics_page/Technologies/0904.html (accessed August 23, 2006).

Ropp, Kevin L. "Robots in the Operating Room." *FDA Consumer*, July/August, 1993, reprinted in 2002. http://www.fda.gov/bbs/topics/CONSUMER/CON00242.html (accessed December 14, 2007).

Samadi, David. "Prostate Cancer Treatment—da Vinci Robotic Surgery." http://roboticoncology.com/Da-Vinci-Robotic-Prostatectomy.php (accessed December 21, 2007).

Schaaf, Tracy. "Robotic Surgery: The Future Is Now." Originally published March, 2001. 2006. http://www.devicelink.com/mx/archive/01/03/0103mx024.html (accessed August 23, 2006).

Schirber, Michael. "NEEMO's Undersea Operations: Making Telemedicine a Long Distance Reality." October 19, 2004. http://www.space.com/scienceastronomy/neemo_surgery_041019.html (accessed December 14, 2007).

Schurr, M. O., G. Buess, and K. Schwarz. "Robotics in Endoscopic Surgery: Can Mechanical Manipulators Provide a More Simple Solution for the Problem of Limited Degrees of Freedom?" Abstract, November 1, 2001. http://www.informaworld.com/smpp/content~db=all~content=a713750297? (accessed December 14, 2007).

"Simulation Development and Cognitive Science Lab." February 24, 2006. http://www.hmc.psu.edu/simulation/equipment/expert/expert.htm (accessed August 23, 2006).

Stiehl, James. "Computer-Assisted Surgery in Adult Reconstruction." 2003. http://64.233.161.104/search?q=cache:gcvMjNmAyyMJ:www.touchbriefings.com/pdf/1680/Steihl.pdf+%E2%80%9CPrimary+and+Revision+Total+Hip+Replacement+Using+Robodoc,%E2%80%9D&hl=en&gl=us&ct=clnk&cd=1/ (accessed August 23, 2006).

"Tagged Surgical Sponges Help Prevent Deadly Problem." July 18, 2006. http://www.medicalnewstoday.com/articles/47583.php (accessed December 14, 2007).

Vaze, Ajit. "Robotic Laparoscopic Surgery: A Comparison of the Da Vinci and Zeus Systems." 2002. http://www.bhj.org/journal/2002_4402_apr/endo_208.htm (accessed August 24, 2006).

Versweyveld, Leslie. "Lower Cost, Portable Surgical Robots Could be Smooth Operators." March 2, 2006. http://www.hoise.com/vmw/06/articles/vmw/LV-VM-04-06-13.html (accessed December 14, 2007).

Versweyveld, Leslie. "Socrates Surgical Mentor Allows Surgeon Experts to Provide Remote Guidance in Complex Procedures." Virtual Medical Worlds, March 8, 2001. http://www.hoise.com/vmw/01/articles/vmw/LV-VM-04-01-8.html (accessed August 24, 2006).

Versweyveld, Leslie. "Thoroscopic Surgery Robots Now FDA-Approved for Use in United States Hospitals." Virtual Medical Worlds, March 6, 2001. http://www.hoise.com/vmw/01/articles/vmw/LV-VM-04-01-12.html (accessed August 24, 2006).

Versweyveld, Leslie. "Undersea Habitat Becomes Experimental Hospital for Remote Medical Care in NEEMO 7 Project." August 11, 2004. http://www.hoise.com/vmw/04/articles/vmw/LV-VM-09-04-8.html (accessed December 14, 2007).

Versweyveld, Leslie. "US Food and Drug Administration Kept Busy Approving Surgical Robots from Various Market Competitors." Virtual Medical Worlds, October 17, 2001. http://www.hoise.com/vmw/01/articles/vmw/LV-VM-11-01-20.html (accessed December 14, 2007).

"Virtual Environments for Surgical Training and Augmentation." February 27, 2001. http://robotics.eecs.berkeley.edu/medical/research.html#sim (accessed December 14, 2007).

RELATED WEB SITES

http://www.cts.usc.edu/videos.html.

CHAPTER 8

Information Technology in Pharmacy

CHAPTER OUTLINE

LEARNING OBJECTIVES

After reading this chapter, the student will be able to

- Describe the Food and Drug Administration (FDA).
- Discuss uncertified medicines as a safety issue.
- Describe the contributions of information technology to the development and testing of drugs.
- Define biotechnology and rational drug design.
- Discuss the significance of the Human Genome Project (HGP) and its contribution to the understanding of genetic diseases.
- List the uses of computers in clinical drug trials.
- Discuss the relationship of the understanding of the molecular basis of a disease to real breakthroughs in treatment.
- List the uses of computer technology in pharmacies including:

- The use of computers in the neighborhood drug store, from the printing drug information for customers, to the full automation of the process of filli prescriptions using robots and barcodes;
- The use of computers in hospital pharmacies
  - in centralized dispensing systems using robots and barcodes;
  - in decentralized point-of-use dispensing units;
  - in computerized IVs.
- Discuss telepharmacy—the linking of pharmacists via telecommunications lin to dispensing units in remote locations such as doctors' offices.
- Discuss the impact of information technology on pharmacy, as it affects pharm cists, patients, and hospital administrators.

KEY TERMS

antisense technology
barcodes
bioinformatics
biotechnology
computer-assisted trial design (CATD)
computerized physician order entry (CPOE) system
DNA (deoxyribonucleic acid)
Food and Drug Administration (FDA)
Human Genome Project (HGP)
PDUFA (Prescription Drug User Fees Act renewed in 1997 and 2002)
Physiome Project
radio frequency identification (RFID) tags
rational drug design
ribonucleic acid (RNA)
RNA interference (RNAi)
scientific visualization
stem cells
telepharmacy

DISCUSSION QUESTIONS

1. Define and briefly discuss biotechnology.
   Biotechnology sees the human body as a collection of molecules and seeks to understan and treat disease in terms of these molecules. It attempts to identify the molecule causing problem and then create another to correct it. Specific drugs are aimed at inhibiting t work of a specific disease-causing agent. In order to be effective, the drug needs to bind its target molecule. It needs to fit, something like a key in a lock. To achieve an exact fit, t precise structure of the target must be mapped. Powerful computers allow scientists to crea graphical models.
2. Discuss rational drug design.
   One way of developing drugs with the help of computers is called rational drug desig Developing drugs by design requires mapping the structure and creating a three-dimension graphical model of the target molecule. Because this involves a huge number of mathem ical calculations, without computers the process took many years; after the calculatio were completed, a wire model of the molecule had to be constructed. Now, supercompute accurately do the calculations in a small fraction of the time, and graphical software pr duces the image on a computer screen.
3. Define bioinformatics.
   The application of information technology to biology is called bioinformatics. This fie seeks to organize biological data into databases. The information is then available researchers who can search through existing data and add new entries of their own.
4. Define the Human Genome Project. Discuss the relationship of computers t the project.
   The Human Genome Project, sponsored in the United States by the National Institutes Health and the Department of Energy, began in 1990 and involved hundreds of scientis all over the world. The goal is to find the location of the 100,000 or so human genes an

to read the entire genetic script, all three billion bits of information, by the year 2005. The project has succeeded in mapping the human genome. One of its goals is an attempt to understand the molecular bases of genetic diseases. This project would be inconceivable without computers and the Internet. Computers are used to keep track of the genes as they are identified; this prevents duplication of effort and ensures that no genes are overlooked. The Internet allows findings to be immediately communicated to scientists working on the project anywhere in the world.

5. What is the relationship between understanding the genetic basis of a disease and treating the disease?
Three to four thousand diseases are caused by errors in genes. Altered genes also contribute to the development of other disorders such as cancer, heart disease, and diabetes. The Human Genome Project expects to be able to identify such genes, which might make prevention, early detection, and treatment possible. Once the gene is identified, drugs can be designed. Treatment may include gene therapy to replace the defective gene or the development of drugs.
6. Comment on recent developments in biotechnology. Refer to Herceptin, Lucentis, and Avastin in your answer.
In September 1998, the U.S. Food and Drug Administration (FDA) approved Herceptin as effective against certain types of metastatic breast cancer. Herceptin can work for patients who have too much of a specific gene in their tumor cells. Clinical trials for Lucentis for the treatment of macular degeneration continued in 2003. Lucentis is an antibody that binds to a protein that is involved in the formation of blood vessels. In 2003, the FDA approved fast track status for the development, testing, and review of Avastin, an antibody that inhibits the protein that plays a role in the maintenance and metastases of tumors.
7. Define RNA interference.
Another new technology aimed at drug development is called RNA interference or RNAi. RNA stands for ribonucleic acid. It is made in the nucleus of a cell but is not restricted to the nucleus. It is a long coiled up molecule whose purpose is to take the blueprint from deoxyribonucleic acid (DNA) and build our actual proteins. RNAi is a process that cells use to turn off genes. The attempt at developing drugs based on RNAi is in its infancy and would, if successful, turn off genes associated with disease. Prior attempts at turning off genes with drugs have not succeeded.
8. Define antisense technology.
Antisense technology is one experimental technology used to develop drugs to shut off disease-causing genes. It has not been very successful. In a large clinical trial of a drug called Genasense, the results were mixed.
9. Comment on the use of computers in drug trials.
Software has been developed that allows companies to simulate clinical trials on a computer before the actual trials begin. A simulated drug trial uses information about the drug's effects from earlier trials, animal studies, or trials of similar drugs. By trying out many "what ifs" on computer models, the actual trials can be more precisely designed, making it more likely that they will be definitive.
10. Describe the Physiome Project.
The Physiome Project is an international project seeking to create mathematical models of human organs—"digital models of every system and anatomical feature of the human body. . . ." It has created a virtual heart using mathematical equations to simulate the processes of the heart. It has been used in studies of irregular heartbeats. A draft of the lungs and skeletal system has been finished. The project is currently working on the digestive system and a database of cellular functions. In the future, the project hopes to model the nervous, endocrine, immune, sensory, skin, kidney–urinary, and reproductive systems. Utilizing these mathematical models, the project hopes to find treatments for conditions such as arthritis and autoimmune disorders. These mathematical models will not only allow the testing of drugs, but "also enable medical engineers to fashion customized

implants . . ." and surgeons to perform "dry runs" of surgeries. The use of these models still far from reality. Computer-assisted drug trials are not a replacement for actual clinic trials; they are a tool to make the trials more effective.

11. What is the purpose of computer-assisted trial design?
    The purpose of computer-assisted trial design (CATD) is to decrease the time and mon spent on the trial phase of drug development.
12. Discuss the effect of computerized warning systems on adverse drug events.
    Computer warning systems can be used to prevent adverse drug events (ADEs). Serio ADEs occur in about 7 percent of patients admitted to hospitals. Many of these are cause by a physician prescribing either the wrong drug or the wrong dosage, because of lack knowledge of either the patient or the drug. In 1994, a computerized warning system w designed and put into place in one hospital. The hospital already had in place a databa with patient information; the existing system warned of a patient's specific drug allerg and of adverse drug interactions. The new alert system added warnings of other like ADEs. In July 2006, "Preventing Medical Errors" stressed that medication errors are sti a serious problem, harming 1.5 million people per year. Several thousand die each yea With the aging population, more medications are prescribed and more errors are mad Like the 1999 Report, "To Err is Human . . . ," the 2006 report recommends the use e-prescribing and electronic health records.
13. Describe a computerized pharmacy that uses robots and bar codes.
    A fully automated dispensing system involves the employment of a robot. In one such sy tem, a prescription is entered into the pharmacy computer; the pharmacy computer, i turn, activates the pharmacy robot, which first determines what size vial is needed for th prescription—from the three available sizes. A robotic arm grips the correct size. One syste has two hundred cells, each containing a different drug. The arm is moved to the corre cell; the tablets or capsules are counted by a sensor and dropped into the vial. The com puter prints a label and puts it on the vial, which is delivered via a conveyer belt to th pharmacist. The pharmacist uses a bar code reader to scan the bar code on the label; a image of the medication and prescription information appears on the screen. The pharma cist puts the lid on and gives the customer the prescription.
14. Describe point-of-use dispensing.
    Some computerized hospital pharmacies are using point-of-use dispensing of drugs— decentralized automated system. A small computer attached to a large cabinet sits at th nursing unit. It is networked to the hospital pharmacy computer. A nurse types a pas word, and the unit displays a list of patients; the nurse selects the patient and enters th drug order, and the computer delivers it by opening the drawer containing the medicatio the nurse enters the name of the drug and closes the drawer. The computer keeps track of a drug transactions, for billing and inventory purposes.
15. What are some of the advantages of point-of-use dispensing over traditiona medication dispensing?
    Point-of-use dispensing has several advantages over traditional manual dispensing. shortens the time between the order for a medication and its delivery to the patien Automating drug distribution improves patient care in other ways too. Drugs are mo likely to be administered on schedule, and significantly fewer doses are missed. Althoug apparently not reducing dispensing errors to zero like centralized robotic systems claim do, one study found that a decentralized system decreased dispensing errors by almost one third. Decentralized computerized drug delivery has a positive financial impact for the hos pital, making it more likely that patients are charged for the medications used. It als decreases the time nurses spend on medication-related activities, such as counting con trolled substances, charting, documentation, and billing.
16. Define telepharmacy.
    Telepharmacy involves using a computer, a network connection, and a drug-dispensin unit to allow patients to obtain drugs outside of a traditional pharmacy, at, for example a doctor's office or clinic.

17. What are some of the advantages of telepharmacy?
Telepharmacy promises to be especially helpful in rural areas and underserved urban neighborhoods where there is no accessible local pharmacy. Using a telepharmacy connection can mean that the patient walks out of the doctor's office with the medication in hand, having already teleconsulted with the pharmacist; neither patient nor pharmacist has to travel. It could prove to be particularly beneficial to populations who cannot travel easily. The elderly, for example, have a poor drug compliance record—due in part to their difficulty traveling. There are several other advantages to telepharmacy. A telepharmacy does not need to fill as many prescriptions as a conventional pharmacy to be cost-effective. Entering prescriptions directly into a computer may cut down on dispensing errors caused by illegible handwriting.
18. What are some of the problems associated with the expansion of telepharmacy?
There are problems with telepharmacy that could slow its expansion. Pharmacy has traditionally been subject to state regulation. Each state has different pharmacy regulations. The National Association of Boards of Pharmacy has model telepharmacy regulations, but only some states have adopted them.
19. Describe the implantable chip that delivers medication.
Newly developed chips with embedded medications can be surgically implanted in the patient. The drug may be released by diffusion. It may be embedded in a biodegradable material that releases as it degrades.
20. Describe some of the potential uses and advantages of using an implanted chip to deliver medication.
Some of the potential uses of the chip include delivering an entire course of medication over a period of months, delivering a series of vaccines at the correct time, and delivering medication that needs to be taken continuously, including painkillers and medications for chronic conditions. This "pharmacy on a chip" is completely biodegradable. One advantage of using chips to deliver medication is that because they bypass the stomach, they avoid stomach upsets.
21. Discuss changes in the FDA funding since 1992.
Since the 1992 passage of PDUFA (Prescription Drug User Fees Act renewed in 1997, 2002, and 2007) that requires drug companies to pay fees to support the drug review process and "companies [to] pay annual fees for each manufacturing establishment and for each prescription drug product marketed," user fees have steadily risen, until in 1992, 51 percent of the FDA's drug review budget came from the companies that the FDA regulates. Between 1996 and 2006, Congressional appropriations to the FDA stayed the same, whereas from 1998 to 2005, user fees doubled. In 2004, the $232 million in fees made up 53 percent of the FDA's new-drug review budget. In 2006, $380 million will come from drug user fees.
PDUFA authorized the FDA to collect fees from companies that produce certain human drug and biological products. Any time a company wants the FDA to approve a new drug or biologic prior to marketing, it must submit an application along with a fee to support the review process. In addition, companies pay annual fees for each manufacturing establishment and for each prescription drug product marketed. Previously, taxpayers alone paid for product reviews through budgets provided by Congress. In the new program, industry provides the funding in exchange for the FDA agreement to meet drug-review performance goals, which emphasize timeliness.
22. Define and discuss stem cells.
Stem cells are cells that can develop into different types of body cells; theoretically, they can repair the body. As a stem cell divides, the new cells can stay a stem cell or become another kind of cell. It is possible that stem cell research may lead to regenerative or rehabilitative medicine. Stem cells are special in a number of ways: "First, they are unspecialized cells that renew themselves for long periods through cell division. The second is that under certain physiologic or experimental conditions, they can be induced to become cells with special functions such as the beating cells of the heart muscle or the insulin-producing cells of the pancreas." Many scientists feel that stem cell research may hold the possibility of future cures, preventions, and therapies.

IN THE NEWS

Prevention: Computer Fails Its Drug Test

by Nicholas Bakalar

According to a study published last week in Archives of Internal Medicine, a computer for hospital physicians reduces errors involving medicines, but it still fails to prevent a large number of "adverse drug events"—defined as overdoses, allergic reactions or other medication-caused problems.

Among 937 randomly selected admissions, researchers at the Salt Lake City Veterans Affairs Medical Center, researchers found 483 drug events that they considered clinically significant.

No evidence suggested that the computerized system was responsible for additional events, but the computer program offered no significant benefits in drug selection, dosage and monitoring, which were largely responsible for the side effects.

Dr. Jonathan R. Nebeker, a V.A. researcher and the lead author, said three-quarters of the adverse drug events were not due to medication error.

"We need to broaden our focus from errors alone," Dr. Nebeker said. "Where computers come in is to help physicians take into account the multiple factors that considered together will make the difference in whether a patient suffers a drug-related injury."

Dr. Steven Rappaport, who oversees computerized systems for the V.A., agrees. "There's a lot more information that a system could provide a doctor," he said. "What's the right dose? What's the right medicine? What's the right kind of lab test to order now that we've started a patient on this medicine?"

Digital Rx: Take Two Aspirins and E-Mail Me in the Morning

by Milt Freudenheim

Doctors may no longer make house calls, but they are answering patient e-mail messages—and being paid for it.

In a move to improve efficiency and control costs, health plans and medical groups around the country are now beginning to pay doctors to reply by e-mail, just as they pay for office visits. While some computer-literate doctors have been using e-mail to communicate informally with patients for years, most have never been paid for that service.

Brian Settlemoir, 39, an accountant in Folsom, Calif., recently sent an e-mail message to his doctor at the Creekside Medical Group to ask if it was time to reduce the dosage of a medicine after his cholesterol level dropped. The prompt answer was "not yet."

"I'm sitting at work," Mr. Settlemoir said. "I've got e-mail open anyway. It's much easier than calling and getting voice-mail prompts and sitting on hold. It's very valuable to me."

Blue Shield of California pays his doctor $25 for each online exchange, the same as it pays for an office visit. Some insurers pay a bit less for e-mailing, and patients in some health plans are charged a $5 or $10 co-payment that is billed to their credit card and relayed to the doctor.

For doctors, the convenience of online exchanges can be considerable. They say they can offer advice about postsurgical care, diet, changing a medication and other topics that can be handled safely and promptly without an office visit or a frustrating round of telephone tag. And surveys have shown that e-mail, by reducing the number of daily office visits, gives physicians more time to spend with patients who need to be seen face to face.

For patients, e-mail allows them to send their medical questions from home in the evening, without missing work and spending time in a doctor's waiting room. In fact, many say exchanges in the more relaxed, conversational realm of e-mail make them feel closer to their doctors.

The patients can also use the e-mail connections, which they reach through secure Web sites, to get X-ray and test results and request prescription renewals. Doctors are not paid for these services, except in time saved in the office.

This shift toward online doctor-patient communication is important for another reason. Physicians and health care technology specialists say they believe that it could help spur the changeover to electronic health care information systems, which government officials and industry leaders say is needed to reduce medical errors and promote better care. Doctors at the clinics of the University of California, Davis, grew accustomed to using e-mail for clinical purposes before the clinics introduced electronic medical records, said Dr. Eric Liederman, medical director of clinical information systems at Davis. The messaging "gave them some comfort and facility with using the computer," he said.

Early research at clinics at the university found that using e-mail improved the productivity of physicians, decreased overhead costs and improved access to doctors for patients, including those who still telephoned. "There was a huge reduction in the number of calls," said Dr. Liederman, who is a big fan of e-mail exchanges.

Doctors and insurers say online consultations can be especially useful for patients who have chronic conditions like diabetes, asthma and heart problems. They have been frequent users and being in touch can help them to comply with regimens to cope with their diseases.

"Patients love this stuff; I love this stuff; the staff loves this stuff," said Dr. Barbara Walters, a senior medical director at Dartmouth-Hitchcock Medical Center in New Hampshire.

One benefit of online messaging—perhaps because it can be done in a setting less harried than a doctor's office—is that it gives patients a greater degree of control.

"The intelligence of our patients never ceases to amaze me," Dr. Walters said. "Patients can describe what's going on with them, if given the chance and given the time." Since last year, several health plans—Anthem Blue Cross, Cigna and Harvard Pilgrim—have been paying Dartmouth-Hitchcock $30 for each online "visit," Dr. Walters said. In some health plans, a co-payment by the patient reduces the insurer's share. The medical center gives participating doctors credits—an e-mail consultation is valued at half an office visit—that increases their pay.

Blue Cross and Blue Shield plans in California, New York, Florida, Massachusetts, New Hampshire, Colorado and Tennessee are beginning to pay doctors similar amounts ($24 to $30, including any co-payment) for online consultations. Blue Cross of California has made the program available to 160,000 of its 6 million health plan members. Last month, Empire Blue Cross and Blue Shield began testing the payment system with New York doctors at the Columbia University and Weill Cornell Medical Centers.

Kaiser Permanente, the nation's largest nonprofit managed care company, has tested patient-physician messaging in the Pacific Northwest and is starting the

(continued)

Digital Rx: Take Two Aspirins and E-Mail Me in the Morning *(continued)*

program this year in Hawaii and Colorado as part of Kaiser's $3 billion information technology program. Kaiser's salaried doctors get credits for messaging, adding to their pay.

System providers say overuse by doctors and fraud have not been problems. RelayHealth, a secure electronic system used by the Blue Cross and Blue Shield plans, for example, provides monthly user reports with names of doctors and patients.

Doctors who use the medical messaging services are advised to limit their replies to appropriate topics, and, under standard rules, the doctors reply only to patients who have already been examined in the office.

The records could even be useful in fending off medical malpractice lawsuits, according to Eric Zimmerman, a senior vice president of RelayHealth, based in Emeryville, Calif., because allegations based on undocumented telephone calls are often hard to rebut. "Good communications with patients is protective," said Frank A. Sloan, an economist at Duke University who has studied malpractice suits. "This kind of interaction is helpful."

Many of the health plans promoting Internet consultations are also introducing electronic systems that keep track of a patient's medical records and send prescriptions to the pharmacy. For doctors in small private practices who have hesitated to invest in computerized systems, the e-mail exchanges are often a first step into the growing world of health care information technology.

Online consulting is "one of the biggest changes to come to health care since the beginning of the electronic medical record itself," said Judith R. Faulkner, chief executive of Epic Systems, a health information technology company based in Madison, Wis., that is working with Kaiser.

The federal Centers for Medicare and Medicaid Systems is sponsoring a study of disease management programs, including payments for online consultations, to help the government decide whether the benefits would justify the cost to Medicare.

Dr. David J. Brailer, the government's health information technology coordinator, said online communications between patients and physicians were "one of 12 strategies to achieve President Bush's goal of widespread adoption of technology" in health care. But he said more experience was needed before asking Medicare to pay for those exchanges.

A bill introduced in the House on Feb. 11 by Charles A. Gonzalez, a Democrat from Texas, and John M. McHugh, a Republican from New York, for the first time included a provision to authorize Medicare to make "bonus payments" to doctors for e-mail consultations.

To comply with federal privacy requirements, medical information technology companies like RelayHealth, Epic and IDX, which is based in South Burlington, Vt., make secure software allowing only the doctor and his staff access to a patient's medical records, including the e-mail exchanges.

Doctors can connect with the secure systems over the Internet from home computers or laptops if they wish, but overnight messages are typically answered the next day.

Some employers are embracing medical e-mailing as a way to help maintain workers' productivity. "Why do I have to leave my office to check out my sore throat?" asked Dr. Jeff Rideout, corporate medical director of Cisco Systems, the big Silicon Valley technology company.

Cisco is paying the Palo Alto Medical Foundation for a one-year trial with the first 500 employees to sign up to see if providing online answers to medical questions eliminates unnecessary appointments for employees. The company's health costs have been rising at 10 percent a year, eroding overall productivity gains, Dr. Rideout said.

Sixty-nine of the foundation's 300 primary care doctors are online in a system provided by Epic. Dr. Paul Tang, the Palo Alto group's chief medical information officer, said it charged $60 a year for patients using the service.

Dr. Tang said most users were people with chronic diseases who were willing to pay for better access to their doctors. But other medical groups said they would prefer that insurers pay for e-mail consultations so there would be no barriers for patients.

The American Medical Association has issued a temporary identification number for online visits in the association's "current procedural terminology" code that doctors and hospitals use in sending bills. But Robert Mills, a spokesman, said the association was waiting for more data on how clinical messaging was being used before issuing code numbers like those for office examinations and follow-up visits that payers refer to in their schedules of fees. "All consumer surveys in the last several years show patients want to be able to communicate through e-mail or messaging," said Dr. Thomas Handler, research director at the Gartner Group, the technology consulting firm. "The problem was, reimbursements for the doctors weren't there."

That is changing quickly. One pleased consumer, Dona Gapp, a schoolteacher in New York, who is expecting her first child in April, said she used e-mail to ask Dr. Richard U. Levine, her obstetrician at the Columbia University Medical Center, if certain vitamins and nonprescription medicines were safe for her.

"It was much easier to have access by e-mail," she said. "When I had a chance to call, it was after 5 o'clock and he was not there." He replied to her e-mail within hours, she said.

Panel Suggests Using Inmates in Drug Trials

by Ian Urbina

PHILADELPHIA, Aug. 7—An influential federal panel of medical advisers has recommended that the government loosen regulations that severely limit the testing of pharmaceuticals on prison inmates, a practice that was all but stopped three decades ago after revelations of abuse.

The proposed change includes provisions intended to prevent problems that plagued earlier programs. Nevertheless, it has dredged up a painful history of medical mistreatment and incited debate among prison rights advocates and researchers about whether prisoners can truly make uncoerced decisions, given the environment they live in.

Supporters of such programs cite the possibility of benefit to prison populations, and the potential for contributing to the greater good.

Until the early 1970's, about 90 percent of all pharmaceutical products were tested on prison inmates, federal officials say. But such research diminished sharply in 1974 after revelations of abuse at prisons like Holmesburg here, where inmates were paid hundreds of dollars a month to test items as varied as dandruff treatments and dioxin, and where they were exposed to radioactive, hallucinogenic and carcinogenic chemicals.

(continued)

Panel Suggests Using Inmates in Drug Trials *(continued)*

In addition to addressing the abuses at Holmesburg, the regulations were a reaction to revelations in 1972 surrounding what the government called the Tuskegee Study of Untreated Syphilis in the Negro Male, which was begun in the 1930's and lasted 40 years. In it, several hundred mostly illiterate men with syphilis in rural Alabama were left untreated, even after a cure was discovered, so that researchers could study the disease.

"What happened at Holmesburg was just as gruesome as Tuskegee, but at Holmesburg it happened smack dab in the middle of a major city, not in some backwoods in Alabama," said Allen M. Hornblum, an urban studies professor at Temple University and the author of "Acres of Skin," a 1998 book about the Holmesburg research. "It just goes to show how prisons are truly distinct institutions where the walls don't just serve to keep inmates in, they also serve to keep public eyes out."

Critics also doubt the merits of pharmaceutical testing on prisoners who often lack basic health care.

Alvin Bronstein, a Washington lawyer who helped found the National Prison Project, an American Civil Liberties Union program, said he did not believe that altering the regulations risked a return to the days of Holmesburg.

"With the help of external review boards that would include a prisoner advocate," Mr. Bronstein said, "I do believe that the potential benefits of biomedical research outweigh the potential risks."

Holmesburg closed in 1995 but was partly reopened in July to help ease overcrowding at other prisons.

Under current regulations, passed in 1978, prisoners can participate in federally financed biomedical research if the experiment poses no more than "minimal" risks to the subjects. But a report formally presented to federal officials on Aug. 1 by the Institute of Medicine of the National Academy of Sciences advised that experiments with greater risks be permitted if they had the potential to benefit prisoners. As an added precaution, the report suggested that all studies be subject to an independent review.

"The current regulations are entirely outdated and restrictive, and prisoners are being arbitrarily excluded from research that can help them," said Ernest D. Prentice, a University of Nebraska genetics professor and the chairman of a Health and Human Services Department committee that requested the study. Mr. Prentice said the regulation revision process would begin at the committee's next meeting, on Nov. 2.

The discussion comes as the biomedical industry is facing a shortage of testing subjects. In the last two years, several pain medications, including Vioxx and Bextra, have been pulled off the market because early testing did not include large enough numbers of patients to catch dangerous problems.

And the committee's report comes against the backdrop of a prison population that has more than quadrupled, to about 2.3 million, over the last 30 years and that disproportionately suffers from H.I.V. and hepatitis C, diseases that some researchers say could be better controlled if new research were permitted in prisons.

For Leodus Jones, a former prisoner, the report has opened old wounds. "This moves us back in a very bad direction," said Mr. Jones, who participated in the experiments at Holmesburg in 1966 and after his release played a pivotal role in lobbying to get the regulations passed.

In one experiment, Mr. Jones's skin changed color, and he developed rashes on his back and legs where he said lotions had been tested.

"The doctors told me at the time that something was seriously wrong," said Mr. Jones, who added that he had never signed a consent form. He reached a $40,000 settlement in 1986 with the City of Philadelphia after he sued.

"I never had these rashes before," he said, "but I've had them ever since."

The Institute of Medicine report was initiated in 2004 when the Health and Human Services Department asked the institute to look into the issue. The report said prisoners should be allowed to take part in federally financed clinical trials so long as the trials were in the later and less dangerous phase of Food and Drug Administration approval. It also recommended that at least half the subjects in such trials be nonprisoners, making it more difficult to test products that might scare off volunteers.

Dr. A. Bernard Ackerman, a New York dermatologist who worked at Holmesburg during the 1960's trials as a second-year resident from the University of Pennsylvania, said he remained skeptical. "I saw it firsthand," Dr. Ackerman said. "What started as scientific research became pure business, and no amount of regulations can prevent that from happening again."

Others cite similar concerns over the financial stake in such research.

"It strikes me as pretty ridiculous to start talking about prisoners getting access to cutting-edge research and medications when they can't even get penicillin and high-blood-pressure pills," said Paul Wright, editor of Prison Legal News, an independent monthly review. "I have to imagine there are larger financial motivations here."

The demand for human test subjects has grown so much that the so-called contract research industry has emerged in the past decade to recruit volunteers for pharmaceutical trials. The Tufts Center for the Study of Drug Development, a Boston policy and economic research group at Tufts University, estimated that contract research revenue grew to $7 billion in 2005, up from $1 billion in 1995.

But researchers at the Institute of Medicine said their sole focus was to see if prisoners could benefit by changing the regulations.

The pharmaceutical industry says it was not involved. Jeff Trewitt, a spokesman for the Pharmaceutical Research and Manufacturers of America, a drug industry trade group, said that his organization had no role in prompting the study and that it had not had a chance to review the findings.

Dr. Albert M. Kligman, who directed the experiments at Holmesburg and is now an emeritus professor of dermatology at the University of Pennsylvania Medical School, said the regulations should never have been written in the first place.

"My view is that shutting the prison experiments down was a big mistake," Dr. Kligman said.

While confirming that he used radioactive materials, hallucinogenic drugs and carcinogenic materials on prisoners, Dr. Kligman said that they were always administered in extremely low doses and that the benefits to the public were overwhelming.

He cited breakthroughs like Retin A, a popular anti-acne drug, and ingredients for most of the creams used to treat poison ivy. "I'm on the medical ethics committee at Penn," he said, "and I still don't see there having been anything wrong with what we were doing."

From 1951 to 1974, several federal agencies and more than 30 companies used Holmesburg for experiments, mostly under the auspices of the University of Pennsylvania, which had built laboratories at the prison. After the revelations about Holmesburg, it soon became clear that other universities and prisons in other states were involved in similar abuses.

In October 2000, nearly 300 former inmates sued the University of Pennsylvania, Dr. Kligman, Dow Chemical and Johnson & Johnson for injuries they said

(continued)

Panel Suggests Using Inmates in Drug Trials *(continued)*

occurred during the experiments at Holmesburg, but the suit was dismissed because the statute of limitations had expired.

"When they put the chemicals on me, my hands swelled up like eight-ounce boxing gloves, and they've never gone back to normal," said Edward Anthony, 62, a former inmate who took part in Holmesburg experiments in 1964. "We're still pushing the lawsuit because the medical bills are still coming in for a lot of us."

Daniel S. Murphy, a professor of criminal justice at Appalachian State University in Boone, N.C., who was imprisoned for five years in the 1990's for growing marijuana, said that loosening the regulations would be a mistake.

"Free and informed consent becomes pretty questionable when prisoners don't hold the keys to their own cells," Professor Murphy said, "and in many cases they can't read, yet they are signing a document that it practically takes a law degree to understand."

During the Holmesburg experiments, inmates could earn up to $1,500 a month by participating. The only other jobs were at the commissary or in the shoe and shirt factory, where wages were usually about 15 cents to 25 cents a day, Professor Hornblum of Temple said.

On the issue of compensation for inmates, the report raised concern about "undue inducements to participate in research in order to gain access to medical care or other benefits they would not normally have." It called for "adequate protections" to avoid "attempts to coerce or manipulate participation."

The report also expressed worry about the absence of regulation over experiments that do not receive federal money. Lawrence O. Gostin, the chairman of the panel that conducted the study and a professor of law and public health at Georgetown University, said he hoped to change that.

Even with current regulations, oversight of such research has been difficult. In 2000, several universities were reprimanded for using federal money and conducting several hundred projects on prisoners without fully reporting the projects to the appropriate authorities.

Professor Gostin said the report called for tightening some existing regulations by advising that all research involving prisoners be subject to uniform federal oversight, even if no federal funds are involved. The report also said protections should extend not just to prisoners behind bars but also to those on parole or on probation.

Professor Murphy, who testified to the panel as the report was being written, praised those proposed precautions before adding, "They're also the parts of the report that faced the strongest resistance from federal officials, and I fear they're most likely the parts that will end up getting cut as these recommendations become new regulations."

Barclay Walsh contributed research for this article.

SOURCES

Ackerman, Kate. "EHR Alerts Reduce Prescription Oversights." ihealthbeat.org, June 2, 2006. http://www.ihealthbeat.org/articles/2006/6/2/EHR-Alerts-Reduce-Prescription-Oversights.aspx?a=1 (accessed December 22, 2007).

"Approved Biotechnology Drugs." 2005. http://www.bio.org/speeches/pubs/er/approveddrugs.asp (accessed August 16, 2006).

Baase, Sara. *A Gift of Fire*. Upper Saddle River, NJ: Prentice Hall: 22–23.

Bakalar, Nicholas. "Medical Errors? Patients May Be the Last to Know." nyt.com, August 29, 2006 (accessed August 30, 2006).

Barker, Kenneth N., Bill G. Felkey, Elizabeth A. Flynn, and Jim L. Carper. "White Paper on Automation in Pharmacy." March 1998. http://www.ascp.com/publications/tcp/1998/mar/ (accessed August 16, 2006).

Binder, A. "Identification of Genes for Complex Trait: Examples from Hypertension." *Current Pharmaceutical Biotechnology* 7, no. 1 (2006): 1–13.

Borel, Jacques, and Karen L. Rascati. "Effect of an Automated, Nursing Unit-Based Drug-Dispensing Device on Medication Errors." *American Journal of Health System Pharmacy* 52 (1995): 1875–9.

Brumson, Bennett. "Consumer Products Produced by Robotics." March 2001. http://www.roboticsonline.com/public/articles/archivedetails.cfm?id=357 (accessed August 17, 2006).

"Cancer Cell 'Executioner' Found." BBC news, August 27, 2006. bbc.co.uk (accessed August 30, 2006).

"Cardinal Health Installs New Point-of-Care Technology System in Huron Valley-Sinai Hospital." pyxis.com, March 6, 2003 (accessed August 17, 2006).

"Cardinal Health Introduces Health Care's First Patient Room Automated Dispensing System for Medications and Supplies." pyxis.com, June 2, 2003 (accessed August 17, 2006).

"Cardinal Health Launches First 'Smart Pump' System to Feature New Bar Code Reader for Safer IV Medication Administration." October 31, 2005. http://www.cardinal.com/content/news/10312005_65252.asp (accessed August 17, 2006).

Cefalu, William T., and William Weir. "New Technologies in Diabetes Care." patientcareonline.com, September 2003 (accessed August 16, 2006).

"Center to Offer Quick, Reliable Source for Genetic Information." National Genome Research Institute. genome.gov (accessed August 17, 2006).

"Center Watch Clinical Trials Listing Service." 2006. www.Centerwatch.com (accessed August 1, 2006).

Chervokas, Jason, and Tom Watson. "Doctors Build a Community Online." CyberTimes, February 6, 1998. http://www.nytimes.com/library/cyber/nation/020698nation.html (accessed August 17, 2006).

Choi, Charles. "RNAi: A New Targeted Silencer?" Thescientist.com, June 27, 2006 (accessed July 27, 2006).

Cohen, Robert. "Uncertified Medicines a 'Serious' Safety Issue." nj.com, July 9, 2006 (accessed July 31, 2006).

"Computer-Aided Drug Design." medfarm.uu.se, 2006 (accessed July 27, 2006).

"Computer-Assisted Trial Design." 2003. http://www.Pharsight.com/ (accessed August 16, 2006).

"Computers: Errors In—Errors Out." August 1995. http://www.usp.org (accessed August 16, 2006).

Darves, Bonnie. "Seven Simple Steps to Prevent Outpatient Drug Errors." American College of Physicians *Observer,* June 2003. acponline.org/cgi-bin/htsearch (accessed August 16, 2006).

Dorchner, John. "Study Finds Healthcare Error Prone." May 6, 2003. http://www.brevardlawyer.com/errorprone.htm (accessed August 16, 2006).

Douglass, Kara. "Rx for Speedy Service." findarticles.com, September 20, 1997 (accessed August 17, 2006).

Dreifus, Claudia. "Saving Lives with Tailor-Made Medication." nyt.com, August 29, 2006 (accessed November 18, 2006).

"FDA Approves Avastin, a Targeted Therapy for First-Line Metastatic Colorectal Cancer Patients." February 26, 2004. http://psa-rising.com/wiredbird/genentech-avastin-feb2004.html (accessed August 16, 2006).

"FDA Approves Herceptin for Breast Cancer." September 29, 1998. http://www.newswise.com/articles/view/?id=hercptn2.ucl (accessed August 16, 2006).

"FDA Approves Xolair, Biotechnology Breakthrough for Asthma." June 20, 2003. http://www.novartis.de/servlet/novartismedia.pdf?id=9793 (accessed August 16, 2006).

"FDA Fails to Protect Americans from Dangerous Drugs and Unsafe Food, Watchdog Groups Say: Agency Captured by Industries It Should be Regulating, According to Rep." Waxman, Public Citizen and CSPI, June 27, 2006. http://www.citizen.org (accessed August 2, 2006).

"FDA Mission Statement." http://www.fda.gov (accessed August 2, 2006).

Fleiger, Ken. "Getting SMART: Drug Review in the Computer Age." *FDA Consumer,* October 1995. http://www.fda.gov/fdac/features/895_smart.html (accessed August 16, 2006).

Fletcher, Amy. "Hospital Drug Delivery Systems Take High-Tech Route." August 8, 2003. http://denver.bizjournals.com (accessed August 16, 2006).

Freierman, Shelley. "Most Wanted: Drilling Down/Online Pharmacies; and No Doctor's Scribble." nyt.com, April 11, 2005 (accessed November 15, 2006).

"From Maps to Medicine: About the Human Genome Research Project." August 9, 2000. whitepapers.zdnet.co.uk/0,39025945,60014727p-39000569q,00.htm (accessed August 16, 2006).

"Gene Breakthrough Heralds Better Prospect For Malaria Solution." sciencedaily.com, July 25, 2006 (accessed August 1, 2006).

"Genentech Presents Positive Preliminary Six-Month Data from Phase Ib/II Study for Lucentis in Age-Related Macular Degeneration (AMD)." gene.com, August 18, 2003 (accessed August 16, 2006).

"Genentech Receives FDA Fast-Track Designation for Avastin." June 26, 2003. http://www.gen com/gene/news/press-releases/detail.jsp?detail=6367 (accessed August 16, 2006).

"Guidelines for Safe Use of Automated Dispensing Cabinets," draft document, posted Octobe 16, 2007, Institute for Safe Medicine Practices, http://www.ismp.org/Tools/guidelines/ labelFormats/comments/default.asp (accessed February 2, 2008).

Gump, Michael D. "Robot Technology Improves VA Pharmacies—U.S. Medicine Interviews. . . July 2001. web.uvic.ca/~h351/online_articles.htm (accessed August 16, 2006).

Harris, Gardiner. "Report Finds a Heavy Toll from Medication Errors." nyt.com, July 21, 200 (accessed July 21, 2006).

"Health Plans for Virtual Human." BBC News, May 17, 1999. news.bbc.co.uk (accessed August 16, 2006).

Henderson, Diedtra. "Drug Makers Lobby US to Hike FDA Funds." Boston Globe, July 13, 2006. globe.com (accessed August 1, 2006).

Henderson, Diedtra. "Study Rebuts Conflict Fears Around FDA Financial Ties of Panels." Boston Globe, April 26, 2006. http://www.mindfully.org (accessed August 2, 2006).

"Hospitals Turn to Robots, Bar Codes to Organize Pharmacies." bizjournals.com, June 3, 2006 (accessed August 1, 2006).

Houlston, Bryan. "Integrating RFID Technology into a Drug Administration System." *Healthcare and Informatics Review Online,* December 1, 2005. hcro.enigma.co.nz (accesse August 2, 2006).

"How RFID Works." technovelgy.com (accessed August 1, 2006).

"Human Genome Resources Fact Sheet." 2003. http://www.nlm.nih.gov/pubs/factsheets/ humangenome.html (accessed August 16, 2006).

"Implanted Chips to Deliver Drugs." reed-electronics.com, March 14, 2006 (accessed August 2006).

Jehlen, Alan. "Preventing Medical Errors." *American Teacher,* May/June 2003. aft.org (accessed August 17, 2006).

Langreth, Robert. "The Suggestive Gene." August 14, 2006. forbes.com (accessed August 1, 2006).

Lawsen, Gary W. "Impact of User Fees on Changes Within the Food and Drug Administration." fdastudy.com, 2005 (accessed July 31, 2006).

Leape, Lucian L., and Donald M. Berwick. "Five Years After To Err Is Human: What Have We Learned?" *Journal of the American Medical Association* 293, no. 19 (2005): 2384–90. http://www.cmwf.org/publications/publications_show.htm?doc_id=278113 (accessed August 17, 2006).

Manning, Margie. "Computers to Replace Docs' Scribbles at Barnes-Jewish: $10 Million System Will Place Orders for Drugs, Tests; Should Be in Place Within Three Years." March 4, 2002. web.uvic.ca/~h351/online_articles.htm (accessed August 17, 2006).

Marietti, Charlene. "Robots Hooked on Drugs: Robotic Automation Expands Pharmacy Services." *Healthcare Informatics,* November 1997. www.ncbi.nlm.nih.gov (accessed August 17, 2006).

"Master Genetic Switch Found for Chronic Pain." sciencedaily.com, January 27, 2006 (accessed January 28, 2006).

"Medical Journal Says It Was Misled Again." AP, July 12, 2006 (accessed August 2, 2006).

"Milestone Demonstrates Pyxis Corporation's Leadership in Development of Automated Medication Technology for Patient Safety." January 10, 2002. web.uvic.ca (accessed August 17, 2006).

Mitchell, Steve. "Scientists Create 'Pharmacy in a Chip.'" October 19, 2003. web.uvic.ca (accessed August 17, 2006).

Murray, Michael D., Pharm.D., M.P.H. "Automated Medication Dispensing Devices," chapter 11 in *Making Health Care Safer: A Critical Analysis of Patient Safety Practices*, prepared for the Agency for Healthcare Research and Quality. contract no. 290-97-0013, 2001, http://www.ahrq.gov/clinic/ptsafety (accessed February 2, 2008).

Neergaard, Lauran. "DNA to Aid in Tailoring Prescription for Patient." *Star-Ledger*, November 3, 2003, 23.

Ouellette, Jennifer. "Biomaterials Facilitate Medical Breakthroughs." American Institute of Physics, October/November 2001. www.aip.org (accessed August 17, 2006).

Page, Douglas. "Drug Topics." addsinc.com, March 20, 2000 (accessed August 17, 2006).

"Penn Researchers Determine Structure of Smallpox Virus Protein Bound to DNA." sciencedaily.com, August 7, 2006 (accessed August 7, 2006).

"Physicians Hospital of El Paso Set to Deploy Pyxis Safetynet Technology to Reduce Medical Errors." pyxis.com, October 10, 2002 (accessed August 17, 2006).

Pollack, Andrew. "Drug Testers Turn to 'Virtual Patients' as Guinea Pigs." nyt.com, November 10, 1998 (accessed August 17, 2006).

Pollack, Andrew. "Merck and Partner Form Alliance to Develop Drugs Based on RNA." nyt.com, September 9, 2003 (accessed September 10, 2003).

Pollack, Andrew. "Mice Deaths Are Setback in Gene Tests." nyt.com, May 25, 2006 (accessed July 31, 2006).

Pollack, Andrew. "Mixed Data Leave Doubts on Cancer Drug." nyt.com, September 12, 2003 (accessed August 17, 2006).

Powell, Jennifer Heldt. "Long-Distance Remedy: ADDS System Indispensible." Boston Herald, June 14, 1999. addsinc.com (accessed August 17, 2006).

"Preventing Death and Injury from Medical Errors Requires Dramatic, System-Wide Changes." The National Academies, November 29, 1999. medicalreporter.health.org/tmr1199/medical_errors.html (accessed August 17, 2006).

Pullan, Andrew, Nicolas Smith, and Peter Hunter. "Creating the Virtual Human." *Healthcare and Informatics Review Online*, 2006. hcro.enigma.co.nz (accessed July 27, 2006).

Raschke, Robert, et al. "A Computer Alert System to Prevent Injury from Adverse Drug Events." *JAMA* 1998: 1317–20.

"RFIDs: The Pros and Cons Every Consumer Needs to Know About Radio Frequency Tags." sixwise.com, June 4, 2005 (accessed August 1, 2006).

Richardson, William C. "To Err Is Human: Building a Safer Health System." news@nas.edu, December 1, 1999 (accessed August 17, 2006).

"The RNA Structure Database." RNABase.org, September 10, 2003 (accessed August 17, 2006).

Sardinha, Carol. "Electronic Prescribing: The Next Revolution in Pharmacy." *Journal of Managed Care Pharmacy* January–February 1998. http://www.amcp.org/jmcp/vol4/num1/spotlight.html (accessed August 17, 2006).

Schwarz, Harold, and Bret Brodowy. "Implementation and Evaluation of an Automated Dispensing System." *American Journal of Health-System Pharmacy* 52 (1995): 823–8. ncbi.nlm.nih.gov (accessed August 17, 2006).

Shah, Nidhi, Andrew C. Seger, and Diane L. Seger. "Computerized Prescribing Alerts Can Be Designed to Be Widely Accepted by Primary." ahcpr.gov, May 2006 (accessed August 11, 2006).

"Significant Milestones in Biotechnology." Genentech Inc., 2000. http://www.gene.com (accessed August 16, 2006).

"Spokane Pharmacists Test Rx Vending Machine Dispensing." February 2002. http://www.telepharmacysolutions.com/news.html (accessed August 16, 2006).

"Stem Cell Basics." nih.gov, August 12, 2005 (accessed August 1, 2006).

"Stem Cell Experiment Yields Heart Valves." nyt.com, November 18, 2006 (accessed November 18, 2006).

"Stem Cell Information." nih.gov, August 12, 2005 (accessed August 1, 2006).

"Stem Cell Research." February 2006. http://www.newsbatch.com (accessed August 1, 2006).

Stephenson, Joan. "Targeting Medical Errors." *JAMA* 283, no. 3 (2000). abs.ca (accessed August 17, 2006).

Tamblyn, R., et al. "The Use of Computers in Health Care Can Reduce Errors, Improve Patient Safety, and Enhance the Quality of Service—There Is Evidence." March 1, 2005 http://www.informatics.nhs.uk (accessed August 17, 2006).

"Tarceva (erlotnib HCl) Phase II Clinical Trials Initiated in Patients with Malignant Glioma. gene.com, August 8, 2003 (accessed August 17, 2006).

"Thompson Approves Demos to Expand Safety-net Patients' Access to Prescription Drugs and Pharmacy Services, Lower Drug Prices." HHS News US Department of Health an Human Services, December 18, 2001. addsinc.com (accessed August 17, 2006).

Thompson, Larry. "User Fees for Faster Drug Reviews Are They Helping of Hurting the Public Health?" Fda.gov, 2000 (accessed July 9, 2006).

Ukens, Carol. "Manuel the Robot Earns His Long-Term Care Keep." July 10, 2006. http://www.drugtopics.com/drugtopics/article/articleDetail.jsp?id=353150 (accessed August 17, 2006).

Ukens, Carol. "New Bar-Code Scanner Simplifies Drug Ordering." August 7, 2006. http://www.drugtopics.com/drugtopics/author/authorDetail.jsp?id=6373 (accessed August 17, 2006).

Ukens Carol. "Pharmacy Shortage Boosts Telepharmacy." addsinc.com, June 3, 2002 (accessed August 17, 2006).

Vanderveen, Tim. "IVs First: A New Barcode Implementation Strategy, Patient Safety and Quality Healthcare." psch.com, May/June 2006 (accessed August 1, 2006).

Wade, Nicholas. "Scientists Discover First Gene Tied to Stroke." nyt.com, September 22, 2003 (accessed August 17, 2006).

"What Is a Helix? And What Is RNA and DNA. . . ." http://www.chemistry-school.info (accessed August 17, 2006).

"What Is RNA?" June 12, 2006. http://www.cancerbackup.org.uk/Aboutcancer/Whatiscancer/Understandingtermsstatistics/related_faqs/QAs/1080223255 (accessed August 17, 2006).

"Which Diseases Will RNAi Drugs be Used to Treat and What Barriers Will RNAi Drugs Nee to Overcome." genengnews.com, July 25, 2006 (accessed July 31, 2006).

Wolfe, Stanley M. "The 100th Anniversary of the FDA: The Sleeping Watchdog Whose Master Is Increasingly the Regulated Industries (HRG Publication #1776)." citizen.org, June 27, 2006 (accessed July 24, 2006).

Zhan, Chunliu, Rodney Hicks, Christopher Blanchette, et al. "Computerized Prescribing May Reduce Some Harmful Errors, but Can Introduce New Errors." ahcpr.gov, July 200 (accessed August 11, 2006).

CHAPTER 9

Information Technology in Dentistry

CHAPTER OUTLINE

LEARNING OBJECTIVES

In this chapter, the student will learn many of the ways that computer technology has impacted on the practice of dentistry. The student will be able to:

- Describe the use of computers in education.
- Discuss the significance of the electronic patient record in integrating practice management and clinical applications.
- Discuss the impact of changing demographics on dental practice.
- Describe the use of computers in endodontics, periodontics, and cosmetic dentistry.
- Define diagnostic tools including the X-ray, digital X-ray, electronic concordance, and the new tools that use light.
- Define minimally invasive dentistry.
- List the uses of computers in dental surgery.
- Describe the trend toward growing specialization.
- Describe the emerging field of teledentistry.

KEY TERMS

bonding
clinical decision-support systems (CDSS)
cosmetic dentistry
demineralize
dental implant
dental informatics
DentSim
digital imaging fiber optic transillumination (DIFOTI®)
electrical conductance
electronic dental chart
endodontics
EXPERTMD
fiber optic camera
fiber optic transillumination
intraoral fiber optic cameras
laser (light amplificatio by stimulated emission of radiation)
light illumination
minimally invasive dentistry
periodontics
remineralize
teledentistry
WAND™

DISCUSSION QUESTIONS

1. Define dental informatics.
Dental informatics combines computer technology with dentistry to create a basis f research, education, and the solution of real-world problems in oral health care using com puter applications. From the time the patient calls the office for an appointment, which recorded in an electronic appointment book, to the services offered, the instruments in us and even the pain the patient senses, digital technology plays a role.
2. Discuss ways that information technology helps in the education of dentists.
Dentists can surf the Web for online information specific to their professional interests an use e-mail to communicate with each other and their patients. Computer generated trea ment plans are used to help educate patients. Virtual reality simulations are beginning be used in the education of dentists and dental surgeons. DentSim is a program that us virtual reality. Its purpose is to teach technical dexterity to dental students.
3. What is the electronic dental chart?
The electronic dental chart will be standardized, easy to search, and easy to read. It wi integrate practice management tasks (administrative applications) with clinical informa tion. It will include all of the patient's conditions and treatments, including images.
4. The surgeon general's report on oral health in 2000 pointed to demographi changes affecting dentistry. Describe them.
In the year 2000, the surgeon general issued a first report on dental health. The repo pointed to changes over the last one hundred years. In the year 1900, most people lost the teeth by middle age. By the middle of the twentieth century, the baby boom generation we taught to take care of their teeth. By the late twentieth century, many children were drink ing fluoridated water, having their teeth regularly cared for, and thus suffering less deca Dental health in general has improved over the last century. These trends—successful pr ventive treatments in middle-class children and an increasing aging population who hav kept their teeth—have changed the conditions dentists are treating and the expectations o patients. Dentists are filling fewer teeth, but increasingly and aggressively treating th more affluent portion of the aging population.
5. What does the current "epidemic of dental disease" mean?
Although dental health in general has improved, decay is epidemic among some popula tions. Victims of this epidemic are low income, minority, and some immigrant popula tions. One study traced the high number of cavities in poor children to increased lead leve in the children's blood, plus shortages in calcium and vitamin C.
6. What is a fiber optic camera?
The fiber optic camera is analogous to the endoscope used in surgery. It is used to view a area that is normally difficult to see. The dentist aims a fiber optic wand at the area of th

mouth to be examined. The image can be viewed on a monitor by the patient and dentist. The image can help the dentist see and diagnose problems at a very early stage.

7. Define endodontics.
   Endodontics is the dental specialty that diagnoses and treats diseases of the pulp.
8. Define periodontics.
   Periodontics is concerned with diagnosing and treating diseases of the gums and other structures supporting the teeth.
9. Define cosmetic dentistry.
   Cosmetic dentistry attempts to create a more attractive smile.
10. List and define two procedures used by cosmetic dentists.
    Bonding involves the application of a material to the tooth that can be shaped and polished. Dental implants can be used to replace missing teeth; computers help plan the exact placement of the implant.
11. List and describe two traditional diagnostic tools.
    A basic diagnostic tool is a clinical examination using a probe. Traditional X-rays have been used for more than a hundred years to diagnose cavities. X-rays are more effective than clinical examination. X-rays can be used because as the mineral content of the tooth decreases, the X-ray shows the cavity as darker. The dentist must then interpret the X-ray correctly. This is not a foolproof method of diagnosis, and may not detect cavities at an early stage when minimal intervention is necessary.
12. Define electrical conductance.
    Electrical conductance is also currently used to diagnose cavities. An electric current is passed through a tooth, and the tooth's resistance is measured. A decayed tooth has a different resistance reading than a healthy tooth. Studies differ on the accuracy of this method, but tend to rate it high in detecting substantial cavities, not early lesions.
13. Briefly describe DIFOTI®.
    Digital imaging fiber optic transillumination (DIFOTI®) diagnoses by using a digital charge-coupled device (CCD) camera to obtain images of teeth illuminated with laser light. The images are analyzed using computer algorithms.
14. Describe the uses of lasers in dentistry.
    There are several uses of lasers in dentistry. Low-level lasers can find pits in tooth enamel that may become cavities. The Food and Drug Administration (FDA) has approved laser machines for drilling and filling cavities; lasers also reduce the bacteria in the cavity. Minimally invasive dentistry uses lasers. Surgical lasers, used in place of drills, burst cells by heating them. One laser works on hard tissue, another on soft tissue. Lasers can quickly harden the material used to fill the tooth, reducing the time it takes to complete a filling. Lasers cannot be used where previous fillings or crowns exist.
15. What is minimally invasive dentistry?
    Minimally invasive dentistry emphasizes prevention and the least possible intervention. Teeth are constantly affected by acids, which demineralize the surfaces (dissolves the enamel). Early lesions beneath the enamel can be treated with calcium, phosphate, and fluoride, which help remineralize teeth. Preventive measures include antibacterial rinses and toothpastes, fluoride, diet, sealants, and the use of sugarless gum to increase saliva. Sealants may be used as a preventative measure.
16. Define air abrasion.
    Air abrasion can remove small amounts of a tooth; it involves aiming high-speed particles at the tooth. It can be used for the removal of cavities, of defects in the enamel, and to detect cavities in fissures by opening them for inspection. It is relatively painless. It removes less of the tooth than a traditional drill.
17. What part do computers play in dental surgery?
    Computers play a part in the delivery of anesthesia and the planning and creation of dental implants. Computerized monitoring devices can keep track of a patient's vital signs. For patients requiring implants, software can create a three-dimensional view of the patient: this allows the dentist to see the exact relationship of the planned implant to the patient's bone. The surgery can be done as a simulation; dental CT scans allow the surgeon to rotate

the implant on the screen so that by the time the patient is operated on, the surgery is plann down to the last detail.

18. Discuss increasing specialization in dentistry.
In the last quarter of the twentieth century, only 10 percent of dentists were specialis This is expected to rise to about 30 percent. This is due in part to the decrease in the nu ber of dentists trained, while the number of specialists trained remains constant, so th specialists form a greater proportion. It is also due to changing demographics. As l expectancy increases and dental health improves, more affluent patients who feel they ne to be attractive will seek cosmetic dentistry. With an aging population, some dentists w specialize in geriatrics. New technologies that allow dental problems to be diagnosed an treated earlier will result in dentists who specialize in diagnostics.
19. Define teledentistry.
Teledentistry programs have been developed to help dentists access specialists, improvi patient care. One system uses the Internet and requires a computer and digital camer The general dentist can e-mail a patient's chart, including images, to the specialist w can suggest both diagnosis and treatment. This saves the patient time and travel, an gives her or him access to expert advice.
20. How do dentists, who use minimally invasive procedures, make use of lasers?
Lasers can be used in place of the drill to fill cavities. The laser vaporizes decay by directi a stream of light at the affected area. The lasers are so precise that they affect only the dec not the tooth.

IN THE NEWS

Taking Care; the New-Age Dentistry

by Andrew H. Malcolm

WHEN TODAY'S ADULTS WERE children, it was a popular pastime to portray what the city of the future would be like—air cars gliding serenely between strange-looking buildings towering over clean streets where vehicular traffic moved efficiently. On a separate level, pedestrians would stroll unmolested by fumes, cars or criminals.

"It's absolutely amazing what's happened," says Dr. Arthur A. Dugoni, past president of the American Dental Association and dean of the School of Dentistry at the University of the Pacific in Stockton, Calif.

What's happened is that technology has swept through one of the oldest and most maligned professions, revolutionizing its approach, its methods and its capabilities, even the personality of its practitioners. And while the image of the dentist's office as a kind of medieval torture chamber filled with strange smells and muffled moans lingers in the nostrils and ears of many middle-aged patients, the modern-day reality for their children is as different as the city of the future that never was. Dental visits now are usually pain free. And, according to public opinion surveys, the nation's estimated 137,000 active dentists, those dour inflicters of dread of yesteryear, now rank right up there in public respect after the clergy, doctors and pharmacists.

For American consumers, who, along with insurance companies, shell out about $42 billion each year to care for their mouths, the dental revolution means, among other things:

O Plastic coatings that thwart even the most diligent efforts of Mean Old Mr. Tooth Decay.

O Live video coverage of the mouth by a camera the size of a finger that presents a magnified picture of the teeth. This enables the dentist to locate areas of decay more easily and allows patients to watch what the dentist is doing.

O Computer-assisted "smile forecasts" that portray on a television screen exactly what a cosmetic procedure, like filling in gaps between teeth, can do to enhance a patient's appearance.

A host of experimental approaches now being studied by researchers promise to keep the dental revolution going. They include:

O Lasers that vaporize, in a flash and a soft pop, even the largest pockets of decay. These could eventually eliminate the need for dreaded dental drilling.

O Time-release fluoride capsules that strap onto a tooth and harden the enamel, protecting the tooth against decay for up to six months.

O "Electronic braces," which can reposition teeth in less than half the time required by conventional orthodontic hardware.

It is all a far cry from the first significant advance in dental work in 1785, when John Greenwood invented a drill run by a foot pedal. With a strong foot a dentist could get that instrument whirling at a donkey-cart speed of 100 revolutions per minute. In the following 160 years, using a complicated series of elastic bands, dentists managed to get the speed up to a jaw-jarring 5,000 times per minute.

In today's jet-age practices, the standard air-driven, water-cooled drill turns a half-million times a minute, although 60 seconds is usually more time than needed to cut through a spot of decay. And dentists are filling cavities with new, more durable materials that are perfectly matched to a patient's own teeth color. In an attempt to make fillings that are even more durable than today's best, researchers are working on isolating the genes that produce natural tooth enamel. The idea would be to use genetic engineering techniques to manufacture large batches of natural enamel, which could be used to repair cavities.

Despite the proliferation of new dental treatments, the number of would-be dentists appears to be declining. After decades of improvement, this year for the first time the American dentist-patient ratio will decrease, albeit only slightly, from the current peak of 60.6 dentists per 100,000 patients. Although more women and minorities are entering the profession, only about 4,000 dental students graduate each year now, down from more than 6,300 in 1979.

Dr. Dugoni sees a shortage of dentists beginning to appear around 1996. By 2020, at current enrollment rates, the dentist-patient ratio is forecast to be 44 dentists per 100,000 patients, the same as it was during World War I. He traces the problem to the fact that much dental work is now discretionary, causing some doubts in the minds of would-be dentists about their future financial security. And, Dr. Dugoni adds, "There has been no glamour in the popular image of dentistry as drilling and filling. Young people have many more attractive alternatives today."

But the current reality of dentistry involves much more than drilling and filling. Dr. Paul Keating, a 34-year-old with a seven-year-old practice in Wilton, Conn., says he now spends only one-third of his time restoring and repairing teeth, primarily replacing old fillings.

Another third of his time goes to preventive work—cleaning teeth and gum lines—and trying to reduce his own tooth repair business by teaching oral hygiene to patients young and old. This includes the traditional lesson about flossing once a day (nine out of ten of us don't do it right), how to brush gently with soft brushes and what to rinse with (plaque-fighting washes with fluoride that have the American Dental Association seal of acceptance). It also includes sealing the vulnerable biting surfaces of teeth, typically children's, with an invisible plastic coating that protects against cavities for five to seven years.

The remaining third of Dr. Keating's workday, the growing third, is devoted to cosmetic work, because of more aware dental consumers and the rapidly evolving

(continued)

Taking Care; the New-Age Dentistry *(continued)*

technology. "We've always had young women concerned about the appearance of their teeth," he says. "But now we're getting a lot more 55-year-old executives who come in here and say, 'Can you do something about my yellow teeth?' Of course, they still have to add, 'My wife says I should do something about it.'"

And what dentists can now do is tantamount to producing the kind of white-capped brilliance once seen beaming only from the expensive smiles of stars on stage during the annual Oscar presentations. Cosmetic procedures are easier and cheaper than ever before. Using new techniques and new or updated materials, such as resins, porcelain and ceramic, dentists can cover stained teeth, rebuild chipped teeth and fill in gaps between teeth, drastically altering smiles to the psychic satisfaction of patients, if not achieving actual dental improvement. This has launched an essentially new cosmetic dental business, which may soon make up 40 percent or more of the dentist's workload.

Years ago, Dr. Randolph Shoup's dental practice in Indianapolis involved perhaps 40 percent fillings and 5 percent cosmetic work. Now fillings are a dwindling 15 percent and cosmetic work is surpassing 35 percent, thanks, in part, to his patients' affluence and to a $30,000 video camera. "It lets me communicate with my patients on an entirely different level," says Dr. Shoup.

The video camera is connected to a computer, which presents two images on a television screen: a picture of the patient's existing smile on one half of the screen, and a picture of how the smile will look after Dr. Shoup has completed the cosmetic procedure. With a tap of his foot on a floor pedal, Dr. Shoup can order the machine to take a Polaroid photo of the split image, producing a record of what patient and doctor both agreed to. Such documentation could also come in handy should the patient's insurance company refuse to pay for the procedure, and as effective evidence in the event of a malpractice suit, another aspect of modern medical life. "It's hard to argue with a photo," says Dr. Shoup. The camera is also helpful for diagnosing dental problems. Dr. Shoup uses its powerful magnification to double-check his own visual examination, often spotting the beginnings of decay that the naked eye might miss. With today's more assertive patients demanding more involvement in treatment decisions than their grandparents, Dr. Shoup can display the troubled area for mutual discussion. "I can say, 'Here's your problem, right here,'" he says. "The kids especially like the camera. They're the video generation and their own mouth is the star of the show."

In some dental practices these days, nearly 50 percent of the orthodontic work occurs in the mouths of adult Americans, up from 10 percent little more than a decade ago. Although orthodontics can take longer in adults than in children, it is increasingly popular in an image-conscious society. To mask the work in progress, orthodontists now have tooth-colored metalwork.

Even among children, however, orthodontia can take years. But experimental "electronic" braces may speed things up considerably. Tiny batteries attached to the teeth deliver a constant low electrical current to the gums. At the same time, braces apply pressure to the teeth to move them into better position. The current accelerates the adjustment of the bone anchoring the teeth, thereby allowing them to be moved more quickly. Studies have shown that electronic braces can realign the teeth in less than half the time required by conventional braces.

LAST SPRING THE Food and Drug Administration approved the use of a new kind of laser for treating periodontal disease, one of the most common dental problems. With this laser, a dentist can vaporize inflamed or infected gum tissue.

The intense beam of laser light instantly cauterizes blood vessels, reducing blood loss, and sterilizes the gum tissue. It is also more precise than scalpels and scraping instruments. Thus, the laser treatment is easier on the patient, less likely to cause complications and results in a less painful recovery. Gum problems, a characteristic of older mouths, often become teeth problems and are expected to become even more frequent as the baby-boom generation reaches middle age and beyond.

Aside from periodontal disease, the dental health of Americans has improved dramatically in recent decades, a trend that companies in the $2 billion-a-year mouth-care business have sought to exploit. A society which once survived using either toothpaste or tooth powder now has a bewildering array of pastes and tastes to choose from—with whiteners, with fluoride, with tartar control, for sensitive teeth and all combinations thereof. Likewise, mouthwashes have specialized. They have existed in one form or another throughout recorded history, from the white wine-anise seed-myrrh mixture used by the Greeks to combat ancient bad breath to the vinegar used by East Indians to the hydrogen peroxide popular in the early 19th century. Although ancients believed that only evil-tasting mouthwashes were powerful enough to overcome evil spirits and humors, modern-day consumers have a wide variety of multipurpose flavored liquids to buy.

Most contain fluoride, a once-controversial additive to community drinking water which the dental association credits with saving more than $2 billion annually in cavity treatments. Surveys indicate that fully half the country's children now get perfect report cards from their dentists, up from 36 percent in 1980.

For reasons that remain a mystery, children in the Northeast and on the Pacific Coast experience more tooth decay than their inland counterparts, and girls more than boys, too. But researchers are working on new weapons. These include a kind of biological warfare, introducing into a patient's mouth neutralizing bacteria that destroy the cavity-producing ones. Another avenue of research is an anticavity vaccine, which stimulates the immune system to destroy the decay-causing bacteria.

All of which has changed the personality of those attracted to dentistry and their training. "Dentistry is much closer to medicine now," says Dr. Dugoni. "It involves more science, technology, psychology, business methods. It requires more education. A lot of training time is spent, for instance, on anticipating patient anxieties and stress." New dental students are also trained much more than their predecessors to involve patients in treatment decisions. "And we're finding a much broader mix of people among dental students," says Dr. Dugoni. One-third of incoming students are now women. And, he says, many students enter dentistry as a second career. The average dentist makes around $90,000 a year, specialists slightly more.

But some things will never change, at least among members of the baby-boom generation, who were raised on some vivid lessons in the "old days" of the 1940's and 1950's. Dr. Keating, who wasn't, sees these memories passed on every Saturday morning and every weekday afternoon (except Friday, which he has set aside for private guitar lessons).

"I get the kids in here and they're great," says the doctor. "We're joking. I'm treating them. They're not afraid. And then the mother comes in and says to her child, 'Oh, my, you're being so brave.' You can see the kid tense up right away. It never occurred to him there was anything to be brave about in here. I guess it'll take us a generation or two to get over all that."

At the Dentist's Office, X-Rays, Root Canals and, Now, Pampering

by Jennifer Alsever

AT her dental appointments, Deann Romanick sips green tea and takes in the scent of lavender and the sounds of New Age music. She gets a free paraffin hand wax treatment, blankets, a warm neck pad and video eyeglasses in which she can watch "Seinfeld" episodes while the dentist works on her teeth.

The pampering eased her through a root canal and a tooth replacement, and now, with her fear of dental work gone, she has moved on to more elective procedures. Ms. Romanick, 34, a graduate student from Germantown, Md., spent $399 for teeth whitening and next plans to straighten her teeth with removable plastic braces, which can cost up to $3,500.

"I was totally afraid of the dentist," she said. "Now I go to the dentist every six months and I just can't wait."

What's that? Enjoy the dentist's office? That is the hope of a growing number of dentists who are turning their practices into "dental spas" that offer such perks as fresh-baked cookies and overstuffed couches and services like body waxing, facials, massage and pedicures.

About 5 percent of the American Dental Association's members have declared their offices as "spas." And their new services may open the door to more elective cosmetic dentistry—an additional revenue source for an industry that historically has been restricted by what patients' insurance will cover.

For dentists, the changes can mean that patients see office visits as more routine.

"Going to the dentist shouldn't be this bad thing," said Dr. Kimberly Baer, who did Ms. Romanick's dental work. "It should be like going to get your hair done."

Dr. Baer opened the Bethesda Dental Spa in North Bethesda, Md., two years ago, installing hardwood floors and waterfalls and decorating in muted lavenders and greens. All patients receive hand waxes before their appointments. For additional fees, they can get follow-up pain treatment from an acupuncturist, and eyebrow waxes from a staff aesthetician. This summer, the office plans to add free 15-minute facials and massages.

"I view it as a marketing expense," Dr. Baer said. "It's what makes other people go back to their office and talk about their dental appointment."

The strategy has paid off. Dr. Baer says the spa receives about 45 new patients a month, with many of them willing to go beyond traditional dentistry and spend $400 to $16,000 out of pocket for various procedures—whitening teeth or attaching porcelain veneers, for example. Sales at the office doubled in the last year, to $1.5 million. she said.

The spa services go hand in hand with the growth of cosmetic dentistry. Dentists surveyed last year by the American Academy of Cosmetic Dentistry reported that the aesthetic procedures in their offices rose by 12.5 percent, on average, in the past five years. Tooth whitening, they said, was the No. 1 requested service. Patients might pay $300 to $600 for it, an expense typically not covered by insurance.

The desire for perfect teeth is not limited to the dental office. Consumers have flocked to over-the-counter teeth-whitening products. Together, sales for Crest Whitestrips and Crest Night Effects, two whitening products from Procter & Gamble, tripled from 2001 to 2005, to $300 million.

"Now more than ever people are looking to improve their smiles," said Dr. Irwin Smigel, a Manhattan dentist and founder and president of the American Society of Dental Aesthetics.

Technology has improved, and reality makeover television shows have helped to make more consumers aware of it. And many people—including baby boomers—have the cash to spend.

"The baby boomer generation has put looking good and feeling good as a priority," said Kimberly Harms, a spokeswoman for the American Dental Association and a dentist in Farmington, Minn. "It goes along with people getting Botox, exercising and dyeing their hair."

Dentists say that when a patient is relaxed, anesthesia works better and procedures move more quickly. And if they enjoy the experience, they'll come back regularly, leading to better overall health, said Lynn Watanabe, a dentist who opened Dental Spa Inc. in Pacific Palisades, Calif.

Dr. Watanabe and her husband, John Chien, started their dental spa in 2002, after watching fearful children run from the office. Since then, they have seen their business and the spa phenomenon grow, even licensing the Dental Spa name to other dentists in San Francisco, New York City and Ann Arbor, Mich., along with the slogan, "Your teeth, body and mind will feel great." The couple also started the International Dental Spa Association—it now has 10 members—and are coming up with guidelines for what services constitute a dental spa. Already, Dr. Watanabe said, they have received interest from dentists in Dubai, South Korea, Russia and Brazil who want to start dental spas.

The trend goes beyond dentistry. Medical spas have become a fast-growing segment of the spa industry. Doctors, including podiatrists, gynecologists and general practitioners, are opening medical spas in malls and hospitals nationwide, offering extras like laser hair removal, Botox injections and facials, said Hannelore R. Leavy, director of the International Medical Spa Association in Union City, N.J. She estimates that there are about 1,500 medical spas worldwide, more than triple the number three years ago.

"This is all cash for the doctor," she said. "There is no insurance, no paperwork. This is a very lucrative business for them."

Citing surveys that say people judge one another by their smiles, dentists now offer a wide range of services.

Dr. Smigel says he has patients who pay up to $40,000 for "nonsurgical face-lifts" that use bonding, veneers, crowns, implants, bridges and even dentures to build out the lower half of the face. "I can build out lips, raise the cheekbones," he said.

Timothy B. Dotson, a dentist in Chicago, offers computerized "smile imaging" at his practice, Perfect Smile Spa. He takes photographs of the patients and then, using a computer, alters the photos to show them what they would look like if they had cosmetic work. His office also gives patients free 10-minute massages in the waiting room and paraffin hand waxes, among other services.

Quickbleach Dental Spa and Boutique, a street-level spa on the East Side of Manhattan, literally offers a menu of services to walk-in customers, including veneers—tooth caps the thickness of a baby's fingernail—at $750 a tooth—and one-hour whitening procedures for $399. Quickbleach is more akin to a trendy store or salon than a dental office, with its modern décor and Latin- and Arabic-influenced music.

"It's serious dentistry with a spa atmosphere," said Jimmy Conlin, 59, a songwriter in New York who saw a flier about Quickbleach and decided to have his teeth whitened there. Mr. Conlin's wife, Carolyn, joined him and received a computerized smile analysis, porcelain veneers, gum recontouring (which evens out the gum tissue), and skin grafting (which patches gums with tissue from other parts of the mouth). The couple spent $7,000.

"It's really a vanity issue, no question about it," Mr. Conlin said. "Our teeth look fabulous. It was all that was promised."

(continued)

At the Dentist's Office, X-Rays, Root Canals and, Now, Pampering *(continued)*

Dr. Jose Souto, a dentist who is Quickbleach's owner, says that since he overhauled his practice, he has doubled his annual revenue, to $3 million, and can accommodate twice as many patients as before.

"When people walk in, they're amazed," Dr. Souto said. "They say, 'This doesn't look like a dentist's office.' Little by little, people will think of the dentist's office as a positive place where they can be more beautiful and not a place where they're going to be punished and lose a couple of teeth."

SOURCES

Alipour-Rocca, L., V. Kudryk, and T. Morris. "A Teledentistry Consultation System and Continuing Dental Education via Internet." *Journal of Medical Internet Research* 1 (1999): e110. http://www.jmir.org/1999/suppl1/e110 (accessed December 27, 2007).

American Association of Cosmetic Dentists. "Not Satisfied with Your Smile? You're Not Alone." July 15, 2002. http://www.aacd.com/press/releases/2002_07_15.asp (accessed December 27, 2007).

American Association of Cosmetic Dentists. "Seniors Benefit from Cosmetic Dentistry." June 2002. http://www.aacd.com/press/releases/2003_06d.asp (accessed December 27, 2007

American Dental Association. "Cosmetic Dentistry." 1995–2003. http://www.ada.org/public/topics/cosmetic.asp (accessed December 27, 2007).

Angier, Natalie. "Dentistry, Far Beyond Drilling and Filling." August 5, 2003. http://www.geocities.com/drkhosla1/News/newsa164.html (accessed August 24, 2006).

Bakalar, Nicholas. "Gum Disease Is Linked to Rates of Early Birth." nyt.com, October 11, 2005. http://www.nytimes.com/2005/10/11/health/11teet.html (accessed December 27, 2007).

Bishop, Alton, Randol Womack, and Mitra Derakhshan. "An Esthetic and Removable Orthodontic Treatment Option for Patients: Invisalign®." *Dental Assistant,* September–October 2002. http://findarticles.com/p/articles/mi_m0MKX/is_5_71/ai_93306390 (accessed December 27, 2007).

Carpenter, S. "Lead and Bad Diet Give a Kick in the Teeth—Poor Children Are Most Susceptible to Lead Toxicity." June 26, 1999. http://findarticles.com/p/articles/mi_m1200/is_26_155/ai_55165309/pg_1 (accessed January 18, 2008).

Clark, Glenn T. "Teledendistry: Genesis, Actualization, and Caveats." *Journal of the California Dental Association* (2000). http://www.cda.org/page/Library/cda_member/pubs/journal/jour0200/intro.html (accessed December 27, 2007).

Cobb, Charles M. "Lasers in Periodontics: A Review of the Literature." *Journal of Periodontal* (April 2006). http://www.perio.org/resources-products/pdf/lr-lasers.pdf (accessed December 27, 2007).

Delrose, Daniel C., and Richard W. Steinberg. "The Clinical Significance of the Digital Patient Record." *JADA* 131 (June 2000): 57s–60s.

Diagnosis and Management of Dental Caries. "Summary." Evidence Report/Technology Assessment: Number 36. AHRQ Publication No. 01-E055. February 2001. http://www.ahrq.gov/clinic/epcsums/dentsumm.htm (accessed August 24, 2006).

Douglas, Chester W., and Cherilyn Sheets. "Patients' Expectations of Oral Health in the 21st Century." *JADA* 131 (June 2000): 3s–7s.

Dove, S. Brent. "Radiographic Diagnosis of Dental Caries." August 29, 2003. http://www.lib.umich.edu/dentlib/nihcdc/abstracts/dove.html (accessed December 27, 2007).

Drisco, Connie H. "Trends in Surgical and Nonsurgical Periodontal Treatment." *JADA*. 131 (June 2000): 31s–38s.

Fonseca, Raymond, Denice Stewart, M. Katie McGee, Noam Arzt, and Jeffery Stewart. "Remote Dental Consultation System." nd. http://64.233.169.104/search?

q=cache:auH6oM1HOfkJ:collab.nlm.nih.gov/tutorialspublicationsandmaterials/telesymposiumcd/5A-3.pdf+Remote+Dental+Consultation+Project&hl=en&ct=clnk&cd=1&gl=us (accessed January 6, 2008).

Forrest, J. L., and S. A. Miller. "Evidence-Based Decision Making in Action: Part 1—Finding the Best Clinical Evidence." *Journal of Contemporary Dental Practice* 3, no. 3 (2002): 010–026. http://www.thejcdp.com/issue011/forrest/forrest.pdf (accessed December 27, 2007).

Freydberg, B. K. "Connecting to Success: Practice Management on the Net." *Journal of Contemporary Dental Practice* 2, no. 3 (2001): 050–061. http://www.thejcdp.com/issue007/freydbrg/freyberg.pdf (accessed December 27, 2007).

Garvin, Jennifer. "Tooth Loss and Cardiovascular Disease." January 4, 2006. http://www.ada.org/prof/resources/pubs/adanews/adanewsarticle.asp?articleid=1735 (accessed December 27, 2007).

Glickman, Gerald N., and Kenneth Koch. "21st-Century Endodontics." June 2000. http://jada.ada.org/cgi/content/abstract/131/suppl_1/39S (accessed August 24, 2006).

Gorman, Jessica. "The New Cavity Fighters." *Science News,* August 19, 2000. http://www.sciencenews.org/articles/20000819/bob9.asp (accessed December 27, 2007).

Goshtasby, A. A. "Intelligent Systems Laboratory." nd. http://www.cs.wright.edu/people/faculty/agoshtas/nih.html (accessed January 6, 2008).

Griffin, Susan. "Virtual Dentistry Becomes Reality in Multimedia Lab." September 27, 2001. http://www.case.edu/pubs/cnews/2001/9-27/dent-sim.htm (accessed August 24, 2006).

Hoyle, Joe. "African-Americans Show Higher Prevalence of Periodontitis: Study." June 15, 2004. http://www.ada.org/prof/resources/pubs/adanews/adanewsarticle.asp?articleid=928 (accessed December 27, 2007).

Hoyle, Joe. "Scientists Sequence Genome of Pathogen Associated with Gum Disease." March 3, 2004. http://www.ada.org/prof/resources/pubs/adanews/adanewsarticle.asp?articleid=805 (accessed December 27, 2007).

Kirshner, M. "The Role of Information Technology and Informatics Research in the Dentist-Patient Relationship." December 2003. http://adr.iadrjournals.org/cgi/content/full/17/1/77 (accessed December 27, 2007).

Kurtzweil, Paula. "Dental More Gentle with Painless 'Drillings' and Matching Fillings." *FDA Consumer,* May–June, 1999. http://www.fda.gov/fdac/features/1999/399_dent.html (accessed December 27, 2007).

"Laser Dentistry." http://floss.com/ (accessed August 24, 2006).

Mendonca, Eneida. "Clinical Decision Support Systems: Perspectives in Dentistry." *Journal of Dental Education* 68, no. 6 (2004): 589–97. http://www.jdentaled.org/cgi/content/full/68/6/589 (accessed December 27, 2007).

"NIH Consensus Statement on Dental Caries Management." ADHA Online, 2003. http://www.adha.org/profissues/nih_consensus_statement.htm (accessed December 27, 2007).

Parks, E. T., and G. F. Williamson. "Digital Radiography: An Overview." *Journal of Contemporary Dental Practice* 3, no. 4 (2002): 023–039. http://www.thejcdp.com/issue012/williamson/index.htm (accessed December 27, 2007).

Scanlon, Jessie. "Say Ahhh (and Watch the Monitor)." nyt.com, September 4, 2003. http://query.nytimes.com/gst/fullpage.html?res=9B00E6D71038F937A3575AC0A9659C8B63 (accessed December 27, 2007).

Schneiderman, A., M. Elbaum, T. Shultz, S. Keem, M. Greenebaum, and J. Driller. "Assessment of Dental Caries with Digital Imaging Fiber-Optic Transillumination (DIFOTI): In Vitro Study." Abstract, 1997. http://www.ncbi.nlm.nih.gov/sites/entrez?db=pubmed&uid=9118181&cmd=showdetailview (accessed December 27, 2007).

Stabholz, A., R. Zeltser, M. Sela, B. Peretz, J. Moshonov, D. Ziskind, and A. Stabholz. "The Use of Lasers in Dentistry: Principles of Operation and Clinical Applications." December 2003. http://www.ncbi.nlm.nih.gov/sites/entrez?cmd=Retrieve&db=PubMed&list_uids=14733160&dopt=AbstractPlus (accessed December 27, 2007).

Stheeman, S. E., P. F. van der Stelt, and P. A. Mileman. "Expert Systems in Dentistry. Past Performance—Future Prospects." April 1992. http://www.ncbi.nlm.nih.gov/sites/entrez?db=pubmed&uid=1564183&cmd=showdetailview (accessed December 27, 2007).

Stookey, George, and Gonzalez-Cabezas. "Emerging Methods of Caries Diagnosis." October 2001. http://www.ncbi.nlm.nih.gov/entrez/query.fcgi?cmd=Retrieve&db=PubMed&dopt=Abstract&list_uids=11699969 (accessed August 24, 2006).

Urbankova, Alice, and Richard Lichtenthal. "DentSim Virtual Reality in Preclinical Operative Dentistry to Improve Psychomotor Skills: A Pilot Study." 2002. http://www.denx.com/research_and_publication_details.asp?id=33 (accessed December 27, 2007).

Valceanu, Anca. "Ultraconservative and Minimally Invasive Esthetic Restoration of Crown Fractures: Case Study." Summer 2006. https://www.aacd.com/downloads/journal/22-2valceanu.pdf (accessed December 27, 2007).

White, Joel M., and W. Stephen Eakle. "Rationale and Treatment Approach in Minimally Invasive Dentistry." June 2000. http://www.ncbi.nlm.nih.gov/entrez/query.fcgi?cmd=Retrieve&db=PubMed&list_uids=10860340&dopt=Abstract (accessed August 24, 2006).

CHAPTER 10

Informational Resources: Computer-Assisted Instruction, Expert Systems, Health Information Online

CHAPTER OUTLINE

LEARNING OBJECTIVES

After reading this chapter, the student will be able to

- List the many informational resources that computer technology and the Internet have made available and their use in the health care fields.
- Describe the use of computer-assisted instruction (CAI) in health care education.
- Discuss the Visible Human Project; many simulation programs use data from this project.
- Describe simulation programs such as ADAM, which make use of text and graphics.
- Describe simulation programs which make use of virtual reality (VR) to teach surgical procedures, dentistry, and other skills.

- Define patient simulators.
- Be aware of the existence of distance learning programs in health care educatio
- Discuss the role of expert systems, such as INTERNIST, MYCIN, and POEMS i health care.
- Describe the resources on the Internet, including medical literature database physicians' use of e-mail, general information and misinformation, and suppo groups, and be able to discuss both the positive and negative consequences using the Internet as a resource for health information.
- Discuss the availability of self-help software.
- Discuss the uses of computers in psychiatry.

KEY TERMS

ADAM
Centerwatch
Composite International Diagnostic Interview (CIDI)
CIDI-AUTO
CINAHL (Cumulative Index to Nursing and Allied Health Literature)
clinical pharmacology
ClinicalTrials.gov
Databank for Cardio-vascular Disease
Explorable Virtual Human
human patient simulators
ILIAD
INTERNIST
KISMET
Medi-Span
MEDLARS (Medical Literature Analysis and Retrieval System)
MEDLINE
Medscape
MYCIN
New Medicines in Development
pediasim
PLATO (Programmed Logic for Automatic Teaching Operation
Postoperative Expert Medical System (POEMS)
SDILINE (Selective Dissemination of Information Online
simulation software
Starbright World
Vesalius Project
Virtual Hospital
Virtual Human
Virtual Human Embryo
Visible Human Project

DISCUSSION QUESTIONS

1. Briefly discuss the Visible Human Project.
   The Visible Human Project is a computerized library of human anatomy at the Nation Library of Medicine. It began in 1986 and is an ongoing project. It has created "comple anatomically detailed, three-dimensional representations of the male and female huma body." The images are accessible over the Internet. Hundreds of people have used the images on computer screens where they can be rotated and flipped, taken apart and p back together. Structures can be enlarged and highlighted. The images, also available o CD-ROM, have been used by students of anatomy, researchers, surgeons, and dentists wh discovered a new face muscle. The Visible Human is available for both teaching an research. Some of the projects using data from the Visible Human include several thre dimensional views of the human body and images of magnetic resonance imaging (MRI and computed tomography (CT) scans. ADAM, a program, which is used to teac anatomy, uses data from the Visible Human.
2. Describe the Virtual Human Embryo.
   A new project called the Virtual Human Embryo is digitizing some of the seven thousan human embryos lost in miscarriages, which have been kept by the National Museum c Health and Medicine of the Armed Forces Institute of Pathology since the 1880s. A embryo develops in twenty-three stages over the first eight weeks of pregnancy. The proje will include at least one embryo from each stage. It will be sectioned and sliced. Each sli will be placed under a microscope and digital images will be created. Users will be able access the images on digital video disks (DVDs) and compact disks (CDs) and manipula and study them.

3. Discuss drill-and-practice and simulation software.
   Computer-assisted instruction (CAI) is used at all stages of the educational process. Drill-and-practice software is used to teach skills that require memorization. Simulation software simulates a complex process. The student is presented with a situation and given choices. The student is then shown what affect that choice would have on the situation. Early simulation programs used text and graphics to describe a situation. Later, animation and sound were added. Today, some programs use virtual reality so that the student actually feels as if he or she were performing a procedure such as administering an epidural.
4. Describe ADAM.
   ADAM teaches anatomy and physiology. It uses two- and three-dimensional images (some of them created from the Visible Human data) and has versions available for both patients and professionals. It is interactive, allowing the user to click away over one hundred layers of the body and see more than four thousand structures! Using multiple windows, the user can compare different views of one anatomical structure.
5. Virtual reality simulations help teach many skills. Discuss several.
   A device using a mannequin and computer imaging allows medical students to practice inserting a bronchoscope into a child's trachea. The epidural simulator allows the student to perform the procedure while feeling the resistance of the tissue, but without endangering a live patient. Students can learn to administer an IV from a simulation program instead of practicing on a rubber arm. In dentistry, virtual reality simulations make use of mannequins to allow students to practice filling cavities while watching both the mannequin and a monitor. The student feels the tooth via the instruments, learning to distinguish between a healthy and a diseased tooth. Virtual reality simulations are being used to train surgeons to perform minimally invasive operations.
6. Describe a human patient simulator.
   Human patient simulators are programmable mannequins on which students can practice medical procedures. The simulator has liquids flowing through its blood vessels, inhales oxygen and exhales carbon dioxide, produces heart and lung sounds, has eyes that open and close, pupils that dilate, a tongue that can swell to simulate an allergic reaction. The student can perform an electrocardiogram, take the pulse, measure blood pressure and temperature. Medications can be administered intravenously; the mannequin reads the bar code and reacts as it has been programmed to react. Students can practice intubations and needle decompression of pneumothorax (accumulation of air or gas in the lung); chest tubes may be inserted. Different types of patients can be simulated including a healthy adult, a woman experiencing problems with pregnancy, and a middle-aged man suffering from hypertension.
7. Briefly discuss expert systems.
   An expert system is an attempt to make a computer an expert in one narrow field. Both facts and rules about how the facts are used to make decisions in the field are entered in the computer. Expert systems are a branch of artificial intelligence, which examines how computers behave like human beings, that is, in "intelligent" ways. Expert systems have been used in medicine since the 1950s. They are meant to be decision support systems, which help, but do not replace, medical personnel. They are especially useful when there is a limited, well-defined area of knowledge needed for a decision, which will be based on objective data. The doctor enters symptoms, test results, and medical history. The computer either asks for more information or suggests a diagnosis, and perhaps treatment. Some systems give the diagnosis in the form of a probability.
8. Describe one suggested code of conduct for health-related Web sites.
   One code of conduct suggests that Web sites disclose any information that consumers would find useful, including who has a monetary interest, that they distinguish scientific information from advertising, attempt to assure the high quality of information, disclose privacy risks, and take steps to ensure privacy.
9. What is the digital divide?
   Access to health-related information on the Internet is not equally distributed through society, but is restricted to those with access to computers, with an Internet connection, and the

knowledge to make use of them. The digital divide refers to the gap between informati haves and have-nots. White and Asian Americans, those with higher incomes and high education, are more likely to have computer and Internet access than low-income, less we educated people and African Americans and Hispanics. People in rural areas have le access to the Internet than people in urban areas. By 2003, 61.8 percent of U.S. hou holds owned computers and of those 87.6 percent were linked to the Internet. The percen age of households with broadband connection grew from 9.1 to 19.9 percent from 2001 2003. Those with broadband connections are more likely to use the Internet than tho with dial-up connections. Although the digital divide is shrinking, it still persists in 200 according to a federal report. Race and ethnicity, family income, and education all infl ence Internet use among students. At school: Among white students, 67 percent use t Internet; this compares to 58 percent for Asian-Americans, 47 percent for African America and native American students, and 44 percent for Hispanic students. At home: 54 perce of white students, 27 percent of African American students, and 26 percent of Hispan students use the Internet. The higher the family income, the more likely a student is to u the Internet (at home or in school). The more education a parent has the higher the Inte net use. Lower use in some ethnic groups is tied to poverty.

10. What is MEDLARS?
    The National Library of Medicine provides a collection of forty computerized databas called medical literature analysis and retrieval system (MEDLARS) containing eightee million references. MEDLARS is available free via the Internet, and can be searched f bibliographical lists or for information.
11. List five of the MEDLARS databases.
    MEDLARS databases include Selective Dissemination of Information Online (SDILINE MEDLINE, AIDSLINE, AIDSTRIALS, and CANCERLIT.
12. Briefly describe ClinicalTrials.gov.
    ClinicalTrials.gov was launched in February 2000; it lists thousands of clinical tria along with their purpose, criteria for participation, location, and contact information. should be noted, however, that the purpose of drug trials is to test the effectiveness an safety of the medication, not to help those patients participating in the trial.
13. What is Starbright World?
    Starbright World is a network linking thirty thousand seriously ill children in one hu dred hospitals and many homes in North America. Children in the network can pl games, chat, send, and receive e-mail. They can also get medical information.
14. Health care providers disagree about the desirability of providing e-mail f patients. Comment.
    Doctors who oppose the use of e-mail cite concerns with liability (a paper trail), privac time, the possibilities of misunderstanding, and the slowness of e-mail compared with co versation. The small percent of doctors who provide e-mail state that patients are calm when they know there is an open line to their physicians, and therefore don't need to co municate as much. Some doctors who provide e-mail for their patients maintain that e-ma has not played a role in any malpractice suit.
15. Briefly describe MEDLINEplus.
    In 1998, the National Library of Medicine introduced MEDLINEplus, which is mea for the general public. In 2001, there were 2.3 hits per month. The information is selecte using strict guidelines to guarantee accuracy and objectivity.
16. Describe the Vesalius project.
    One goal of the Visible Human was to allow the use of three-dimensional anatomical mo els in education. The Vesalius project (Columbia University) is creating these mode (called maximal models) of anatomical regions and structures to be used in teachi anatomy.
17. Discuss the use of computers in psychiatry.
    Computers play a part in psychiatry from diagnosis to treatment. The first uses of compute in psychotherapy were in testing; later studies found the online tests comparable to tradition testing. Some studies found that some people are more open with a computer-administere

interview and more people were willing to participate in a computer-administered interview. A series of studies in 2004 found that computers and the Internet were helpful aids to therapy. The Web-Based Depression and Anxiety Test was found effective in diagnosing anxiety disorders and depression. Several programs that are effective include: Fear Fighter for phobias and panic, BTSteps for obsessive-compulsive disorder (OCD), Cope and Overcoming Depression Course for depression, and Balance for general anxiety disorder. Two programs have been found helpful for drinking: Behavioral Self-Control Program for Windows and Drinker's Checkup. Beating the Blues for depression and anxiety was found more effective than live therapy, and computer-aided therapy is cheaper. Although patients using computer-aided therapies are in some phone contact with live therapists, computers apparently do a good job at some sorts of therapies. There is computer-aided self-help for phobia, panic, nonsuicidal depression, and OCD.

Later studies tended to confirm the 2004 studies. Online screening programs for anxiety and mood disorders have been "generally equivalent" to assessment by a therapist. Some self-help programs on computers have been shown to be effective; on the Internet users can get feedback, making the programs more helpful. Internet-based treatment was found to be as effective as face-to-face treatment in a number of randomized clinical trials. Virtual reality is useful in treating certain phobias and has also been tested in randomized clinical trials and found effective. Virtual reality is being used to treat soldiers returning from Iraq with posttraumatic stress disorder. Internet therapy (Interapy) for those suffering from posttraumatic stress disorder was found to be very effective through self-reports. Interapy is also being tried for work-related stress. Interapy was found to be ineffective in treating insomnia. The Internet-based treatment was cognitive behavior therapy in all cases studied. Anxiety disorders have been treated for many years with controlled exposure to whatever provokes the anxiety. Investigations are being performed to see whether the exposure can be done using virtual reality technology.

IN THE NEWS

Correcting the Errors of Disclosure

by Benedict Carey

By now, tales of scientific conflict of interest have become all too familiar. In recent weeks, two top medical journals have been in the news for failing to disclose the financial ties of the academic authors of published papers, one involving antidepressant drugs, the other a medical device approved to treat depression.

But nondisclosure is only part of the story. Companies don't just hire doctors to do research—a practice that in theory ought to help keep businesses scientifically honest—they also trade on the researchers' names. Like producers shopping a new a movie, they go for star power, an A-list cast with names that themselves sell a product, and pull other doctors along, even when the evidence for a treatment is not strong.

Last week, an influential psychiatry journal, Neuropsychopharmacology, said it would print a correction, after revelations that it did not disclose the financial ties of authors of a paper reviewing a new treatment for depression. The treatment, a $15,000 chest implant that sends pulses of electricity to the brain, was approved for depression in 2005 after intense debate over its effectiveness.

At least as important as the failure to disclose financial ties were the authors themselves, and other consultants that the device manufacturer, Cyberonics Inc. of Houston, had hired.

(continued)

Correcting the Errors of Disclosure *(continued)*

Among them are Dr. Charles Nemeroff, one of the nation's most influential research psychiatrists and the editor of Neuropsychopharmacology; Dr. Dennis S. Charney, of the Mount Sinai School of Medicine, the editor of Biological Psychiatry; and Dr. A. John Rush of the University of Texas Southwestern Medical Center, who led the largest-ever long-term government study on depression.

These are precisely the sorts of experts the field relies on to help evaluate highly disputed data, like those Cyberonics has presented for the treatment.

In a bitter debate over the interpretation of these results, more than 20 experts at the Food and Drug Administration opposed the approval of the device for depression before being overruled by a senior official, according to a Senate Finance Committee investigation.

The device begged for some more public analysis. But few if any outside experts knew the data well enough to raise questions. And the scientists who did know the science and the data were all on the company's payroll.

"This is what companies do, try to get top researchers to accept large grants for research, or to consult, because they know those names make them look more legit," said Dr. Daniel Carlat, editor in chief of The Carlat Psychiatry Report, a well-regarded monthly newsletter, who in January reviewed the evidence for the implant and found it unconvincing.

The very presence of those names on papers reviewing the treatment, he said, "is a big part of the salesmanship that comes after getting approval."

One of the company's primary consultants, Harold Sackeim, a professor of psychiatry and radiology at Columbia, said that if device makers could not hire the field's top experts, effective new devices would never be approved. "This is not like pharmaceuticals, where the companies are much bigger and have their own experts," he said.

He added that he and other academic doctors advising the company "are a pretty small group, we all know each other, and the gestalt in the group carries a lot of weight."

By the time Cyberonics published its data widely—in Biological Psychiatry, the journal edited by Dr. Charney—the product was already approved and the game over. Doctors around the country are now discussing using the implant for chronically depressed patients, who are thought to number more than four million.

The company has focused on promotion, as have some of its consultants. At an American Psychiatry Association meeting in May, Dr. Rush sat in the Cyberonics booth, describing the benefits of the therapy to curious psychiatrists. In one of several presentations about the device, doctors reviewed its use for obesity, anxiety and Alzheimer's disease, purposes for which it is not approved.

And the recent review article that appeared without full disclosure was not focused on whether the device worked for depression, or for whom. It was a speculative essay about its mechanism of action—about how it worked.

One of the supposed strengths of American science is that it is decentralized and diverse: there are dozens of top researchers who are competitive and critical, enforcing a high standard. But when many or most of the leading figures are playing for the same team—an all-star team—that lineup itself may carry the day, regardless of the science.

SOURCES

"2001 Report to Congress on Telemedicine." February 2001. http://www.hrsa.gov/telehealth/pubs/report2001.htm (accessed December 29, 2007).

ADAM. 2006. http://www.adam.com (accessed August 24, 2006).

AIMS Industry Council. "What Is Medical Simulation?" 2006. http://www.medsim.org/what_medsim.asp (accessed December 28, 2007).

Aschoff, Susan. "A Diehard Patient." sptimes.com, April 30, 2002. http://www.sptimes.com/2002/04/30/Floridian/A_diehard_patient.shtml (accessed December 28, 2007).

Association of Schools of Public Health Distance Programs. 2003. asph.org (accessed August 24, 2006).

Beamish, Rita. "Computers Now Helping to Screen for Troubled Teen-Agers." *New York Times,* December 17, 1998, G9.

Bergfeld, Carlos. "A Dose of Virtual Reality." businessweek.com, July 26, 2006. http://www.businessweek.com/technology/content/jul2006/tc20060725_012342.htm?chan=top+news_top+news (accessed December 28, 2007).

Bitzer, Maryann D., and Martha C. Boudreaux. "Using a Computer to Teach Nursing." In *Computers in Nursing.* Edited by Rita D. Zielstorff, 171–85. Rockville, MD: Aspen, 1982.

Borowitz, Stephen, and Jeffrey Wyatt. "The Origin, Content, and Workload of E-mail Consultations." *JAMA* 280 (1998): 1321–4.

"Chapter 2. Review of the Literature." 2003. http://herkules.oulu.fi/isbn9514270215/html/c216.html (accessed January 6, 2008).

Choi, James J. "Viewing Virtual Hospital Content on a Personal Digital Assistant." March 2004. http://lib.cpums.edu.cn/jiepou/tupu/atlas/www.vh.org/welcome/help/vhpdausers.html (accessed August 24, 2006).

"CIDI Composite International Diagnostic Interview." 1999. http://www.hcp.med.harvard.edu/wmhcidi/ (accessed January 18, 2008).

Classen, D. C. "Clinical Decision Support Systems to Improve Clinical Practice and Quality of Care." *JAMA* 280 (1998): 1360–1.

"Digital Divide Still Separates Students." eschoolnews.com, September 6, 2006. http://www.eschoolnews.com/news/top-news/index.cfm?i=41296&CFID=2272416&CFTOKEN=83744007 (accessed December 28, 2007).

Eisenberg, Anne. "The Virtual Stomach (No, It's Not a Diet Aid)." nyt.com, October 31, 2002. http://query.nytimes.com/gst/fullpage.html?res=9807EFDC103FF932A05753C1A9649C8B63 (accessed December 28, 2007).

Emmelkamp, Paul M. G. "Technological Innovations in Clinical Assessment and Psychotherapy." *Psychotherapy and Psychosomatics,* 2005. http://content.karger.com/ProdukteDB/produkte.asp?Doi=87780 (accessed December 28, 2007).

Eng, Thomas R., et al., "Access to Health Information and Support: A Public Highway or a Private Road?" *JAMA* 280 (1998): 1371–5.

Epstein, Randi Hutter. "Sifting Through the Online Medical Jumble." nyt.com, January 28, 2003. http://query.nytimes.com/gst/fullpage.html?res=9901EED81239F93BA15752C0A9659C8B63 (accessed December 28, 2007).

"Evaluating Medical Information on the Web." November 17, 2003. http://www.ornl.gov/sci/techresources/Human_Genome/posters/chromosome/evaluate.shtml (accessed August 24, 2006).

"eXpert Laparoscopic Trainer." February 24, 2006. http://www.hmc.psu.edu/simulation/equipment/expert/expert.htm (accessed August 24, 2006).

"Fact Sheet." The Visible Human Project, February 16, 2001. http://www.nlm.nih.gov/research/visible/visible_human.html (accessed December 28, 2007).

Ferguson, Tom. "Digital Doctoring—Opportunities and Challenges in Electronic Patient-Physician Communication." *JAMA* 280 (1998): 1361–2.

Fisk, Sandra. "Doc in a Box a Home Health Software Guide." *Better Homes and Gardens,* August 1995, 44–52.

Gallagher, Anthony G., E. Matt Ritter, Howard Champion, Gerald Higgins, Marvin P. Fried, Gerald Moses, C. Daniel Smith, and Richard Satava. "Virtual Reality Simulation for the Operating Room." 2005. http://www.pubmedcentral.nih.gov/articlerender.fcgi?&pubmedid=15650649 (accessed January 18, 2008).

Griffith, Susan. "Virtual Dentistry Becomes Reality in Multimedia Lab." 2001. http://www.cwru.edu/pubs/cnews/2001/9-27/dent-sim.htm (accessed August 24, 2006).

Guernsey, Lisa. "A Dissent on the Digital Divide." nyt.com, September 18, 2003. http://query.nytimes.com/gst/fullpage.html?res=9F0DE7D6153AF93BA2575AC0A96 9C8B63 (accessed December 28, 2007).

Hafner, Katie. "'Dear Doctor' Meets 'Return to Sender.'" nyt.com, June 6, 2002. http://query.nytimes.com/gst/fullpage.html?res=9C0CE1DC1F3AF935A35755C0A96 9C8B63 (accessed December 28, 2007).

Hamilton, Robert A. "FDA Examining Computer Diagnosis." *FDA Consumer Magazine*, September 1995. http://www.fda.gov/fdac/features/795_compdiag.html (accessed August 24, 2006).

"Health Information On-Line." *FDA Consumer Magazine*, June 1996, revised January 1998. http://www.fda.gov/fdac/features/596_info.html (accessed August 24, 2006).

Hersh, William, and David Hickam. "How Well Do Physicians Use Electronic Information Retrieval Systems? A Framework for Investigation and Systematic Review." *JAMA* 280 (1998): 1347–52.

"How to Evaluate Health Information on the Internet: Questions and Answers." August 28, 2002. http://www.cancer.gov/cancertopics/factsheet/Information/internet (accessed December 28, 2007).

Imielinska, Celina, and Pat Molholt. "Incorporating 3D Virtual Anatomy into the Medical Curriculum, Communications of the ACM." *CACM* 48, no. 2 (2005): 49–54.

"Internet Pharmacy Doctors Charged." nyt.com, August 2, 2006 (accessed August 6, 2006).

"The 'Karlsruhe Endoscopic Surgery Trainer': A 'Virtual Reality' based Training System for Minimally Invasive Surgery," http://www.kismet.iai.fzk.de/TRAINER/mic_trainer1.html (accessed February 2, 2008).

Kolata, Gina. "Web Research Transforms Visit to the Doctor." nyt.com, March 6, 2000. http://query.nytimes.com/gst/fullpage.html?res=9D03E1D61538F935A35750C0A966 C8B63 (accessed December 28, 2007).

Kühnapfel, U., Ch. Kuhn, M. Hübner, H.-G. Krumm, H. Maaß, and B. Neisius. "The Karlsruhe Endoscopic Surgery Trainer as an Example for Virtual Reality in Medical Education." http://www-kismet.iai.fzk.de/KISMET/docs/UKMITAT.html (accessed January 12, 2008).

Le, Tao. "Medical Education and the Internet: This Changes Everything." *JAMA* 285, no. 6 (2001): 809.

Lindberg, Donald A. B. "The National Library of Medicine's Web Site for Physicians and Patients." *JAMA* 285, no. 6 (2001): 806.

Maddox, Peggy Jo. "Ethics and the Brave New World of E-Health." November 21, 2002. http:// www.nursingworld.org/MainMenuCategories/ANAMarketplace/ANAPeriodicals/OJIN/Columns/Ethics/Ethicsandehealth.aspx (accessed December 28, 2007).

Marriott, Michel. "Digital Divide Closing as Blacks Turn to Internet." nyt.com, March 31, 2006. http://www.nytimes.com/2006/03/31/us/31divide.html (accessed November 13, 2006).

"Medical Databases." 2003. medic8.com (accessed August 24, 2006).

"Medical Databases." March 19, 2002. allhealthnet.com (accessed August 24, 2006).

Morrow, David J. "Safety Data from F.D.A." nyt.com, September 10, 1998. http://query.nytimes.com/gst/fullpage.html?res=9B0DEED7103EF933A2575AC0A96E958260 (accessed December 28, 2007).

Mott, Ken. "Cancer and the Internet." *Newsweek*, August 19, 1996, 19.

The National Library of Medicine. "The Visible Human Project®." September 11, 2003. http:// www.nlm.nih.gov/research/visible/visible_human.html (accessed August 24, 2006).

Newman, Michelle G. "Technology in Psychotherapy: An Introduction." *JCLP* 60, no. 20 (2004): 141–5. http://www3.interscience.wiley.com/cgi-bin/abstract/106570982/ABSTRACT?CRETRY=1&SRETRY=0 (accessed December 28, 2007).

O'Connor, Anahad. "Images of Preserved Embryos to Become a Learning Tool." nyt.com, March 25, 2003. http://query.nytimes.com/gst/fullpage.html?res= 9C07E6DF1730F936A15750C0A9659C8B63 (accessed December 28, 2007).

"Patient Simulator Program: HPS Capabilities." http://www.cscc.edu/nursing/pspcapabilities.htm (accessed December 28, 2007).

Patsos, Mary. "The Internet and Medicine: Building a Community for Patients with Rare Diseases." *JAMA* 285, no. 6 (2001): 805.

"PediaSim Capabilities." http://www.cscc.edu/nursing/pspedsimcap.htm (accessed August 2 2006).

Prutkin, Jordan. "Cybermedical Skills for the Internet Age." *JAMA* 285, no. 6 (2001): 808.

"Psych Screen, Inc." psychscreen.com (accessed August 24, 2006).
"Public Health Workforce Development." May 12, 2003. http://www.phf.org/phworkforce.htm (accessed December 28, 2007).
Rajendran, Pam R. "The Internet: Ushering in a New Era of Medicine." *JAMA* 285, no. 6 (2001): 804–5.
"Robertson Janice Guidelines for Physician-Patient Electronic Communications." December 6, 2004. http://www.ama-assn.org/ama/pub/category/2386.html (accessed August 24, 2006).
Rubin, Rita. "Prescribing On Line . . . Industry's Rapid Growth, Change Defy Regulation." *USA Today,* October 2, 1998, 1, 2.
Scerbo, Mark. "Medical Reality Simulators: Have We Missed an Opportunity?" 2005. http://www.hfes.org/web/BulletinPdf/bulletin0505.pdf (accessed August 9, 2006).
Speilberg, Alissa. "On Call and Online, Sociohistorical, Legal and Ethical Implications of E-mail for the Patient-Physician Relationship." *JAMA* 280, no. 15 (1998): 1353–9.
"Starbright World." starbright.org (accessed August 24, 2006).
Termen, Amanda. "Closing the Digital Divide with Solar Wi-Fi." News.com, August 2, 2006. http://news.zdnet.com/2100-1035_22-6101071.html (accessed December 28, 2007).
Terry, Nicolas. "Access vs Quality Assurance: The e-Health Conundrum." February 14, 2001. http://jama.ama-assn.org/cgi/content/full/285/6/807 (accessed August 24, 2006).
Trowbridge, Robert, M.D., and Scott Weingarten, M.D., M.P.H., "Clinical Decision Support Systems," chapter 53 in *Making Health Care Safer: A Critical Analysis of Patient Safety Practices,* prepared for the Agency for Healthcare Research and Quality, contract no. 290-97-0013, 2001, http://www.ahrq.gov/clinic/ptsafety (accessed February 2, 2008).
"Virtual Hospital." 2008. http://www.uihealthcare.com/vh/ (accessed January 12, 2008).
"Virtual Reality Simulation Technology Improves Carotid Angiography Skills." Medical Studies/Trials, May 3, 2006. http://www.news-medical.net/?id=17717 (accessed December 29, 2007).
"The Visible Human Project: From Data to Knowledge." May 3, 2001. nlm.nih.gov/research/visible/data2knowledge.html (accessed August 24, 2006).
Urbankova, Alice, and Richard Lichtenthal. "DentSim Virtual Reality in Preclinical Operative Dentistry to Improve Psychomotor Skills: A Pilot Study." 2002. http://www.denx.com/research_and_publication_details.asp?id=33 (accessed December 29, 2007).
U.S. Department of Commerce. "A Nation Online: Entering the Broadband Age." September, 2004. http://www.ntia.doc.gov/reports/anol/index.html (accessed November 13, 2006).
"Web Site to Rate Content of Health Care News." *Star-Ledger,* April 17, 2006.
"What's New on Virtual Hospital?" 2004. http://lib.cpums.edu.cn/jiepou/tupu/atlas/www.vh.org/welcome/whatsnew/index.html (accessed August 24, 2006).
Winker, Margaret A., Annette Flanagin, Bonnie Chi-Lum, John White, Karen Andrews, Robert L. Kennett, Catherine D. DeAngelis, and Robert A. Musacchio. "Guidelines for Medical and Health Information on the Internet." August 7, 2001. http://www.ama-assn.org/ama/pub/category/1905.html (accessed August 24, 2006).
Zuger, Abigail. "HEALTH: Hospital, Clinic, Practice: 3 Views of Doctors and the Web; Reams of Information, Some of It Even Useful." nyt.com, October 25, 2000. http://query.nytimes.com/gst/fullpage.html?res=9D04E2DF1E3CF936A15753C1A9669C8B63&sec=&spon=&pagewanted=all (accessed December 29, 2007).

RELATED WEB SITES

The Federal Trade Commission (FTC) looks into complaints about false health claims on the Internet. Their Web page can help consumers evaluate claims. http://www.ftc.gov/bcp/conline/edcams/cureall is the Federal Trade Commission's *Operation Cure-all* page.

The Food and Drug Administration (FDA) regulates drugs and medical devices. *Buying Medicines and Medical Products Online* is at http://www.fda.gov/oc/buyonline.

The National Cancer Institute is located at http://cancer.gov.

The Harvard School of Public Health provides consumers with *Ten Questions to Help Make Sense of Health Headlines* at http://www.health-insight.com.

The Journal of the American Medical Association is available at http://jama.ama-assn.org.

The National Library of Medicine provides access to Medline and Medline*plus* at http://www.nlm.nih.gov.

CHAPTER 11

Information Technology in Rehabilitative Therapies: Computerized Medical Devices, Assistive Technology, and Prosthetic Devices

CHAPTER OUTLINE

Learning Objectives
Overview
Computerized Medical Instruments and Devices
- *Computerized Devices in Optometry/Ophthalmology*

Assistive Devices
- *Augmentative Communications Devices*
- *Environmental Control Systems*

Prosthetic Devices
Computerized Functional Electrical Stimulation Technology
Risks Posed by Implants
Computers in Rehabilitative Therapies
Conclusion
In the News
Chapter Summary
Key Terms
Review Exercises
Sources
Related Web Sites

LEARNING OBJECTIVES

After reading this chapter, you will be able to

- Describe the contribution made to the design of medical devices by information technology and be able to discuss the advantages of computerized medical monitoring systems over their predecessors.
- Describe the use of computerized devices in delivering medications.
- Discuss the Americans with Disabilities Act of 1990 and be able to discuss the impact digital technology has had on assistive devices for people with physical challenges.
  - List assistive devices for those with impaired vision, speech, hearing, and mobility.
  - Discuss speech-recognition devices, speech synthesizers, and screen readers.
- Describe the contributions computer technology has made to the development of prosthetics.
  - Discuss the contribution of computer technology to the improvement of myoelectric limbs.
  - Discuss the contributions computer technology has made to improving sight for the blind and hearing for the deaf.

- Define functional electrical stimulation.
  - List its uses in implanted devices such as pacemakers.
  - Discuss its use in simulating physical workouts for paralyzed muscles and resto ing movement to paralyzed limbs.
- Discuss the risks posed by implants.
- Discuss the uses of computers in rehabilitative therapies.

KEY TERMS

adaptive technology
Americans with Disabilities Act of 1990
arrhythmia monitors
assistive technology
augmentative communication device
biomicroscopes
Biomove 3000
BrainGate Neural Interface System
computerized functional electrical stimulation (CFES or FES)
computerized medical instrument
corneal topography
environmental control systems
EYESI surgical simulator
fetal monitors
GDx Access
head mouse
Heidelberg retinal tomograph (HRT)
HELEN (HELp Neuropsychology)
microdialysis
motion monitor
myoelectric limb
neonatal monitors
Neuromove
neuroprosthesis
optical biometry
Optomap Panoramic2(
osseointegration
page scanners
physiological monitoring system:
prosthetic devices
puff straws
pulmonary monitors
screen reader software
smart glasses
speech recognition
speech synthesizer
text telephones
tonometers
Tracey visual function analyzer
vision replacement therapy

DISCUSSION QUESTIONS

1. Define computerized medical instruments.
   Computerized medical instruments are electronic devices equipped with microprocesso They provide direct patient services such as monitoring and administering medication treatment.
2. Describe the insulin pump.
   Computerized drug delivery systems are used to give medications. Insulin pumps include battery-operated pump and a computer chip. The pump is not automatic. However, the ch allows the user to control the amount of insulin administered. Insulin is administered via plastic tube inserted under the skin; the tube is changed every two or three days. The pun is worn externally and continually delivers insulin according to the user's program.
3. Define three computerized monitoring systems.
   Computerized physiological monitoring systems analyze blood, arrhythmia monitors mon tor heart rates, and pulmonary monitors measure blood flow through the heart and resp ratory rate.
4. Are computerized devices more accurate than their predecessors?
   Computerized instruments are both more accurate and more reliable than their predece sors. For example, an infusion pump can be set at the desired rate and that rate will maintained. Its predecessor, whose flow had to be estimated, could have its rate changed l the patient's movements. Computerized cardiac monitors are able, unlike their predece sors, to distinguish between cardiac arrest and a wire coming loose.
5. Where are networked devices most likely to be found in a hospital?
   Networked equipment is most common in emergency rooms, operating rooms, and critic and intensive care units. Because a network makes patient information immediate available anywhere in the hospital and allows a specialist to consult with the emergen room online, it can reduce response time in emergencies.

6. Define ophthalmologist and optometrist.
   An ophthalmologist is a doctor who treats eye diseases. An optometrist examines the eye and prescribes glasses.
7. Briefly describe smart glasses.
   The lenses are two flat pieces of glass; between them in a 5-micron space is liquid crystal. The liquid crystal is coated with a transparent electrode that transmits light. At present, the prototype glasses need to be switched on and off before they will change focus. Soon they will automatically adjust (like a camera lens). In the future, you will not need prescriptions for new glasses, just a new program.
8. Define the Americans with Disabilities Act of 1990.
   The Americans with Disabilities Act of 1990 prohibits discrimination against people with disabilities and requires that businesses with more than fifteen employees provide "reasonable accommodation" to allow the disabled to perform their jobs.
9. Describe two adaptive mice.
   Other input devices include the head mouse, which moves the cursor according to the user's head motions. Puff straws allow people to control the mouse with their mouths.
10. What is an augmentative communication device?
    An augmentative communication device is any device that helps a person communicate. Medicare began covering these devices in 2002. Those who lack the ability to speak or whose speech is impaired can have a computer speak for them. The device should allow the user to communicate basic needs, carry on conversations, work with a computer, and complete assignments for work or school.
11. Briefly describe an environmental control system.
    Environmental control systems help physically challenged people control their environments. Speech-recognition technology can be used in the home to control appliances. One system understands and obeys voice commands. Using this system, one can control home appliances with voice commands. It also acts as a speaker phone that will dial or answer calls on command. Other environmental control systems allow the installation of a single switch to control the operation of several appliances (including other controllers). Environmental control systems can be used to control any electrical appliance in the home. This would include lights, telephones, computers, appliances, infrared devices, security systems, sprinklers, doors, curtains, and electric beds. Voice, joysticks, or switches may control the system. This may enable physically challenged people to live independently at home.
12. Define myoelectric limb.
    Myoelectric limbs are artificial limbs containing motors and responding to the electrical signals transmitted by the residual limb to electrodes mounted in the socket.
13. Describe the C-leg.
    The C-leg (computerized leg) is a lower leg prosthesis. It includes a prosthetic knee and shin system controlled by a microprocessor. It is made of lightweight carbon fiber and gets its power from a rechargeable battery. With a traditional prosthesis, the user has to think about each step. But the C-leg analyzes gait fifty times per second; it anticipates movement and thus thinks for the patient. It is supposed to adjust to uneven ground by itself, but results from studies are mixed. It requires less energy for walking at speeds slower or faster than usual, but not at the walker's usual speed; the user does not have to think about changing walking speed.
14. Describe the uses of CFES technology.
    Computerized functional electrical stimulation (CFES or FES) directly applies low-level electrical stimulation to muscles that cannot receive these signals from the brain. CFES technology was originally developed by NASA. FES has been used for many years in pacemakers and other implanted devices. It is now used to strengthen paralyzed muscles with exercise. It can be used to simulate a full cardiovascular workout for people who are paralyzed, reducing the secondary effects of paralysis. FES even makes it possible to restore movement to some limbs paralyzed by stroke and spinal injury.
15. What are some of the risks of implants?
    Implants pose some risks including rejection of the implant and infection at the site. Some implants can cause blood clots and require the user to take anticlotting medications.

16. Briefly describe BrainGate.
    BrainGate involves implanting a chip in the brain that will convert brain cell impulses computer signals. In 2006, in the pilot clinical trial, "A man with paralysis of all fo limbs could directly control objects around him . . . using only his thoughts." BrainGate surgically implanted. It includes a sensor that records brainwaves and interprets them. Ti patients with the implants who suffered from spinal cord injuries can now hold a convers tion and control a cursor at the same time. One of them was able to control a robotic ar From the first, the patients were able to move limbs by thinking about the motion.
17. Briefly describe neuromodulation.
    Neuromodulation is a new field that may help treat disorders of the central nervous syste including chronic pain. It. ". . . involves implanting an electrode within the nervous syste such as on or below the surface (cortex) of the brain, the spinal cord or the peripheral nerve. pacemaker-like device called a neurostimulator is implanted in the upper chest and connecte under the skin to the electrode. The device is programmed to deliver an electrical current stimulate targeted nerve cells and nerve fibers in the brain, spinal cord and peripheral nerve.
18. Describe HELEN.
    HELEN (HELp Neuropsychology) contains diagnostic analyses that keep track of speci tests and tasks performed by the stroke patient. The tasks and methods of solving them a kept in a database. HELEN also contains a rehabilitative module. Tasks are provided f the patient. The methods used to solve the task is information for the neuropsychologi Interactive procedures allow the patient to try different solutions to the problem. Defic can be pinpointed, and problems that engage the intact portion of the brain can be pr sented. The patient can control the pace of rehabilitation.
19. What is vision replacement therapy (VRT)?
    Vision replacement therapy (VRT) retrains the brain. Using dots on a computer screen, t aim is to stimulate peripheral vision. This therapy can be effective years after a stro occurred. It is based on the fact that the brain is not fixed, but can rewire itself.
20. How can virtual reality be used to control phantom pain experienced by a amputee?
    Virtual reality is being used experimentally to help people with amputations control pha tom pain. The system gives the illusion that the amputated limb is still there. Using a hea set, the patient sees himself or herself with two arms or legs. They are able to use the physic limb to control the virtual limb. Five patients have tried the system. "Four out of the fi patients report[ed] improvement in their phantom limb pain."

IN THE NEWS

Paralyzed Man Uses Thoughts to Move a Cursor

by Andrew Pollack

A paralyzed man with a small sensor implanted in his brain was able to control a computer, a television set and a robot using only his thoughts, scientists reported yesterday.

Those results offer hope that in the future, people with spinal cord injuries, Lou Gehrig's disease or other conditions that impair movement may be able to communicate or better control their world.

"If your brain can do it, we can tap into it," said John P. Donoghue, a professor of neuroscience at Brown University who has led development of the system and was the senior author of a report on it being published in today's issue of the journal Nature.

In a variety of experiments, the first person to receive the implant, Matthew Nagle, moved a cursor, opened e-mail, played a simple video game called Pong and drew a crude circle on the screen. He could change the channel or volume on a television set, move a robot arm somewhat, and open and close a prosthetic hand.

Although his cursor control was sometimes wobbly, the basic movements were not hard to learn.

"I pretty much had that mastered in four days," Mr. Nagle, 26, said in a telephone interview from the New England Sinai Hospital and Rehabilitation Center in Stoughton, Mass. He said the implant did not cause any pain.

Mr. Nagle, a former high school football star in Weymouth, Mass., was paralyzed below the shoulders after being stabbed in the neck during a melee at a beach in July 2001. He said he had not been involved in starting the brawl and did not even know what had sparked it. The man who stabbed him is now serving 10 years in prison, he said.

Implants like the one he received had previously worked in monkeys. There have also been some tests of a simpler sensor implant in people, as well as systems using electrodes outside the scalp. And Mr. Nagle has talked before about his experience.

But the paper in Nature is the first peer-reviewed publication of an experiment in people with a more sophisticated implant, able to monitor many more brain neurons than earlier devices. The paper helps "shift the notion of such 'implantable neuromotor prosthetics' from science fiction towards reality," Stephen H. Scott, professor of anatomy and cell biology at Queen's University in Ontario, wrote in a commentary in the journal.

The sensor measures 4 millimeters by 4 millimeters—less than a fifth of an inch long and wide—and contains 100 tiny electrodes. The device was implanted in the area of Mr. Nagle's motor cortex responsible for arm movement and was connected to a pedestal that protruded from the top of his skull.

When the device was to be used, technicians plugged a cable connected to a computer into the pedestal. So Mr. Nagle was directly wired to a computer, somewhat like a character in the "Matrix" movies.

Mr. Nagle would then imagine moving his arm to hit various targets. The implanted sensor eavesdropped on the electrical signals emitted by neurons in his motor cortex as they controlled the imaginary arm movement.

Obstacles must be overcome, though, before brain implants become practical. For one thing, the electrodes' ability to detect brain signals begins to deteriorate after several months, for reasons not fully understood. In addition, the implant would ideally transmit signals wirelessly out of the brain, doing away with the permanent hole in the head and the accompanying risk of infection. Further, the testing involving Mr. Nagle required recalibration of the system each day, a task that took technicians about half an hour.

Still, scientists said the study was particularly important because it showed that the neurons in Mr. Nagle's motor cortex were still active years after they had last had a role to play in moving his arms.

The implant system, known as the BrainGate, is being developed by Cyberkinetics Neurotechnology Systems Inc. of Foxborough, Mass. The company is now testing the system in three other people, who remain anonymous: one with a spinal cord injury, one with Lou Gehrig's disease and one who had a brain stem stroke.

Timothy R. Surgenor, president and chief executive, said Cyberkinetics hoped to have an implant approved for marketing as early as 2008 or 2009. Dr. Donoghue, the chief developer, is co-founder and chief scientist of Cyberkinetics. Some of the paper's other authors work at the company, while still others are from academic or medical institutions including Massachusetts General Hospital.

Like his performance in other tasks, Mr. Nagle's control of the computer cursor was not particularly smooth. When his goal was to guide the cursor from the center of the screen to a target on the perimeter, he hit the target 73 to 95 percent of the time. When he did, it took 2.5 seconds on average, but sometimes

(continued)

Paralyzed Man Uses Thoughts to Move a Cursor *(continued)*

much longer. And the second patient tested with the implant had worse control than he, the paper said.

By contrast, healthy people moving the cursor by hand hit the target almost every time, and in only one second.

Dr. Jonathan R. Wolpaw, a researcher at the New York State Department of Health, said the BrainGate performance did not appear to be substantially better than that of a noninvasive system he is developing using electroencephalography, in which electrodes are placed outside the scalp.

"If you are going to have something implanted into your brain," Dr. Wolpaw said, "you'd probably want it to be a lot better."

Dr. Donoghue and other proponents of the implants say they have the potential to be a lot better, because they are much closer to the relevant neurons than are the scalp electrodes, which get signals from millions of neurons all over the brain.

One way to improve implant performance was suggested by another paper in the same issue of Nature. In a study involving monkeys, Krishna V. Shenoy and colleagues at Stanford University eavesdropped not on the neurons controlling arm movement but on those expressing the intention to move, which occurs earlier and would make the system work faster.

"Instead of sliding the cursor out to the target, we can just predict which target would be hit and the cursor simply leaps there," said Dr. Shenoy, an assistant professor of electrical engineering and neurosciences. He said the system could operate at the equivalent of typing 15 words a minute, about four times as fast as the devices produced by Cyberkinetics and Dr. Wolpaw.

After more than a year, Mr. Nagle had his implant removed so he could undergo another operation, which allowed him to breathe without a ventilator. He can control a computer by voice, so he does not really need the implant. But he said he was happy he had volunteered for the experiment.

"It gave a lot of people hope," he said.

Growing Debate as Doctors Train on New Devices

by Barry Meier

Last summer, rival cardiologists in Rock Hill, S.C., decided to learn how to perform a lucrative new procedure, implanting a defibrillator, a device that protects against fatal heart rhythms.

One doctor attended weekend classroom sessions sponsored by a professional medical organization, passed a daylong written test given by that group and implanted defibrillators in 10 patients while an expert observed.

But by then, four other doctors at a competing practice had left him in the dust, implanting 75 devices. They chose a separate training program, provided free and tailored to their liking by a little-known device maker named Biotronik. Only one of the four doctors so far has taken the recommended daylong competency test. The training also apparently had unorthodox elements: two doctors sometimes trained together on one patient, a technique that experts called highly unusual.

The different training regimens like the ones followed by the Rock Hill physicians are at the center of a growing and often contentious debate. As companies develop more sophisticated devices like advanced pacemakers and carotid artery stents, medical experts are asking how doctors should best be trained— and who should train them—to implant such devices without compromising patient safety.

The growing use of the costly defibrillators is drawing particular attention. Until recently, such units were typically implanted by highly trained heart device specialists. But since last year, when the government agreed to pay for tens of thousands more patients annually to get such devices, many new practitioners like those in Rock Hill have entered the field. One result is that patients do not realize that the training and experience of doctors can vary widely.

"A patient does not know whether they are a doctor's third implant or their 300th," said Dr. Charles E. Swerdlow, a heart device expert in Los Angeles who advocates rigorous training standards.

To meet patient demand, the Heart Rhythm Society, a professional group that represents experts like Dr. Swerdlow, adopted so-called fast-track training guidelines two years ago for doctors who had not implanted defibrillators before. But those guidelines, of which the daylong written test is one part, are voluntary. No one knows what percentage of physicians who have recently begun to put in defibrillators are following the guidelines.

At the same time, makers of the devices have jumped into the mix by offering free schooling. That has prompted concerns about possible conflicts of interest, since doctors may return the favor when deciding which company's units to implant in patients.

Separately, federal officials started collecting data last year to determine, among other things, if the rate of complications from implant surgery differs between heart device specialists and other doctors. Such specialists, who are known as electrophysiologists, are cardiologists who undergo a year or more of added training at a teaching hospital in the treatment of abnormal heart rhythms, including device use.

That reporting has just started. Patient deaths during defibrillator implants are extremely rare. Recent government data indicates they occur at a rate of about .03 percent. An analysis by The New York Times of the first 45,000 implants reported into the Medicare database indicates that the death rate for patients of nonelectrophysiologists was 1.5 times that for patients of the specialists, and that the complication rate was slightly higher as well. Medical statisticians cautioned that such raw data would have to be analyzed further to determine whether significant differences existed.

It is in places like Rock Hill, a city of 50,000 people, located 30 miles south of Charlotte, N.C., that the broader national debate over physician training, and the role of device makers in it, has been playing out.

The tab for Biotronik for training the four physicians, for example, could total $50,000 or more, according to a consultant's contract and company data. But since last year, Biotronik has more than recouped those costs in sales of defibrillators, which sell for about $20,000 each.

By their own accounting, those doctors estimated that, with only a few exceptions, all of their 100 defibrillator patients got a Biotronik device. That provided the company, which has a scant 1 percent market share nationwide, with an estimated $2 million in revenue.

The doctors, who belong to a practice called Carolina Cardiology Associates, said in an interview that they used Biotronik devices because they thought they were superior, and not because of the free training. They also say they have a strong patient safety record.

(continued)

Growing Debate as Doctors Train on New Devices *(continued)*

"No one can buy my business," said Dr. Jugalkishor K. Shah, the president of Carolina Cardiology. "I think that Biotronik has very good technology."

But in March, a partner of their Rock Hill competitor sent a letter to federal health care fraud officials urging them to investigate whether Biotronik intended to influence physicians when it paid to train doctors in Rock Hill and other areas.

"It is a way that they have actually bought their way into these hospitals," that physician, Dr. Paul G. Colavita, wrote, referring to Biotronik. Dr. Colavita is the president of the Sanger Clinic, a large cardiology practice based in Charlotte, N.C.

A Biotronik executive, Jake Langer, rejected that assertion, saying that doctors whose training is underwritten by the company are not obligated to use its products.

The scramble by doctors to get quickly trained in defibrillator use was accelerated in January 2005 when the federal government sharply increased the number of patients for whom it will pay to get such a device, potentially bringing the figure to 500,000 people. Physicians have responded. Since then, for example, more than 900 doctors have paid $700 each to attend weekend sessions about defibrillators offered by the Heart Rhythm Society.

For all involved, there is big money in heart devices. And Biotronik is not the only company courting new practitioners. One manufacturer, St. Jude Medical, has sent about a dozen cardiologists over the last year to a Mexico City hospital for hands-on training. Another big maker, Medtronic, has turned three tractor-trailers into traveling mock operating rooms in which physicians can learn how to use cardiac resynchronization devices.

To implant a defibrillator, a tissue "pocket" is created under a patient's skin near the shoulder, and electrical cables, known as leads, are threaded through veins to connect the unit to the heart. Implant complications include blood clots, infections and, in a small number of cases, death.

Many doctors now implanting defibrillators, like those in Rock Hill, have previously put in pacemakers, devices that regulate a heart that is beating too slowly. While the skills used to implant the two devices are similar, electrophysiologists said that managing defibrillator patients was complex.

"The follow-up of these patients is different, the indications are different, the troubleshooting is different," said Dr. Anne B. Curtis of the University of South Florida who, until recently, was president of the heart society.

That group, which represents electrophysiologists, has been split over nontraditional training. In 2004, it issued fast-track training recommendations, citing growing patient demand, a lack of specialists in rural areas and reports that device companies were running their own programs. Last year, after members complained, it toughened those guidelines.

Some cardiologists say they think electrophysiologists are most concerned about another issue—their incomes. More than two decades ago, they say, surgeons raised safety issues when cardiologists started implanting pacemakers; today, cardiologists implant most of them.

"This is about protecting turf," said Dr. Sushil Singhi, who practices with Carolina Cardiology.

Whatever the case, some newcomers have homework to do. Last summer, 250 doctors took a daylong written exam given by the heart society to test their knowledge of defibrillators. One in three failed.

All heart device makers, including Biotronik, say they support the heart society's training guidelines. But as events in Rock Hill suggest, that support may be equivocal at times. They also show that doctors can take whatever training route they choose. The head of Carolina Cardiology, Dr. Shah, arrived in Rock Hill about 22 years ago as the town's first full-time cardiologist. About six years later, the Sanger Clinic in Charlotte opened a satellite office there.

Before last year, heart patients needing a defibrillator had to travel to Charlotte or to Columbia, S.C., 70 miles south. But as patient demand increased in 2005, local cardiologists decided it made more sense to do the procedures at a Rock Hill hospital, Piedmont Medical Center.

"Most of these people are old and sick, so they don't like to travel," said Dr. Nathaniel C. Edwards, who works in the Sanger Clinic's Rock Hill office.

Dr. Edwards said he decided to follow the heart society's guidelines both to improve his skills and to protect himself from liability. "If anything goes wrong in an implant and I get sued, it protects me legally," he said.

Across town, Dr. Shah said that his efforts in recent years to hire an electrophysiologist for his practice were unsuccessful. He added that both he and several colleagues were convinced that they could be properly trained without following all of the society's recommendations.

"I feel that the best learning procedure is to have someone standing there and showing you how he does it," said Dr. Shah, adding he had learned many new techniques during his long career.

At first, Dr. Shah reached out to Medtronic, the nation's biggest heart device maker, rather than Biotronik, for help in defibrillator training. And that request set off events that have resulted in bitter feelings and a string of accusations, like Dr. Colavita's claim that Biotronik is trying to tie implant training to device sales.

Last summer, Dr. Shah asked the local Medtronic sales representative, Robert Gray, if the company could provide an expert to teach him and his colleagues how to implant defibrillators. At that time, Carolina Cardiology was primarily using Medtronic pacemakers.

Dr. Shah said he was told by Mr. Gray that Medtronic typically did not supply such experts. But Mr. Gray and other Medtronic officials later told doctors with the Sanger Clinic that they had turned down Dr. Shah for other reasons, too.

A Medtronic spokesman, Robert Clark, said that Dr. Shah made it clear to company officials that he did not intend to follow the heart society's guidelines and wanted training brought to him. In addition, the cardiologist told them that if Medtronic did not do what he wanted, he would switch his business to a company that would, Mr. Clark said.

"There was nothing unclear in our sales representatives' minds" about what Dr. Shah meant, Mr. Clark said.

The doctor denied tying his business to training. "I did not threaten anyone," Dr. Shah said.

Whatever occurred, Biotronik stepped in. The company put on classroom sessions especially for the Carolina Cardiology doctors at a Charlotte-area restaurant, the Providence Bistro, and a nearby hotel. One of the speakers was Dr. G. Conrad Bauknight Jr., a electrophysiologist based in Columbia, who was hired last August by Biotronik and its local distributor to oversee the physicians' hands-on training.

Both Dr. Bauknight and the distributor, R. Kenyon Wells, declined to be interviewed for this article, as did Mr. Langer, the Biotronik executive.

The Heart Rhythm Society has stated that classroom courses used for fast-track training "cannot be provided directly" by the industry because of the potential for conflicts of interest. In a written response, Mr. Langer of Biotronik maintained that it was "always explicitly" stated at company-sponsored events that they did not meet

(continued)

Growing Debate as Doctors Train on New Devices *(continued)*

the heart society's requirements. Dr. Singhi, who attended those sessions, said he never heard such disclaimers.

He added that about a dozen of the hands-on patient implants supervised by Dr. Bauknight were "doubles," or cases in which two doctors trained on one patient. Several experts like Dr. Swerdlow in Los Angeles said they were puzzled by the approach, because doctors were supervised to see if they could handle a new procedure alone.

"You don't get a driver's license if one guy does the turns and the other one parallel parks," Dr. Swerdlow said.

Dr. Bauknight did not respond to inquiries about Dr. Singhi's description of some training implants. In an earlier letter, he stated that he trained new implanters according to the heart society's guidelines.

In addition to defibrillators, the majority of the pacemakers now implanted by doctors at Carolina Cardiology are also made by Biotronik. Dr. Shah and others there insist that they are using the units because they have superior features that automatically alert a doctor to possible problems.

They also said that Dr. Bauknight provided excellent training and pointed out that Medtronic had also hired him to teach one member of their group how to implant a specific type of defibrillator. Mr. Clark, the Medtronic spokesman, confirmed that Medtronic had done so but said that thus far it had used Dr. Bauknight's services for one day.

Ultimately, hospitals decide how much experience a doctor needs to perform a procedure like a defibrillator implant. At some facilities, none of the Rock Hill doctors would have made the cut because those hospitals give credentials only to formally trained electrophysiologists. When Piedmont Medical set its defibrillator standards last August, it set ones that were less stringent than those recommended by the heart society, both Dr. Edwards and Dr. Shah said.

Piedmont Medical, which is owned by Tenet Healthcare, said in a statement that it set rigorous standards but declined to release them, stating in the letter that the guidelines are "protected by the peer review privilege." With respect to the hospital's complication rate, Myra Joines, a hospital spokeswoman, added that that were there no significant differences between the complication rates of Dr. Edwards' and Dr. Shah's group.

For its part, the Heart Rhythm Society plans to drop support in 2008 for fast track training, saying that by then there should be plenty of implanters to meet patient needs. It is also around then that Medicare officials should have enough data to know whether those new implanters were any better or worse for patients.

Study Finds High Rate of Recalls of Heart Devices Used in Emergencies

by Barry Meier

BOSTON, May 17—As the use of life-saving emergency defibrillators has proliferated over the last decade, so have recalls of the devices because of their potential to fail, according to data to be presented Thursday at a medical meeting here.

A study based on Food and Drug Administration records from the last 10 years found that about 164,000 emergency defibrillators—or about one out of every five units sold during the period—had been subject to an agency recall or alert.

During that period, the F.D.A. also received 370 reports of deaths in which defibrillators or critical components malfunctioned during attempts to resuscitate patients in cardiac arrest, researchers reported. It is not clear how many of those patients might have been saved had the devices functioned properly.

The study's lead author, Dr. William H. Maisel of Beth Israel Deaconess Medical Center in Boston, said the growing use of emergency external defibrillators—portable devices like those used by paramedics and in hospitals that shock failed hearts back into normal rhythms—has led to thousands of saved lives.

But Dr. Maisel, who is a consultant to the F.D.A., said the data raised questions about the reliability of external defibrillators and how quickly users are learning about recalls.

"Many failures occurred during life-threatening circumstances," Dr. Maisel said. "It does not mean that every one of these people could have been saved, but these are very high-risk malfunctions." The study did not address internal defibrillators, which are surgically implanted into the chests of heart patients who are at risk of cardiac arrest.

For F.D.A. officials, the issue of how to alert owners of external defibrillators about problems is particularly complex because the devices have increasingly moved outside traditional medical settings into places like hotels, schools and homes. That trend has meant defibrillators are readily available when needed, but it also means alerting users to problems has become more problematic.

A separate report to be presented Thursday at a meeting here of the Heart Rhythm Society, a group that represents doctors who implant devices like defibrillators, found a far lower rate of complications from device replacements than a recent medical journal had reported.

Such complications can occur when an implanted heart device is removed because of a recall or to replace the batteries.

All patients who use internal defibrillators have those units replaced about every five years when the batteries wear out.

In the latest study, researchers from the Mayo Clinic said a five-year review of complications like infections and blood clots at that center found a rate of about 1.24 percent, which is consistent with previous estimates of such risks.

A study by Canadian researchers published last month in The Journal of the American Medical Association found that 5.8 percent of patients in that country who underwent replacement procedures because their defibrillators were the subject of recalls experienced serious complications. Put another way, the Canadian complication rate, which received widespread attention, was four times that found at the Mayo Clinic.

Dr. David L. Hayes, a professor of medicine at the Mayo Clinic College of Medicine in Rochester, Minn., said it was difficult to compare the Mayo findings with those of the Canadian researchers because, among other things, his study was performed at one center and the Canadian data reflected outcomes at hospitals throughout that country. Still, the divergent findings suggest that patients

(continued)

Study Finds High Rate of Recalls of Heart Devices Used in Emergencies *(continued)*

may face far different levels of risk depending on where the replacement procedure is performed.

The surgical risks related to device replacement appear to be the same whether a unit is replaced on a normal schedule or prematurely because of a defect. Most experts agree that devices should be replaced early only in patients who have health problems that make them dependent on the device.

With respect to the new data on external defibrillators, Dr. Maisel and a colleague, Dr. Jignesh S. Shah, conducted their study by reviewing all recall notices and safety alerts contained in weekly F.D.A. reports from 1996 to 2005. During that period, sales of the units increased on an annual basis about tenfold, growing to 200,000 last year from about 20,000 in 1996, researchers said.

Over that time, the agency issued 52 advisories about malfunctions in either emergency units or their critical components, like the cables used to connect a unit to a patient's chest. The annual number of alerts issued by the agency grew significantly over the period, the researchers said.

Dr. Maisel and Dr. Shah also reviewed so-called adverse event reports filed with the F.D.A. over the period and found 370 episodes in which a defibrillator reportedly malfunctioned during efforts to revive a patient with a particular type of deadly heart rhythm. Such devices are designed to treat that rhythm, known as ventricular fibrillation, which causes the heart to beat so rapidly that blood is not pumped out and cardiac arrest occurs.

Dr. Maisel said the number of episodes in which an external defibrillator malfunctioned might be significantly higher because the F.D.A. had received 801 adverse-event reports associated with a death. However, he said that he and Dr. Shah had decided to use the lower 370 figure because that number represented the number of cases in which an emergency worker or a manufacturer had confirmed a malfunction.

Dr. Maisel said he had been unable to correlate the number of malfunctions with devices that had been recalled because there was not enough information in public records to make that connection.

Universal ID Systems Urged for Medical Devices

by Barnaby J. Feder

Spurred by repeated problems monitoring malfunctions in medical devices after they have been approved for sale, federal regulators are moving toward requiring the industry and hospitals to adopt a universal system for using bar codes or other technology to identify individual devices.

Such a regulation would follow up on identification requirements adopted in 2004 by the Food and Drug Administration for drugs and biological agents like vaccines under a rule being phased in. A proposal to include devices in the 2004 rule was defeated under pressure from the industry.

Device makers argued in 2004 that the approaches being considered were impractical for their far more diversified industry, which makes everything from disposable bandages and needles to implants meant to function inside the body for decades. And unlike drugs, some devices are sterilized for reuse.

Since then, F.D.A. regulators have been criticized for their inability to gather reliable data on the role of various devices in patient injuries and deaths. And regulators have been concerned about how difficult it has often been for hospitals and clinics to identify particular lots of devices that pose continuing risks to patients once a recall has been announced, said Larry G. Kessler, director of the Office of Science and Engineering Laboratories in the agency's Center for Devices and Radiological Health.

The F.D.A.'s concerns and the proposed strategy for identification rules for devices are scheduled to be published today in the Federal Register. The notice will begin a 90-day comment period. A final regulation is not expected before 2007, Mr. Kessler said.

Mr. Kessler said that a universal identification system might address a range of product compatibility challenges. Many hospitals routinely refuse to use advanced magnetic resonance imaging scanning equipment on patients with metal or battery-powered implants because they have no easy way of identifying whether such patients—or their particular implant—could be harmed by the radiation from the scanner.

SOURCES

"$3.1 Million NIH Grant Funds Research to Help Stroke Patients." October 17, 2002. http://www.udel.edu/PR/UDaily/01-02/NIHgrant101702.html (accessed August 24, 2006).

Agarwal, S., R. Kobetic, S. Nandurkar, and E. B. Marsolais. "Functional Electrical Stimulation for Walking in Paraplegia: 17-Year Follow-up of 2 Cases." Abstract, Spring 2003. http://www.ncbi.nlm.nih.gov/sites/entrez?db=pubmed&uid=12830975&cmd=showdetailview (accessed December 27, 2007).

ALS Association. Patient & Family Services >> Assistive Technology." 2004. http:// www.alsinfo.org/ (accessed November 20, 2006).

Anderson, Annalee. "Language Learning Using Infrared Toys." 2003 Conference Proceedings. www.csun.edu/cod/conf/2003/proceedings/68.htm (accessed August 24, 2006).

Anderson, Sandra. *Computer Literacy for Health Care Professionals.* New York: Delmar, 1992.

Begley, Sharon. "Wall Street Journal Feature: NovaVision™ VRT™ Research & Improvements for Stroke Vision Loss Patient." novavision.com, February 1, 2005. http://www.novavision.com/wall-street-journal-feature-novavision-vrt-research-improvements-for-stroke-vision-loss-patient-nid-61.html (accessed December 27, 2007).

Berck, Judith. "Tools for Blind Students." nyt.com, August 6, 1995. http://query.nytimes.com/gst/fullpage.html?res=990CE7D9143DF935A3575BC0A963958260 (accessed December 27, 2007).

Bhattacharjee, Yudhijit. "Smart Wheelchairs Will Ease Many Paths." nyt.com, May 10, 2001. http://www.nytimes.com/2001/05/10/technology/10NEXT.html?ex=1198904400&en=49d403d1d3597ed8&ei=5070 (accessed December 27, 2007).

Bhattacharjee, Yudhijit. "So That's Who's Talking: A Hearing Aid Points to the Sound." nyt.com, September 27, 2001. http://query.nytimes.com/gst/fullpage.html?res=9D03E1D6133AF934A1575AC0A9679C8B63 (accessed December 27, 2007).

Biersdorfer, J. D. "A Scanner-Reader to Take Along Anywhere." nyt.com, July 13, 2006. http://www.nytimes.com/2006/07/13/technology/13blind.html?ex=1310443200&en=a9311e255a6b8d11&ei=5090&partner=rssuserland&emc=rss (accessed December 27, 2007).

"Biomove 3000 System." January 27, 2005. http://www.fda.gov/cdrh/pdf4/k042650.pdf (accessed December 27, 2007).

Boch, Otto. "C-Leg: New Generation Leg System Revolutionizes Lower Limb Prostheses." http://www.ottobockus.com/products/lower_limb_prosthetics/c-leg_article.asp (accessed December 27, 2007).

Bowers, Cynthia. "New Device Gives Hope to Paralyzed." cbsnews.com, July 17, 2006. http:/ www.cbsnews.com/stories/2006/07/17/earlyshow/health/main1808040.shtml (accessed December 27, 2007).

Calacanis, Catherine. "FDA Approves Research to Study Brain Chip for ALS." August 3, 2005. www.telemedicineinsider.com (accessed August 3, 2005).

Carroll, Linda. "Doctors Look Ahead to 'Pacemakers for the Brain.'" February 18, 2003. http://www.mindcontrolforums.com/news/pacemakers-for-brain.htm (accessed August 24, 2006).

"Cochlear Implants." August 16, 2006. http://www.nidcd.nih.gov/health/hearing/coch.as (accessed December 27, 2007).

"Computer Display on Glasses Helps to Overcome Tunnel Vision." September 11, 2006. http://www.mtbeurope.info/news/2006/609009.htm (accessed January 6, 2008).

"The Dasher Project." August 2, 2006. http://www.inference.phy.cam.ac.uk/dasher/ (accessed August 2, 2006).

"Early Infection and Rejection Detection: Microdialysis Technique May Help Implants Stay Put Longer." July 28, 2003. http://www.rpi.edu/web/Campus.News/july_03/july_28/ stenken.htm (accessed December 27, 2007).

Eisenberg, Anne. "Analog over Digital? For a Better Ear Implant, Yes." nyt.com, May 29, 200 http://query.nytimes.com/gst/fullpage.html?res=9901E7DE1F31F93AA15756C0A965 C8B63 (accessed December 27, 2007).

———. "Beyond Voice Recognition, to a Computer That Reads Lips." nyt.com, September 11, 2003. http://query.nytimes.com/gst/fullpage.html?res=9401E3DC 133BF932A2575AC0A9659C8B63 (accessed December 27, 2007).

———. "A Chip That Mimics a Retina but Strains for Light." nyt.com, August 9, 2001. http:// query.nytimes.com/gst/fullpage.html?res=9F0DE3D7163FF93AA3575BC0A9679C8B6 (accessed December 27, 2007).

———. "A Gaze That Dictates, with Intuitive Software as the Scribe." nyt.com, September 1 2002. http://query.nytimes.com/gst/fullpage.html?res=9B0CEED81531F931A2575 AC0A9649C8B63 (accessed December 27, 2007).

———. "The Kind of Noise That Keeps a Body on Balance." nyt.com, November 14, 2002. http://query.nytimes.com/gst/fullpage.html?res=9F01E6D61F31F937A25752C1 A9649C8B63 (accessed December 27, 2007).

———. "What's Next: A Chip That Mimics Neurons, Firing Up the Memory." nyt.com, June 2, 2002. http://query.nytimes.com/gst/fullpage.html?res=9906E3D9173 FF933A15755C0A9649C8B63 (accessed December 27, 2007).

———. "What's Next: Glasses So Smart They Know What You're Looking At." nyt.com, Jun 28, 2001. http://www.nytimes.com/2001/06/28/technology/28NEXT. html?ex=1198904400&en=1d794cee7a240466&ei=5070 (accessed December 27, 2007)

———. "When the Athlete's Heart Falters, a Monitor Dials for Help." nyt.com, January 9, 2003. http://query.nytimes.com/gst/fullpage.html?res=9B03E0DE113EF93AA35752 C0A9659C8B63 (accessed December 27, 2007).

"Environmental Control Systems for People with Spinal Injuries." 1999. http://www. abilitycorp.com.au/ftp/research/environmental_controls_systems_report.pdf (accessed January 18, 2008).

"FDA Approves Electronic Capsule for Stomach Disorder." ihealthbeat.org, July 21, 2006. http://www.ihealthbeat.org/articles/2006/7/21/FDA-Approves-Electronic-Capsule-fo Stomach-Disorder.aspx?topicID=53 (accessed December 27, 2007).

"FDA Approves New Glucose Test for Adult Diabetics." FDA News, March 22, 2001. http:// www.fda.gov/bbs/topics/NEWS/2001/NEW00758.html (accessed December 27, 2007).

Felton, Bruce. "Technologies That Enable the Disabled." nyt.com, September 14, 1997. http://query.nytimes.com/gst/fullpage.html?res=9A0CE3D81139F937A2575AC0A96 58260 (accessed December 27, 2007).

Gallagher, David. "For the Errant Heart, a Chip That Packs a Wallop." nyt.com, August 16, 2001 (accessed August 24, 2006).

Garibaldi, Matthew. "Myoelectric Prostheses Offer Advantages." Winter 2006. http://www. ucsfhealth.org/common/pubs/ortho/winter2006/myoelectric/index.html (accessed December 27, 2007).

Glassman, Mark. "A Braille Phone Organizer Connects the Dots and the User." nyt.com, April 17, 2003. http://query.nytimes.com/gst/fullpage.html?res=9C0DEFDD163AF9 34A25757C0A9659C8B63 (accessed December 27, 2007).

Grady, Denise. "Digital Hearing Aids Hold New Promise." nyt.com, June 4, 1997. http://query.nytimes.com/gst/fullpage.html?res=9C07E2D6123DF937A35755C0A961958260 (accessed December 27, 2007).

Hales, Dianne. "New Help for Hearing Loss." May 14, 2006. http://www.parade.com/articles/editions/2006/edition_05-14-2006/Hearing_Loss (accessed December 27, 2007).

Happ, Mary, Kathryn Garrett, and Tricia Roesch. "Feasibility of an Augmentative Device for Head and Neck Cancer Patients." May 15, 2002. http://www.ons.org/research/funding/SummaryReports/summaryReportsSm.shtml (accessed January 18, 2008).

Henkel, John. "Parkinson's Disease: New Treatments Slow Onslaught of Symptoms," US FDA, 1998. http://www.fda.gov/Fdac/features/1998/498_pd.html (accessed December 27, 2007).

Hochberg, Leigh, Mijail D. Serruya, Gerhard M. Friehs, Jon A. Mukand, Maryam Saleh, Abraham Caplan, Almut Branner, David Chen, Richard Chen, Richard Penn, and John P. Donoghue. "Neuronal Ensemble Control of Prosthetic Devices by a Human with Tetraplegia." *Nature* 442 (2006): 164–71. http://www.nature.com/nature/journal/v442/n7099/abs/nature04970.html (accessed December 27, 2007).

Junker, Andrew H. "A Revolutionary Approach to Computer Access: Coherent Detected Periodic Brainwave Computer Control." 2003. http://brainfingers.com/ (accessed November 20, 2006).

Klonoff, David C. "Diabetes and Telemedicine: Is the Technology Sound, Effective, Cost-effective, and Practical?" 2003. http://care.diabetesjournals.org/cgi/content/full/26/5/1626 (accessed January 6, 2008).

Krcmar, Stephen. "The Stuff of Dreams." April 2006. http://www.rehabpub.com/features/42006/7.asp (accessed August 24, 2006).

Krieg, Lawrence. "Introduction to Computerized Medical Instrumentation." February 2004. http://courses.wccnet.edu/computer/mod/mod-m.htm (accessed December 27, 2007).

Lanyi, Cecelia Sik, Julianna Szabo, Attila Pall, and Ilona Pataky. "Computer Controlled Cognitive Diagnostics and Rehabilitation Method for Stroke Patients." ERCIM News No. 61, April 2005. http://www.ercim.org/publication/Ercim_News/enw61/lanyi.html (accessed December 27, 2007).

Lazzaro, John. *Adaptive Technologies for Learning and Work Environments.* Chicago, IL: American Library Association, 1993.

Marriott, Michel. "Wired by a Kindred Spirit, the Disabled Gain Control." nyt.com, April 24, 2003. http://query.nytimes.com/gst/fullpage.html?res=9A01E3D71F3AF937A15757C0A9659C8B63 (accessed December 27, 2007).

"Medicare to Pay for FES Walking System." 2002. http://sci.rutgers.edu/forum/archive/index.php/t-47354.html (accessed December 27, 2007).

Meier, Barry. "FDA Plans to Intensify Oversight of Heart Devices." nyt.com, April 7, 2006. http://www.nytimes.com/2006/04/07/business/07device.html (accessed December 27, 2007).

"The Neurostimulator: Pacemaker for the Brain." September 2006. http://www.froedtert.com/HealthResources/ReadingRoom/FroedtertToday/September2006Issue/PacemakerfortheBrain.htm (accessed December 27, 2007).

"New Device Approval: GlucoWatch® Automatic Glucose Biographer—P990026." March 22, 2001. http://www.fda.gov/cdrh/pdf/P990026.html (accessed December 27, 2007).

"New Device Approvals: Medtronic Model 7250 Jewel®AF Implantable Cardioverter Defibrillator System—P980050/S1." April 1, 2001. http://www.fda.gov/cdrh/mda/docs/p980050s001.pdf (accessed December 27, 2007).

"New, Light Prosthetics Helping Amputees Function Better: Computerized Prosthetics Offer Better Fit." March 2005. http://www.wnbc.com/print/2267223/detail.html (accessed January 6, 2008).

Norwood, Robert. "NASA Technologies Contribute to Medical Breakthroughs." *Advanced Technologies,* March–April, 1998.

Nussbaum, Debra. "Bringing the Visual World of the Web to the Blind." *New York Times,* March 26, 1998, G8.

Ouellette, Jennifer. "Biomaterials Facilitate Medical Breakthroughs." American Institute of Physics, October/November 2001. http://www.aip.org/tip/INPHFA/vol-7/iss-5/p18.pdf (accessed December 27, 2007).

"A Pacemaker for the Brain." 2005. http://www.clevelandclinic.org/health/health-info/docs/1900/1937.asp?index=8782&src=news&ref=1900/1937.asp?index=8782 (accessed December 27, 2007).

"Pacemaker for the Brain May Offer Hope for Parkinson's Disease." 2006. http://mentalhealt about.com/library/sci/0102/blparkins0102.htm (accessed December 27, 2007).
Rachkesperger, Tracy. "Growing Up with AAC." 2006. http://www.asha.org/public/speech disorders/GrowingUpAAC.htm (accessed December 27, 2007).
Rainwater, Steven. "Heroic Cyborg to Receive Medal." February 2006. http://robots.net/article/1826.html (accessed December 27, 2007).
"Rechargeable Spinal Cord Stimulators for Chronic Pain." spine-health.com, 2006. http://www.spine-health.com/research/stim/stim01.html (accessed December 27, 2007).
Roberts, Dan. "Microchip Implantation." February 10, 2007. http://www.mdsupport.org/library/chip.html (accessed December 27, 2007).
Senn, Jim. *Information Technology in Business: Principles, Practices, and Opportunities.* 2nd ed. Upper Saddle River, NJ: Prentice Hall, 1998.
Skillings, Jonathan. "Prosthetics Go High Tech." cnetnews.com, August 3, 2005. http://www.news. com/Prosthetics-go-high-tech/2008-1082_3-5816267.html (accessed December 27, 2007).
"Some Biomove 3000 Questions." http://biomoveusa.com/FAQ-Biomove-3000.htm (accessed August 8, 2006).
Taub, Eric. "Typing with Two Hands, No Fingers." nyt.com, May 1, 2003. http:// query.nytimes.com/gst/fullpage.html?res=9C0CE5D81F3DF932A35756C0A9659C8B63 (accessed December 27, 2007).
"UA Optical Scientists Develop Switchable Focus Eyeglass Lenses." innovations-report.com April 4, 2004. http://www.innovations-report.com/html/reports/medical_technology report-57456.html (accessed December 27, 2007).
"VA Technology Assessment Program Project Report—Patient Summary on Computerized Lower Limb Prosthesis." March 2000. http://www.va.gov/vatap/patientinfo/prosteticlimb.htm (accessed December 27, 2007).
"Virtual Reality Gaining Acceptance in Ophthalmic Surgical Training Programs." August 1 2006. http://www.med.nyu.edu/communications/news/pr_190.html (accessed December 27, 2007).
"Virtual Reality Lets Amputees 'Control' Missing Limbs." sciencedaily.com, November 15, 2006. http://www.sciencedaily.com/releases/2006/11/061115093227.htm (accessed December 27, 2007).
Weingarten, Marc. "For an Irregular Lens, an Optical Blueprint." nyt.com, September 12, 200 http://query.nytimes.com/gst/fullpage.html?res=9D02E2D81531F931A2575AC0A9649C B63 (accessed December 27, 2007).
"What Is an Insulin Pump and How Does It Work." February 1, 2005. http://www.banting.com/tcenter/pump101.html (accessed December 27, 2007).
Wiener, Jon. "USC Ophthalmologists Announce Launch of Permanent Retinal Implant Study." April 30, 2002. http://www.eurekalert.org/pub_releases/2002-04/uosc-uoa_1043002.php (accessed January 18, 2008).
"Zynex Medical's NeuroMove™ System Cited in New Clinical Study of Stroke Recovery Therapies." *Business Wire,* October 26, 2005. http://findarticles.com/p/articles/mi_m0EIN/is_2005_Oct_26/ai_n15736093 (accessed January 6, 2008).

RELATED WEB SITES

http://www.alsinfo.org
http://www.fda.gov
http://www.nih.gov
http://www.patientcareonline.com
http://www.telemedicineinsider.com
http://www.va.gov

CHAPTER 12

Security and Privacy in an Electronic Age

CHAPTER OUTLINE

LEARNING OBJECTIVES

After reading this chapter, you will be able to

- Define security and privacy.
- Discuss threats to information technology, including crimes, viruses, and the unauthorized use of data.
- Discuss security measures including laws, voluntary codes of conduct, restriction of access to computer systems, and the protection of information on networks.
- Describe the Real ID Act of 2005.
- Describe the impact of information technology on privacy, including the existence of large computerized databases of information kept by both government and private organizations, some of which are on networks linked to the Internet.
- Describe the relationship of privacy and security to health care and appreciate the importance of the privacy of electronic medical records.
- Discuss the Health Insurance Portability and Accountability Act of 1996 (HIPAA) and the USA Patriot Act (2001), specifically their effects on privacy protections.
- Discuss the lack of enforcement of HIPAA.

KEY TERMS

adware
biometric keyboard
biometric method
body odor sensor
codes of conduct
data accuracy
database
DNA
Electronic Communications Privacy Act of 1986
encryption
facial structure scan
facial thermography
Fair Credit Reporting Act of 1970
fingerprint
firewalls
fraud
fraudulent dialer
hacker
hand print
Health Insurance Portability and Accountability Act (HIPAA)
Homeland Security Act
identity theft
iris scan
keylogging
lip print
malware
Medical Information Bureau
password
personal identification number (PIN)
privacy
Real ID Act of 2005
retina scan
security
software piracy
Spybot Search and Destroy software
spyware
theft of information
theft of service
USA Patriot Act
Verichip
virus
voice recognition

DISCUSSION QUESTIONS

1. Discuss two violations concerning medical privacy.
In March 2003, the following appeared in The Centre Daily Times *(Texas): "In Kentuc state computers put up for sale as surplus . . . contained confidential files naming tho sands of people with AIDs and sexually transmitted diseases. The oversight was discover when the state auditor's office purchased eight of the computers. Thousands of state-own computers may still be out there. . . ."*
In August 2006, a Department of Veterans Affairs containing data on 38,000 patie at Pennsylvania VA hospitals disappeared.
2. Name at least two threats to information technology.
Threats to information technology include hazards to hardware, software, networks, a data including information stored in electronic databases. Data accuracy and security a what is most relevant to the use of computerized medical records. However, computer har ware, software, and data can be damaged by anything from simple carelessness to pow surges, crime, and computer viruses. Computer systems, like any other property, can hurt or destroyed by disasters such as floods and fires.
3. Define and discuss software piracy, theft of services, and theft of information.
Crimes involving computers can be crimes using computers and/or crimes against compu systems. Many times they are both—using computers to harm computer systems. Computer cri includes committing fraud and scams over the Internet, unauthorized copying of software p tected by copyright (called software piracy), and theft of services such as cable TV. Software pira costs the software industry billions of dollars a year. According to the Business Softwa Alliance, over 30 percent of software is pirated. Theft of information, including breaking into medical database and gaining access to medical records, is also considered a crime.
4. Give two examples of how viruses can damage hardware and software.
Viruses can damage hardware, software, and data. A virus is a program that attach itself to another program and replicates itself. A virus may do damage to your hardware destroy your data or it may simply flash an annoying message. Most states and the feder government make it a crime to intentionally spread a computer virus. Federal law makes a felony to do $1,000 or more worth of damage to any computer involved in interstate co merce; this includes any personal computer connected to the Internet. The penalties f damaging computer systems have been severely increased by the USA Patriot Act and t Homeland Security Act. Spreading viruses is a kind of high-tech vandalism. Virus dete tion software can find and get rid of many but not all viruses.

5. Define identity theft. Is identity theft rising? What is the negative impact of identity theft? Comment.
Identity theft involves someone using your private information to assume your identity. Identity theft rose between 2000 and 2003; however, it has now stabilized: "Identity fraud victims as a percent of the United States adult population . . . declined slightly from 4.7% to 4.0% between 2003 and 2006." Although identity theft predates computers, the existence of computer networks, the centralization of information in databases, and the posting of public information on the Internet make information much easier to steal. However, currently 68 percent of victims do not experience any financial loss. Many identity thieves start from home; according to a study by the Federal Trade Commission, among those who find out who stole their identity, half are members of the family or household (partners, roommates, children, and parents). An identity thief needs only a few pieces of information (such as Social Security number and mother's maiden name) to steal your identity. Under this false identity—your identity—the thief can take out credit cards, loans, buy houses, and even commit crimes. Identity theft is extremely difficult to prosecute. It is also not easy for the victim to correct all the negative information that the thief has created. False negative information may keep appearing in response to every routine computer check. Currently, some cities are putting all public records including property and court records on the Internet, making identity theft even easier to commit. Think of the information (including your signature) on the ticket you were issued last month.
6. Define the following: spyware, adware, fraudulent dialer, keylogging, malware, and Spybot Search and Destroy software.
Spyware is software that can be installed without the user's knowledge to track their actions on a computer. Adware may display unwanted pop-up advertisements on your monitor; the advertisements may be related to the sites you search on the Web or even the content of your e-mail. A fraudulent dialer can connect the user with numbers without the user's knowledge; the dialer may connect the user's computer to an expensive 900 number. The user will be totally unaware until he or she receives their telephone bill. A dialer is usually installed with free software. Keylogging can be used by anyone to track anyone else's keystrokes. Malware includes different forms of malicious hardware, software, and firmware. Spybot Search and Destroy software can remove malware, adware, spyware, dialers, and keyloggers from your computer.
7. Describe implanted RFID tags. Comment on privacy implications.
A new threat to personal privacy may come from implanted radio frequency identification (RFID) tags (Verichips), according to privacy advocates. The tags are radio transmitters that give off a unique signal, which can be read by a receiver. The person with the tag implanted does not need to know it is being read. Tags have been used in pets and products. The FDA has approved the tags for medical use. In 2006, two employees of an Ohio company had RFID tags embedded in their arms. The company said "it was testing the technology as a way of controlling access to a room."
However, Verichips are very easily counterfeited—". . . you could have a chip implanted, and then your front door would unlock when your shoulder got close to the reader. Let us imagine that you did this; then, I could sit next to you on the subway, and read your chip's ID. This takes less than a second. At this point I can let myself in to your house, by replaying that ID. So now you have to change your ID; but as far as I know, you cannot do this without surgery."
8. List some methods used to restrict access to computers?
Many organizations restrict access to their computers. This can be done by requiring authorized users to have personal identification numbers (PINs) or use passwords. Locking computer rooms and requiring employees to carry ID cards and keys are also used to restrict access. Biometric methods including fingerprints, hand prints, retina or iris scans, lip prints, facial thermography, and body odor sensors also help make sure only authorized people have access to computer systems. Biometric technology can use facial structure to identify individuals. Biometric keyboards can identify a typist by fingerprints. None of these methods is foolproof. Even biometric methods, which for a time were seen as more reliable, are far from perfect. PINs and passwords can be forgotten or shared, and ID cards and keys can be lost or stolen. Biometric methods also pose a threat to privacy, because

anyone who can gain access to the database of physical characteristics gains access other, possibly private information about you. Some biometric measures are inherently d ferent than other security measures. In more traditional methods, such as fingerprintin you are aware that your identity is being checked. However, iris and retina scans, fac thermographs, facial structure scans, and body odor sensors allow your identity to checked without your knowledge, cooperation, or consent. This can be seen as an invasi of privacy. Now there is the possibility of implanted RFID tags as a security measure.

9. Describe the Fair Credit Reporting Act of 1970 and the Privacy Act of 1974.
   1970—Fair Credit Reporting Act regulates credit agencies. It allows you to see your cre reports to check the accuracy of information and challenge inaccuracies. Amended seve times, Fair and Accurate Credit Transaction Act of 2003 preempts some state privacy p tections but mandates that you can have a free credit report each year.
   1974—Privacy Act prohibits disclosure of government records to anyone except the in vidual concerned, except for law enforcement purposes. It also prohibits the use of inf mation except for the purpose for which it was gathered. It deals with the use a disclosure of Social Security numbers.
10. Briefly describe the USA Patriot Act of 2001 and The Homeland Security Act of 20(
    The USA Patriot Act gives law enforcement agencies greater power to monitor electronic a other communications, with fewer checks. It allows increased sharing of information betwe the states, the FBI, and the CIA. The law expands the authority of the government to all roving wiretaps, which intercept communications, wherever the person is. Both e-mail a voice mail may be seized under a search warrant. The government may track Web surfi and request information from Internet service providers (ISPs) about their subscribers. T law establishes a DNA database that will include anyone convicted of a violent crime.
    The Homeland Security Act expands and centralizes the data gathering allowed under t Patriot Act. A new federal department of Homeland Security is established to analyze data c lected by other agencies. The law includes expanded provision for the government to moni electronic communications and authority for the government to mine databases of person information, at the same time that it limits Congressional oversight. Any government body any level can now request information from your ISP without a warrant or probable cause, long as there is a "good faith" belief that national security is involved. Your local library required to turn over any records to the FBI, if asked. The act limits an individual's access information under the Freedom of Information Act. If a business states that its activities a related to security, that information will be kept secret. The law gives government committe more freedom to meet in secret. It limits liability for companies producing antiterrorism pro ucts including vaccinations, at the same time that the government would gain wider power declare national health emergencies, quarantines, and order forced vaccinations.

IN THE NEWS

THE CONSUMER; How Patients Can Use the New Access to Their Medical Records

by Mary Duenwald

At one time, polite people never asked to look at their own medical records. To do so would indicate a lack of trust in your physician. Besides, doctors were so resistant to the practice that getting hold of your records could require a subpoena.

But that way of thinking is a relic of old-fashioned medicine, as out of date as the house call and the black medical bag.

Since last April, federal law has required that doctors, clinics and hospitals provide patients with access to their records on demand. As it turns out, many people want to see them, and if you know what you are looking for, medical records can be easy to decipher. Reading them can also be a good way to become more involved in your own medical care.

Doctors once suspected that patients who wanted to see their own charts were distrustful or, worse, planning to sue, said George J. Annas, chairman of the health law, bioethics and human rights department at Boston University School of Public Health. And some doctors argued that patients lacked the expertise to understand their own charts.

"They'd say, you can't possibly understand because it's written in medical language," Mr. Annas said. "You won't know that S.O.B. stands for shortness of breath."

But in this era of consumer medicine and increasing safeguards on personal privacy, Mr. Annas said, "it is considered a basic privacy principle that if anybody has personal information about you, you should have access to that information, too."

The new federal rules, part of the Health Insurance Portability and Accountability Act, or Hipaa, give patients the right to inspect and copy all their records. Parents are also entitled to their children's medical records.

An exception is made for notes from psychotherapy, which are thought to be especially sensitive or likely to be misinterpreted as critical of the patient. With a doctor's permission, patients can view therapy records in the doctor's presence.

Access to medical records will soon be very easy for anyone with a personal computer, as hospitals and clinics switch to electronic record-keeping. But even with paper records, obtaining access is easy. Patients need merely telephone their doctor's office or a hospital's records office and ask, said Carol Ann Quinsey, a professional practice manager for the American Health Information Management Association, a professional organization.

Typically, the office manager or the records administrator will schedule an appointment for the patient to come in and examine the records. Once there, the patient may be asked to sign a form authorizing the release of the records.

Or the patient can send a written request to have the records photocopied and sent by mail. The doctor's office or hospital may charge a fee for photocopying and postage.

Ideally, when looking through the file, the patient should be able to ask a doctor or other informed medical professional questions about anything that seems confusing or hard to understand.

Deciphering handwriting is another challenge, insurmountable in some cases.

"It isn't just that the patients can't read it," Mr. Annas said. "Sometimes, nobody can."

(continued)

THE CONSUMER; How Patients Can Use the New Access to Their Medical Records *(continued)*

What pieces of the record are most interesting and important?

The ones that a patient might need to provide to future physicians, said Dr. Jinnet B. Fowles, vice president of research for the Park Nicollet Institute, a health research center in Minneapolis. Those might include the dates of immunizations and regular screenings like mammograms, P.S.A. tests and cholesterol checks; the dates of any surgeries and the hospitals where they were performed; a record of all allergies; accounts of any serious medical illnesses; and descriptions of current medical problems and medications.

Dr. Fowles found that reviewing her own records gave her a starkly realistic view of how her weight had increased over the years and how her blood pressure and blood sugar numbers had "moved in the wrong direction." The revelation inspired her to lose 30 pounds.

Patients may want to photocopy the pertinent pages and save them in a file, said Ms. Quinsey of the information management association. Or they may want to transfer the key details to a health history record form. (Her group offers such a form on its Web site at www.myphr.com/maintaining/index.asp.) Some patients may want to carry a partial record of their medical profile with them at all times.

"I'm allergic to penicillin, sulfa and tetracycline," Ms. Quinsey said. "All those drugs are essentially deadly to me, so I keep that information on a piece of paper that stays in my billfold."

People who suffer from chronic conditions like diabetes or high blood pressure are advised to keep that information with them also, Ms. Quinsey said.

It is important to check for inaccuracies: misfiled pages from another patient's chart, for example, or incorrect notations about allergies or medications.

Sometimes, Ms. Quinsey said, a patient disagrees with a doctor's description of a medical situation: "A patient will say, 'I didn't say that I'd had five drinks and crashed my car.'"

If the doctor will not change the chart, patients are entitled to write down their versions of the events and attach them to the record.

Contrary to patients' expectations, the doctors' notations are typically not all that interesting, Ms. Quinsey said. "If they think there's gossip in their chart, they are usually disappointed," she said. "Most doctors don't write comments like 'She was very short-tempered,' or 'She was really nasty to me.'"

Naturally, the trend toward greater openness with patients has discouraged doctors from jotting down ill-considered comments. "They are encouraged to stick to the facts and not characterize patients as 'fat' or 'shabbily dressed,'" Mr. Annas said.

Your Life as an Open Book

by Tom Zeller Jr.

Privacy advocates and search industry watchers have long warned that the vast and valuable stores of data collected by search engine companies could be vulnerable to thieves, rogue employees, mishaps or even government subpoenas.

Four major search companies were served with government subpoenas for their search data last year, and now once again, privacy advocates can say, "We told you so."

AOL's misstep last week in briefly posting some 19 million Internet search queries made by more than 600,000 of its unwitting customers has reminded many Americans that their private searches—for solutions to debt or bunions or loneliness—are not entirely their own.

So, as one privacy group has asserted, is AOL's blunder likely to be the search industry's "Data Valdez," like the 1989 Exxon oil spill that became the rallying cry for the environmental movement?

Maybe. But in an era when powerful commercial and legal forces ally in favor of holding on to data, and where the surrender of one's digital soul happens almost imperceptibly, change is not likely to come swiftly.

Most of the major search engines like Google, Yahoo and MSN collect and store information on what terms are searched, when they were queried and what computer and browser was used. And to the extent that the information can be used to match historic search behavior emanating from a specific computer, it is a hot commodity.

As it stands now, little with regard to search queries is private. No laws clearly place search requests off-limits to advertisers, law enforcement agencies or academic researchers, beyond the terms that companies set themselves.

"This is a discussion that we as a society need to have," said Kevin Bankston, a lawyer with the Electronic Frontier Foundation, a rights organization based in San Francisco.

Mr. Bankston's group, which is spearheading a class-action lawsuit against AT&T for sharing consumer phone records with the National Security Agency, issued an alert this week calling the AOL incident a "Data Valdez," asserting that it may be in violation of the Electronic Communications and Privacy Act, which regulates some forms of online communications.

"I am very skeptical of any claims that the monetary worth of this information to these companies is worth the privacy trade-off to millions of people," Mr. Bankston said.

That is not to say that marketers are not keenly interested in being able to push ads to a particular computer based on the types of searches coming from that address over time. For users who register as members with some search engines, including Yahoo, this is already happening—although consumers are unlikely to realize it.

Which is why privacy advocates question whether such advertising models are appropriate in the first place.

"In many contexts, consumers already have the expectation that information about their cultural consumption will not be sold," said Chris Jay Hoofnagle, a senior researcher at Boalt Hall School of Law at the University of California, Berkeley. "They understand that the library items that they check out, the specific television shows that they watch, the videos that they rent are protected information."

Indeed, legislation like the Cable TV Privacy Act of 1984 and the Video Privacy Protection Act of 1988 were tailored to keep the specific choices consumers make in their daily diet of cultural ephemera off limits.

(continued)

Your Life as an Open Book *(continued)*

There are exceptions: video "genre preferences," for instance, may be disclosed for marketing purposes.

And of course, such fare as magazine subscription lists and club membership information are bought and sold for marketing purposes all the time.

But how to characterize a search engine's vast catalog, not of what an individual bought, rented or subscribed to, but merely what he or she was curious about—perhaps only for a moment in time—for reasons that are impossible to know?

That's one thing that the culture and the law need to address fully, Mr. Hoofnagle suggested. And simply relying on the terms of service posted by Internet companies to sort things out, he said, is not enough.

"The problem with the consent model is that users don't read the terms and it's hard to comprehend what the effect of storing the data over time will be," Mr. Hoofnagle said. "And there's a corresponding promise that the company will protect the data," he added, "and sometimes, obviously, those promises are broken."

Indeed, AOL's publication of user search data comes in a social context that is newly sensitive about data leaks.

"Part of this conversation should be about the responsibility of companies to maintain data securely," said Mr. Hoofnagle, who was among several privacy advocates who were critical of ChoicePoint, the large commercial data broker, in the months before the disclosure in February last year that criminals had foiled its screening protocols and gained access to consumer information.

"The longer companies hold onto information, the greater the risk," Mr. Hoofnagle said.

The ChoicePoint debacle, in fact, was a watershed moment for data security law, at least at the state level, with at least 30 states enacting some form of breach-notification legislation requiring businesses to notify consumers if their information is compromised.

Numerous bills have been proposed in Congress as well, but pitched battles between privacy advocates, who seek comprehensive data protections for consumers, and the financial industry, which wants to limit any onerous legislation and pre-empt tougher state laws, have stalled progress.

It is not surprising, then, that a bill by Representative Edward J. Markey, Democrat of Massachusetts, that seeks to force Web sites, including search engines, to purge old data, has not moved since its introduction in February.

"Corporate negligence with consumers' personal information shouldn't be tolerated by average Americans, the financial markets, or the federal government," Representative Markey said in an e-mail message.

The bill was inspired by the Justice Department's subpoenas for search data held by MSN, Yahoo, AOL and Google this year—a move aimed at bolstering the government's efforts to uphold an online child pornography law. Google was alone in resisting the subpoena in federal court, which mostly sided with the company, granting the government access only to information on Web site addresses returned in Google searches, rather than search terms entered by users.

And yet the vast data troves held by search engines and Internet companies of all stripes continue to present an irresistible investigatory target, particularly in an era of terrorist plots like the one that seriously disrupted British airports, and much of the rest of global aviation this week.

In December, the European Parliament passed sweeping data retention rules aimed at the telecommunications and Internet industries, requiring that fixed-line and cellphone records, e-mail and Internet logs be stored for up to two years. The measure was lauded by law enforcement groups but decried by privacy advocates and even industry, which would have to find space—and money—to store it all.

Congress, too, has toyed with the idea of drafting data retention legislation, and Attorney General Alberto R. Gonzales has signaled on numerous occasions that he would like to see that happen.

Speaking at the Search Engine Strategies 2006 Conference and Expo in San Jose, Calif., on Wednesday, Google's chief executive, Eric E. Schmidt, suggested that government interest in the sort of information Google archives remains a chief concern for his company.

"I've always worried that the query stream was a fertile ground for governments to randomly snoop on people," he said.

In a public forum with Danny Sullivan, the editor of Search Engine Watch, an online news blog, and the San Jose event's organizer, Mr. Schmidt was asked about the AOL incident. "It's obviously a terrible thing, and the data as released was obviously not anonymized enough," Mr. Schmidt said.

Mr. Schmidt also said his company, which stores every query its visitors make, deploys numerous safeguards to protect and keep that data anonymous, and that he was confident that "this sort of thing would not happen with Google—although," he added, "you can never say never."

That might be the battle cry of privacy advocates, who wonder why any company that doesn't have to, and that wants to maintain the faith of its customers, would bother to hang onto so much data.

"This AOL breach is just a tiny drop in the giant pool of information that these companies have collected," Mr. Bankston said. "The sensitivity of this data cannot be overemphasized."

A similar sentiment was at the heart of an e-mail message sent to employees by AOL's own chief executive, Jonathan F. Miller, on Wednesday.

"We work so hard to protect this kind of information, and yet it was made public without review by our privacy experts, undermining years of industry leadership in a single act," Mr. Miller wrote. "The reaction has been a powerful reminder of how quickly a company such as AOL can forfeit the good will we have worked for years to engender."

SOURCES

109th U.S. Congress (2005–2006). "H.R. 82 [109th]: Social Security Online Privacy Protection Act." http://www.govtrack.us/congress/bill.xpd?bill=h109-82 (accessed December 28, 2007).

109th U.S. Congress (2005–2006). "H.R. 84 [109th]: Online Privacy Protection Act of 2005." http://www.govtrack.us/congress/bill.xpd?bill=h109-84 (accessed December 28, 2007).

"Another Veterans Affairs Computer with Sensitive Data Is Missing." privacy.org, August 8, 2006. http://www.privacy.org/archives/2006_08.html (accessed December 28, 2007).

"Answers to Frequently Asked Questions About Government Access to Personal Medical Information (Under the USA Patriot Act and the HIPAA Regulations)." American Civil Liberties Union, May 30, 2003. http://www.aclu.org/privacy/medical/15222res20030530.html (accessed December 28, 2007).

Austen, Ian. "A Scanner Skips the ID Card and Zooms In on the Eyes." nyt.com, May 15, 2003. http://query.nytimes.com/gst/fullpage.html?res=9907E0D71F3FF936A25756C0A9659C8B63 (accessed December 28, 2007).

Baase, Sara. *A Gift of Fire: Social, Legal, and Ethical Issues in Computing.* Upper Saddle River, NJ: Prentice Hall, 1996.

Beekman, George. *Computer Confluence: Exploring Tomorrow's Technology.* 5th ed. Upper Saddle River, NJ: Prentice Hall, 2003.

Bernstein, Nina. "Personal Files Via Computer Offer Money and Pose Threat." *New York Times,* June 12, 1997, A1, B14.

"A BILL: To Establish a Department of Homeland Security, and for Other Purposes." 2002, http://www.whitehouse.gov/deptofhomeland/bill/ (accessed December 28, 2007).

Burton, Brenda K., and Erik Kangas. "HIPAA Email Security Management in Email Communications, Secure Email White Paper." 2006. http://luxsci.com/info/hipaa-email.html (accessed December 2, 2006).

"Cegavske Targets 'Video Voyeurism.'" February 17, 2005. http://www.reviewjournal.com/lvrj_home/2005/Feb-17-Thu-2005/news/25883310.html (accessed November 29, 2006).

Chaddock, Gail Russell. "Security Act to Pervade Daily Lives." *Christian Science Monitor,* November 21, 2002. http://www.csmonitor.com/2002/1121/p01s03-usju.html (accessed November 30, 2006).

"A Chronology of Data Breaches." Privacy Rights Clearinghouse, August 5, 2006. http://www.privacyrights.org/ar/ChronDataBreaches.htm (accessed August 9, 2006).

Clymer, Adam. "Conferees in Congress Bar Using a Pentagon Project on Americans." February 12, 2003. http://foi.missouri.edu/totalinfoaware/conference.html (accessed December 1, 2006).

"Computer Fraud and Abuse Act." 2003. http://legal.web.aol.com/resources/legislation/comfraud.html (accessed November 29, 2006).

"The Computer Fraud and Abuse Act (as Amended 1994 and 1996)." http://www.panix.com/~eck/computer-fraud-act.html (accessed November 29, 2006).

Cronin, Anne. "Census Bureau Tells Something About Everything." *New York Times,* December 1, 1997, D10.

"Demo: Cloning a Verichip." July 2006. http://cq.cx/verichip.pl (accessed December 1, 2006

Donovan, Larry. "Privacy Law Update." 2001. http://library.findlaw.com/2001/Feb/1/129062.html (accessed December 28, 2007).

"Driver Privacy Protection Act (DPPA)." 2005. http://www.maine.gov/informe/subscriber/dppa.htm (accessed December 28, 2007).

"EFF Analysis of the Provisions of the USA Patriot Act That Relate to Online Activities (October 31, 2001)." October 27, 2003. http://w2.eff.org/Privacy/Surveillance/Terrorism/20011031_eff_usa_patriot_analysis.php (accessed December 1, 2006).

"Electronic Communications Privacy Act." http://www.usiia.org/legis/ecpa.html (accessed November 29, 2006).

Electronic Privacy Information Center. "Latest News." epic.org, December 2, 2006 (accesse December 2, 2006).

Electronic Privacy Information Center. "Medical Privacy." April 3, 2006. http://www.epic.org/privacy/medical (accessed December 1, 2006).

"Face Recognition." January 19, 2006. http://epic.org/privacy/facerecognition/ (accessed December 28, 2007).

"Fair Credit Reporting Act and the Privacy of Your Credit Report." October 7, 2005. http://epic.org/privacy/fcra/ (accessed December 28, 2007).

Feder, Barnaby J., and Tom Zeller Jr. "Identity Chip Under Skin Approved for Use in Healt Care." nyt.com, October 14, 2004. http://www.nytimes.com/2004/10/14/technology/14implant.html (accessed December 28, 2007).

Fein, Esther B. "For Many Physicians, E-Mail Is the High-Tech House Call." *New York Times,* November 20, 1997, A1, B8.

Fitzgerald, Thomas J. "A Trail of Cookies? Cover Your Tracks." nyt.com, March 27, 2003. http://query.nytimes.com/gst/fullpage.html?res=9407E6DC1E30F934A15750C0A965 C8B63 (accessed December 28, 2007).

Glass, Andrew. "Computer Industry Adopts Internet Privacy Code." Accessmylibrary.com, 1997, 1–2. http://www.accessmylibrary.com/coms2/summary_0286-5567738_ITM (accessed December 28, 2007).

"Gramm-Leach Billey." 2005. http://www.cleo.com/about/glb.asp (accessed December 28, 2007

Guernsey, Lisa. "What Did You Do Before the War." nyt.com, November 22, 2001. http://query.nytimes.com/gst/fullpage.html?res=9B0CE6DE173AF931A15752C1A9679C8B6 (accessed December 28, 2007).

Hafner, Katie. "'Dear Doctor' Meets 'Return to Sender.'" nyt.com, June 6, 2002. http://query.nytimes.com/gst/fullpage.html?res=9C0CE1DC1F3AF935A35755C0A9649C8B6 (accessed December 28, 2007).

HHS Fact Sheet. "Protecting the Privacy of Patients' Health Information." July 6, 2001. http://www.nchica.org/HIPAAResources/Samples/privacylessons/P-110%20Article%20-%20HHS%20Fact%20Sheet%20-%20July%206%202001.doc (accessed January 7, 2008).

HIPAA Advisory, June 2006 News Archives, Phoenix Health Systems, http://www.hipaadvisory.com/News/NewsArchives/2006/jul06.htm (accessed February 2, 2008).

"HIPAA Security Series." June 6, 2005. http://64.233.169.104/search?q=cache:BK34bm5c668J:www.cms.hhs.gov/EducationMaterials/Downloads/SecurityStandardsAdministrative Safeguards. pdf+HIPAA+Security+Series&hl=en&ct=clnk&cd=1&gl=us (accessed January 18, 2008).

Holtzman, David. "Homeland Security and You." CNET News.com, January 21, 2003. http://www.news.com/2010-1071-981262.html (accessed December 28, 2007).

"How to Comply with the Children's Online Privacy Protection Rule." 1999. http://www.ftc.gov/bcp/conline/pubs/buspubs/coppa.htm (accessed November 29, 2006).

Hubler, David. "GAO Finds Holes in Privacy Laws." FCW.com, July 26, 2006. http://www.fcw.com/online/news/95427-1.html (accessed December 28, 2007).

Klitzman, Robert. "The Quest for Privacy Can Make Us Thieves." nyt.com, May 9, 2006. http://www.nytimes.com/2006/05/09/health/09essa.html?_r=1&oref=slogin (accessed December 28, 2007).

Klosek, Jacqueline. *The War on Privacy*. Westport, CT: Praeger, 2007.

Leary, Warren E. "Panel Cites Lack of Security on Medical Records." *New York Times,* March 6, 1997, A1, B11.

Lee, Jennifer. "Dirty Laundry, Online for All to See." nyt.com, September 5, 2002. http://query.nytimes.com/gst/fullpage.html?res=9A04E4D9173EF936A3575AC0A9649C8B63 (accessed December 28, 2007).

Lee, Jennifer. "Identity Theft Complaints Double in '02, Continuing Rise." nyt.com, January 23, 2003. http://query.nytimes.com/gst/fullpage.html?res=9F04EFD61130F930A15752C0A9659C8B63 (accessed December 28, 2007).

Lee, Jennifer. "Welcome to the Database Lounge." nyt.com, March 21, 2002. http://query.nytimes.com/gst/fullpage.html?res=980DE5DE1038F932A15750C0A9649C8B63 (accessed December 28, 2007).

Leland, John. "Identity Thief Is Often Found in Family Photo." nyt.com, November 13, 2006. http://www.nytimes.com/2006/11/13/us/13identity.html (accessed December 28, 2007).

Lewis, Peter H. "Forget Big Brother." *New York Times,* March 19, 1998, G1, G6.

Lichtblau, Eric. "Republicans Want Terror Law Made Permanent." CommonDreams.org, April 2003. http://www.commondreams.org/headlines03/0409-01.htm (accessed December 28, 2007).

Lohr, Steve. "I.B.M. to Put Genetic Data of Workers Off Limits." nyt.com, October 10, 2005. http://www.nytimes.com/2005/10/10/business/10gene.html (accessed December 28, 2007).

Markoff, John. "Guidelines Don't End Debate on Internet Privacy." *New York Times,* December 18, 1997.

Martin, Georgia A., and Jason F. Kaar. "Telehealth: Consulting Across Borders." *Georgia Nursing.* http://findarticles.com/p/articles/mi_qa3925/is_200105/ai_n8948046 (accessed January 7, 2008).

McCullagh, Declan. "Bush Signs Homeland Security Bill." CNET News.com, November 25, 2002. http://www.news.com/Bush-signs-Homeland-Security-bill/2100-1023_3-975305.html (accessed December 28, 2007).

McCullagh, Declan. "FAQ: How Real ID Will Affect You." CNET News.com, May 6, 2005. http://www.news.com/FAQ-How-Real-ID-will-affect-you/2100-1028_3-5697111.html (accessed December 28, 2007).

McCullagh, Declan, and Robert Lemos. " 'Perfect Storm' for New Privacy Laws?" CNET News.com, March 1, 2005. http://www.news.com/Perfect-storm-for-new-privacy-laws/2100-1029_3-5593225.html (accessed December 28, 2007).

"Medicine and the New Genetics." 2006. http://genome.gsc.riken.jp/hgmis/medicine/medicine.html (accessed December 28, 2007).

Mitchell, Mitch. "Medical Privacy Law Stirs Controversy." Star Telegram, February 23, 2003. http://www.gardere.com/Content/hubbard/tbl_s31Publications/FileUpload137/498/Star-Tel.Hoffman-02-23-03.pdf (accessed December 1, 2006).

Murphy, Dean E. "Librarians Use Shredder to Show Opposition to New F.B.I. Powers." Originally in the nyt.com, April 7, 2003. http://www.commondreams.org/headlines03/0407-03.htm (accessed December 1, 2006).

"National ID Cards and REAL ID Act." November 29, 2006. http://www.epic.org/privacy/id_cards/default.html (accessed December 1, 2006).

"National Information Infrastructure Protection Act of 1996." http://epic.org/security/1996_computer_law.html (accessed December 28, 2007).

"New Research Shows Identity Fraud Contained and Consumers Have More Control Than They Think." bbbonline.com, January 2006. http://www.bbbonline.org/IDTheft/safetyQuiz.asp (accessed December 28, 2007).

"The New Threat to Your Medical Privacy." ConsumerReports.org, 2006. http://www.consumerreports.org/cro/health-fitness/health-care/electronic-medical-records-306/overview/index.htm (accessed December 28, 2007).

Newman, Andy. "Those Dimples May Be Digits." nyt.com, May 3, 2001. http:// query.nytimes.com/gst/fullpage.html?res=9E04E2DE1538F930A35756C0A9679C8B63 (accessed December 28, 2007).

"Office for Civil Rights—HIPAA: Medical Privacy—National Standards to Protect the Privacy of Personal Health Information." 2006. http://www.os.dhhs.gov/ocr/hipaa/finalreg.html (accessed January 7, 2008).

"Overview of the Privacy Act of 1974, 2004 Edition Computer Matching." http://www.usdoj.gov/oip/1974compmatch.htm (accessed November 29, 2006).

Parsons, June, Dan Oja, and Stephanie Low. *Computers, Technology, and Society.* Cambridge, MA: ITP, 1997.

Pear, Robert. "Bush Acts to Drop Core Privacy Rule on Medical Data." nyt.com, March 22, 2002. http://query.nytimes.com/gst/fullpage.html?res= 9C0DEFD61E38F931A15750C0A9649C8B63 (accessed December 28, 2007).

———. "Health System Warily Prepares for Privacy Rules." nyt.com, April 6, 2003. http://query.nytimes.com/gst/fullpage.html?res=9B06E2DC1238F935A35757C0A965C8B63 (accessed December 28, 2007).

———. "Vast Worker Database to Track Deadbeat Parents." *New York Times,* September 22, 1997.

"Real ID Act of 2005 Driver's License Title Summary." 2006. http://www.ncsl.org/standcomm/sctran/realidsummary05.htm (accessed January 18, 2008).

Reuters. "Senate Rebuffs Domestic Spy Plan." *Wired News,* January 23, 2003. http://www.wired.com/politics/law/news/2003/01/57386 (accessed December 28, 2007).

"The Right to Financial Privacy Act." 2003. http://epic.org/privacy/rfpa/ (accessed December 28, 2007).

Safire, William. "You Are a Suspect." nyt.com, November 14, 2002. http://query.nytimes.com/gst/fullpage.html?res=9F0CE6D71630F937A25752C1A9649C8B63 (accessed December 28, 2007).

Schwaneberg, Robert. "Questions Leave 'Smart Card' in Limbo for Now." *Star-Ledger,* June 30, 1998, 11, 14.

———. "Smart Cards Take a Step in Legislature." *Star-Ledger,* June 23, 1998, 11, 15.

Schwartz, John. "Threats and Responses: Surveillance; Planned Databank on Citizens Spurs Opposition in Congress." nyt.com, January 16, 2003. http://query.nytimes.com/ gst/fullpage.html?res=940CE4D61131F935A25752C0A9659C8B63 (accessed December 28, 2007).

Seelye, Katharine Q. "A Plan for Database Privacy, but Public Has to Ask for It." *New York Times,* December 18, 1997, A1, A24.

Shelley, Gary, and Cashman, Thomas. *Discovering Computers a Link to the Future.* Cambridge, MA: ITP, 1997.

"Spotlight on Surveillance." 2005. http://epic.org/privacy/surveillance/spotlight/ (accessed December 28, 2007).

"Statement of Barry Steinhardt, Director of the ACLU Technology and Liberty Program, on RFID Tags Before the Commerce, Trade and Consumer Protection Subcommittee of the House Committee on Energy and Commerce." July 14, 2004. http://www.aclu.org/privacy/spying/15744leg20040714.html (accessed January 7, 2008).

Stein, Rob. "Medical Privacy Law Nets No Fines." washingtonpost.com, June 5, 2006. http://www.washingtonpost.com/wp-dyn/content/article/2006/06/04/AR2006060400672.html (accessed December 28, 2007).

"Surfer Beware: Personal Privacy and the Internet." Report of the Electronic Privacy Information Center, Washington, DC, June 1997. http://www.epic.org/Reports/surfer-beware.html (accessed December 1, 2006).

"Telehealth Update: Final HIPAA Privacy Rules." February 20, 2001. http://www.hrsa.gov/telehealth/pubs/hippa.htm (accessed December 28, 2007).

"The USA Patriot Act." November 17, 2005. http://epic.org/privacy/terrorism/usapatriot/ (accessed December 28, 2007).

"The Video Privacy Protection Act (VPPA)." 2002. http://epic.org/privacy/vppa/ (accessed December 28, 2007).

Waters, Richard. "US Group Implants Electronic Tags in Workers." FT.com, February 12, 2006. http://www.ft.com/cms/s/2/ec414700-9bf4-11da-8baa-0000779e2340.html (accessed December 28, 2007).

Wayner, Peter. "Code Breaker Cracks Smart Cards' Digital Safe." *New York Times,* June 22, 1998, D1–D2.

Weinstein, Lauren. "Taking Liberties with Our Freedom." Wired News, December 2, 2002. http://www.wired.com/politics/law/news/2002/12/56600 (accessed December 28, 2007).

"What Is the Privacy Act?" http://www.fs.fed.us/im/foia/pa.htm (accessed November 29, 2006).

Yegyazarian, Anush. "Tech.gov: Real ID's Real Problems." washingtonpost.com, October 11, 2006. http://www.pcworld.com/article/id,127419-c,techrelatedlegislation/article.html (accessed December 28, 2007).

Zeller, Tom, Jr. "Breach Points Up Flaws in Privacy Laws." nyt.com, February 24, 2005. http://www.nytimes.com/2005/02/24/business/24datas.html (accessed December 28, 2007).

RELATED WEB SITES

http://www.biometrics.dod.mil/

http://www.dol.gov

http://www.eff.org

Electronic Privacy Information Center (http://www.epic.org) is a research organization concerned with privacy issues. It keeps a Privacy Archive with "an extensive collection of documents, reports, news items, policy analysis and laws relating to privacy issues."

http://www.ftc.gov

http://www.govtrack.us/congress/billsearch.xpd lists 202 bills under the USA Patriot Act (2007–2008)

http://www.hhs.gov

http://www.hipaaadvisory.com/news

http://www.mib.com

http://www.patientprivacyrights.org

http://www.privacyrights.org

Answer Key to the Student Text

Chapter One Multiple Choice

1. D
2. D
3. A
4. B
5. B
6. D
7. D
8. C
9. C
10. D
11. B
12. B
13. C
14. C
15. B

Chapter One True/False

1. True
2. True
3. False
4. True
5. True
6. False
7. True
8. True
9. False
10. True
11. False
12. True
13. True
14. True
15. False

Chapter Two Multiple Choice

1. C
2. C
3. A
4. B
5. B
6. B
7. A
8. B

9. D
10. C
11. D
12. C
13. A
14. B
15. B

Chapter Two True/False

1. False
2. True
3. False
4. True
5. True
6. True
7. True
8. False
9. True
10. True

Chapter Three Multiple Choice

1. B
2. C
3. D
4. D
5. B
6. D
7. A
8. B
9. C
10. D
11. C
12. C
13. A
14. A
15. B

Chapter Three True/False

1. True
2. False
3. True
4. True
5. False
6. True
7. True
8. True
9. False
10. True

Chapter Four Multiple Choice

1. D
2. C
3. D

4. C
5. D
6. D
7. C
8. D
9. C
10. C
11. B
12. A
13. D
14. A
15. B

Chapter Four True/False

1. True
2. False
3. True
4. False
5. True
6. True
7. False
8. False
9. True
10. True

Chapter Five Multiple Choice

1. C
2. A
3. C
4. A
5. B
6. D
7. A
8. B
9. C
10. D
11. D
12. C
13. D
14. D
15. C

Chapter Five True/False

1. True
2. True
3. False
4. True
5. False
6. True
7. True
8. True
9. True
10. False

Chapter Six Multiple Choice

1. B
2. D
3. C
4. B
5. C
6. D
7. D
8. D
9. C
10. B
11. A
12. B
13. D
14. B
15. A

Chapter Six True/False

1. True
2. False
3. False
4. True
5. False
6. True
7. False
8. False
9. True
10. True

Chapter Seven Multiple Choice

1. C
2. A
3. A
4. D
5. B
6. D
7. A
8. C
9. D
10. D

Chapter Seven True/False

1. False
2. True
3. False
4. True
5. False
6. False
7. True
8. True
9. True
10. False

Chapter Eight Multiple Choice

1. B
2. D
3. C
4. D
5. B
6. A
7. B
8. C
9. D
10. B

Chapter Eight True/False

1. True
2. True
3. True
4. False
5. True
6. True
7. True
8. True
9. True
10. False

Chapter Nine Multiple Choice

1. C
2. B
3. A
4. C
5. D
6. B
7. D
8. C
9. A
10. D

Chapter Nine True/False

1. True
2. True
3. True
4. False
5. True
6. True
7. True
8. False
9. True
10. True

Chapter Ten Multiple Choice

1. C
2. B
3. D

4. B
5. A
6. D
7. D
8. B
9. B
10. C

Chapter Ten True/False

1. True
2. True
3. True
4. False
5. True
6. True
7. True
8. True
9. False
10. False

Chapter Eleven Multiple Choice

1. C
2. B
3. D
4. A
5. A
6. C
7. D
8. D
9. B
10. A

Chapter Eleven True/False

1. False
2. False
3. True
4. True
5. True
6. False
7. True
8. True
9. True
10. True

Chapter Twelve Multiple Choice

1. D
2. B
3. B
4. D
5. C
6. B
7. A
8. D

9. C
10. B
11. C
12. A
13. A
14. B
15. B

Chapter Twelve True/False

1. True
2. False
3. False
4. True
5. False
6. True
7. True
8. False
9. False
10. False
11. True
12. True
13. True
14. False
15. True

Test Bank

CHAPTER ONE EXAM

Name ____________________________________

MULTIPLE CHOICE Choose the one alternative that best completes the statement or answers the question.

1. Information technology includes the use of computers, communications ______________, and computer literacy.
   A. groups C. networks
   B. tags D. None of the above
2. An electronic device that can accept data as input, process it according to a program, store it, and produce information as output is called a ________________.
   A. calculator C. multiplication table
   B. adding machine D. computer
3. Step-by-step instructions are called a ________________.
   A. menu C. hardware
   B. program D. None of the above
4. Small hand-held computers used throughout the health care system today are called ________________. They can hold reference manuals or be used to write prescriptions.
   A. supercomputers C. mainframes
   B. personal digital assistants (PDAs) D. None of the above
5. A tiny ____________ can be put into a human being and can dispense medication among other things.
   A. supercomputer C. embedded computer
   B. personal digital assistant (PDA) D. minicomputer
6. ________________ take data that humans understand and digitize it, that is, translate it into binary form of ones and zeroes.
   A. Output devices C. Storage devices
   B. Input devices D. None of the above
7. A/An ________________ manipulates data, doing arithmetic or logical operations on it.
   A. output device C. storage device
   B. input device D. processing unit
8. ______________________ can take complex mathematical data and create simulations of epidemics, pandemics, and other disasters.
   A. Supercomputers C. Embedded computers
   B. Personal digital assistants (PDAs) D. Minicomputers

9. ________________ are used in business for input/output intensive purpos such as generating paychecks or processing medical insurance claims.
   A. Supercomputers
   B. Personal digital assistants (PDAs)
   C. Mainframes
   D. None of the above

10. ______________________ identify people by their body parts. It includes fi gerprints, hand prints, face recognition, and iris scans.
   A. Biometrics
   B. All security systems
   C. Both A and B
   D. None of the above

CHAPTER ONE EXAM

Name ______________________________

FILL-INS Write the word or phrase that best completes each statement or answers the question.

1. The term ____________ includes knowledge of computers, the Internet, and computer literacy.
2. A computer manipulates data by following step-by-step instructions called a ____________.
3. ____________ are the largest and most powerful computers at any time. They are used for weather forecasting and scientific research.
4. ____________ devices take data that humans understand and input it into the computer in digital form of ons and offs, ones and zeroes that the computer can process.
5. ____________ are the second largest computers at any time. They are used for input/output intensive operations like generating payroll.
6. Small handheld computers known as ____________ originally could hold a notepad, calendar, and an address book. Today, sophisticated handhelds are used throughout the health care world.
7. The embedded computer is a single-purpose computer on a ____________ of silicon.
8. In a digital computer, all information including text, music, animation, graphics, smell, and sound is represented by combinations of ones and zeroes, called ____________.
9. The physical components of a computer are called ____________.
10. ____________ is changeable, temporary, volatile memory.
11. ____________ or firmware contains basic start-up instructions, which are burned into a chip at the factory; you cannot change the contents.
12. ____________ refers to the programs—the step-by-step instructions that tell the hardware what to do.
13. The ____________ is a group of programs that manages and organizes the resources of the computer.
14. ____________ is a wireless technology that can connect digital devices from computers to medical devices to cell phones.
15. Transmission over networks is governed by sets of technical standards or rules called ____________.

CHAPTER TWO EXAM

Name ______________________________

MULTIPLE CHOICE Choose the one alternative that best completes t statement or answers the question.

1. ______________ refers to the use of computers to organize information health care.
   A. Computer informatics
   B. Medical computing
   C. Medical informatics
   D. None of the above

2. __________________ uses computers to solve biological problems.
   A. Biological informatics
   B. Bioinformatics
   C. Computerized biology
   D. Biological computing

3. __________________ refers to the connection of people and diverse co puter systems.
   A. Interoperability
   B. Systemic computerization
   C. Intersystemology
   D. None of the above

4. ______________ is the use of computers and software to enter prescriptio and send them to pharmacies electronically.
   A. Computer prescription
   B. Elemental prescribing
   C. E-prescribing
   D. None of the above

5. __________________ was passed by the U.S. Congress and signed into law 1996. Its goal was to make health insurance portable from one job to anoth and to secure the privacy of medical records.
   A. HIPAA
   B. HIPPA
   C. The Americans with Disabiliti Act
   D. None of the above

6. Scrambling data, so that no one can see it without a key, is called ____________
   A. scrambling
   B. biometrics
   C. a firewall
   D. encryption

7. What information is included in the patient information form?
   A. Name
   B. Insurance information
   C. Medical history
   D. All of the above

8. The federal government has set a goal of the year __________ for univers adoption of electronic records.
   A. 2009
   B. 2010
   C. 2013
   D. 2014

9. Which of the following is true?
   A. A fully developed electronic health record sends a warning to doctors of adverse drug reactions
   B. Most doctors now use electronic health records
   C. Most hospitals now use electron health records
   D. None of the above

10. Which of the following are obstacles in the way of adopting electronic record
    A. Cost
    B. Privacy concerns
    C. Lack of interoperability
    D. All of the above

CHAPTER TWO EXAM

Name ________________________________

FILL-INS Write the word or phrase that best completes each statement or answers the question.

1. The emphasis in ______________ is on the use of technology to organize information in health care.
2. ______________________ uses computers to solve biological problems.
3. The U.S. Government is attempting to make the EHR and e-prescribing universal by _________________.
4. One of the obstacles in the way of introducing the EHR is ___________.
5. Regional cooperation is being fostered through the establishment of _________________ in which data could be shared within a region.
6. The _________________________ is the infrastructure that would allow communication between RHIOs.
7. The goal of the HIT decade is fully _________________ EHRs, that is, health care computers and EHRs that can talk to each other nationally (or even internationally).
8. ____________________________________ of the Department of Health and Human Services of the federal government has developed an electronic health record with a graphical user interface.
9. The first information systems introduced into hospitals (in the 1960s) were used for _________________ purposes (managing finances and inventory).
10. A __________ information system is concerned with the financial details of running a hospital.
11. A ________ information system uses computers to manage clinical information.
12. ____________ information systems monitor drug allergies and interactions and fill and track prescriptions. They also track inventory and create patient drug profiles.
13. ___________________ information systems are supposed to improve care by using computers to manage charting, staff scheduling, and the integration of clinical information.
14. ______________________________ manages radiological images in digital form in hospitals.
15. ___________________ information systems use computers to manage both laboratory tests and their results.

CHAPTER THREE EXAM

Name ______________________________

MULTIPLE CHOICE Choose the one alternative that best completes t statement or answers the question.

1. The ____________ use of computers includes anything that has to do w direct patient care, such as diagnosis, monitoring, and treatment.
   A. clinical
   B. special purpose
   C. administrative
   D. None of the above
2. ________________ applications include the use of computers in educatio research, and some aspects of pharmacy.
   A. Clinical
   B. Special purpose
   C. Administrative
   D. None of the above
3. ______________ applications include office management, scheduling, a accounting tasks.
   A. Clinical
   B. Special purpose
   C. Administrative
   D. None of the above
4. Medical offices must use ____________ billing to accommodate two or thr insurers, who must be billed in a timely fashion before the patient is billed.
   A. super
   B. partial
   C. bucket
   D. None of the above
5. An organized collection of related data is called a ________________.
   A. relational database
   B. program
   C. bill
   D. None of the above
6. ________________ software allows the user to enter, organize, and sto huge amounts of data and information.
   A. Word processing
   B. Database management
   C. Spreadsheet
   D. Graphics
7. In a database, a ___________ holds all related information on an entity, f example, a medical practice.
   A. field
   B. record
   C. file
   D. None of the above
8. A table is made up of related ____________; each holds all the informatio on one item in the table.
   A. fields
   B. records
   C. files
   D. keys
9. Each record is made up of related ____________. One holds one piece information.
   A. fields
   B. records
   C. files
   D. keys
10. The ___________ field uniquely identifies each record in a table.
    A. field
    B. record
    C. file
    D. key

CHAPTER THREE EXAM

Name ______________________________

FILL-INS Write the word or phrase that best completes each statement or answers the question.

1. The ______________ uses of computers include anything that has to do with direct patient care, such as diagnosis, monitoring, and treatment.
2. ______________ applications include the use of computers in education and some aspects of pharmacy.
3. ______________ applications include office management, scheduling, and accounting tasks.
4. ______________—the delivery of health care over telecommunications lines—includes clinical, special purpose, and administrative applications.
5. Medical offices use ______________ billing to accommodate two or three insurers, who must be billed in a timely fashion before the patient is billed.
6. A ______________ is an organized collection of related data; information input in one part of the program can be linked to information in another part of the program.
7. A ______________ allows the user to enter, organize, and store huge amounts of data and information.
8. A database ______________ holds all related information on an entity, for example, a medical practice.
9. Within each file, there can be several ______________, each of which holds related information.
10. A table is made up of related ______________, each of which holds all the information on one item in a table, for example, one patient.
11. Each record is made up of related ______________, one of which holds one piece of information, such as patient's last name or Social Security number or chart number.
12. The ______________ field uniquely identifies each record in a table.
13. A standard grouping system is ______________ on which hospital reimbursement by private and government insurers is based.
14. Services including tests, laboratory work, examinations, and treatments are coded using ______________.
15. Charges, payments, and adjustments are called ______________.

CHAPTER FOUR EXAM

Name ___________________________________

MULTIPLE CHOICE Choose the one alternative that best completes t statement or answers the question.

1. ______________ uses computers and telecommunications equipment to deliv medical care at a distance.
   A. Medical informatics
   B. Telemedicine
   C. Computer informatics
   D. None of the above

2. The Department of ________________ of the United States has spent millio of dollars on telemedicine equipment and installation.
   A. Veterans Affairs
   B. Defense
   C. Education
   D. Health

3. ______________ treats skin rashes at a distance.
   A. TeleStroke
   B. Telecardiology
   C. Teleoncology
   D. Teledermatology

4. __________________ technology involves sharing information in a time- an place-independent way over the Internet.
   A. Store and send
   B. Send and store
   C. Store and forward
   D. Interactive videoconferencing

5. ____________________ or teleconferencing allows doctors to consult wi each other and with patients in real time, at a distance.
   A. Store and send
   B. Send and store
   C. Store and forward
   D. Interactive videoconferencing

6. ______________ involves the sending of radiological images in digital for over telecommunications lines.
   A. Teleradiology
   B. Telekinetics
   C. Both A and B
   D. None of the above

7. In __________, the pathologist sees images on a monitor instead of under microscope.
   A. teleradiology
   B. telepathology
   C. interactive radiology
   D. None of the above

8. _________________ technology can link devices such as a pacemaker and a ce phone.
   A. Wi-Fi
   B. Satellite
   C. Bluetooth
   D. None of the above

9. ______________________ saves patients by speeding diagnosis, so that tPA ca be given within a few hours if appropriate.
   A. TeleStroke
   B. Teleoncology
   C. Telecardiology
   D. Telepsychiatry

10. ____________________ involves the delivery of therapy using teleconferencin
    A. TeleStroke
    B. Teleoncology
    C. Telecardiology
    D. Telepsychiatry

CHAPTER FOUR EXAM

Name ______________________________

FILL-INS Write the word or phrase that best completes each statement or answers the question.

1. ______________ uses computers and telecommunications equipment to deliver medical care at a distance.
2. ______________ involves sharing information in a time- and place-independent way over the Internet. The information is stored, digitized, and then sent.
3. Interactive videoconferencing or ______________ allows doctors to consult with each other and with patients in real time, at a distance.
4. ______________ technology can link devices such as a pacemaker and a cell phone.
5. A victim of a stroke caused by a clot (determined by a CT scan) may be helped by the administration of ______________, a clot-busting drug, if it is given within a few hours.
6. ______________ involves the delivery of therapy using teleconferencing.
7. A ______________ system can be used at home by asthmatic patients; it is designed to transmit over the telephone to a remote location.
8. A miniature ECG telemetry system allows wireless remote ______________ monitoring.
9. A ______________ weighs 135 pounds, is only 5 inches high, and includes a respirator, heart machine, and intravenous drugs, and monitors that transmit all the data they gather immediately to the hospital.
10. ______________ involves the monitoring of vital signs from a distance via telecommunications equipment and the replacement of home nursing visits with videoconferences.
11. ______________ is usually used to manage chronic conditions such as congestive heart failure and diabetes.
12. The stated reasons for introducing telemedicine into ______________ are cost-containment, security, and enhanced medical care.
13. ______________ purpose was to compare high-risk, premature infants receiving traditional care with an experimental group, which in addition to traditional care received a telemedicine link to the hospital while the babies were hospitalized and for six months after.
14. In Vermont, a ______________ project links trauma surgeon's homes with hospital emergency departments, providing immediate expert service at any time.
15. Medical personnel are required to be licensed by the ______________ in which they practice.

CHAPTER FIVE EXAM

Name ______________________________

MULTIPLE CHOICE Choose the one alternative that best completes t statement or answers the question.

1. ______________ refers to "the study of diseases in populations by collecti and analyzing statistical data."
   A. Pandemic
   B. Epidemic
   C. Epidemiology
   D. None of the above

2. ______________ supports public health practice and research with inform tion technology.
   A. Medical informatics
   B. Health care informatics
   C. Public health informatics
   D. None of the above

3. Public health is affected by social factors such as poverty and soc ______________.
   A. inequality
   B. style
   C. Both A and B
   D. None of the above

4. Information technology can help infection control practitioners in the task ______________.
   A. surveillance
   B. outbreak monitoring
   C. reporting
   D. All of the above

5. Computers can create what-if scenarios or ______________ of what wou happen to an infectious disease if something else happened (e.g., if air trav increased/decreased or the temperature rose or fell; if there was an adequa supply of antiviral drugs, if a vaccine existed or did not exist).
   A. let us pretend
   B. spreadsheets
   C. simulations
   D. None of the above

6. ______________ models are the programs that create the simulations
   A. What-if
   B. Computational
   C. Computer
   D. Disease

7. Currently, a program called ______________ is modeling flu.
   A. Socrates
   B. MIDAS
   C. AESOP
   D. None of the above

8. A/An ______________ is "an excess in the number of cases of a given heal problem. . . ."
   A. pandemic
   B. epidemic
   C. small outbreak
   D. outbreak

9. ______________ are organized "system[s] for the collection, storag retrieval, analysis, and dissemination of information" on people with a disease, predisposition toward a disease, and an exposure to anything thought to cau ill health.
   A. Registries
   B. Offices
   C. Bureaus
   D. None of the above

10. ______________ uses "health-related data that precede diagnosis and si nal a sufficient probability of a case or an outbreak."
    A. Counting
    B. Syndromic surveillance
    C. Computer surveillance
    D. None of the above

11. In developing countries in Asia and Africa, __________ PDAs are used for the collection and dissemination of information, warnings, education. . . .
    A. SATTELIFE
    B. LIFESAVE
    C. Save-a-Life
    D. None of the above
12. ______________________ will be a national electronic surveillance system that would allow epidemics to be identified quickly.
    A. National Email Disease Initiative
    B. New Electronic Disease Initiative
    C. National Electronic Disease Initiative
    D. None of the above
13. A/An ______________ is a global outbreak of disease to which every individual in the world is susceptible.
    A. epidemic
    B. pandemic
    C. Both A and B
    D. None of the above
14. ______________ is a microbiology information system developed at Brigham and Women's Hospital in Massachusetts.
    A. WHONET
    B. WHATNOT
    C. WHOBIO
    D. None of the above
15. Some of the effects of global warming are ______________.
    A. more intense storms and heat waves
    B. There are no effects
    C. drought in the developing world
    D. Both A and C

CHAPTER FIVE EXAM

Name ______________________________

FILL-INS Write the word or phrase that best completes each statement or answe the question.

1. ______________________ is a microbiology information system dev oped at Brigham and Women's Hospital in Massachusetts. It is used to monit antibacterial resistance.
2. ______________ is already having a devastating effect on the earth and affecting agricultural production in some places.
3. One of the concrete steps that could be taken to slow global warming is cutti ________ emissions.
4. Hurricane ______________ flooded New Orleans both because it was "monster hurricane" and because the levees failed.
5. In the early twentieth century, epidemic ______________ struck in Ne York for the first time.
6. ______________ attacks the immune system, leading to susceptibility opportunistic infection.
7. ____________________ informatics integrates "health-related data on levels, such as molecule, cell, tissue, organ, people and the entire population.
8. ____________________ appeared in 2002, first in China. The epidem was caused by the corona virus.
9. The first human cases of ______________ flu were confirmed in 199 The virus, called H5N1 or A(H5N1), which causes the disease currently pre ents itself in the animal population.
10. WHO stands for ______________________.
11. ______________ virus first appeared in the 1930s. It is a form of encepha tis or brain inflammation.
12. ______________ disease is a progressive neurological disorder of catt that results from infection. Cows contract this by eating infected food.
13. ______________ surveillance can be used for example in shelte where there are no medical personnel; people can look out for signs and sym toms (for instance diarrhea) and report them.
14. The ________________________ (part of the Public Health Informatio Network) will promote "integrated surveillance systems that can transfer . . public health, laboratory and clinical data . . . over the internet." This would b a national electronic surveillance system.
15. ____________ virus was first identified in Zaire in 1976.

CHAPTER SIX EXAM

Name ______________________________

MULTIPLE CHOICE Choose the one alternative that best completes the statement or answers the question.

1. Radiology is increasingly concerned with treating disease. Radiologists who treat disease are called ____________ radiologists.
   A. interventional
   B. treating
   C. medical
   D. None of the above

2. Digital images ____________________.
   A. are immediately available on a network
   B. do not have to be developed
   C. can be transmitted over telephone lines
   D. All of the above

3. If a doctor suspects that you have a broken bone, which of the following imaging techniques is likely to be used?
   A. X-ray
   B. PET scan
   C. Ultrasound
   D. MRI

4. __________________ is used to examine a moving fetus.
   A. X-ray
   B. PET scan
   C. Ultrasound
   D. Computerized tomography (CT) scan

5. ________________________ uses X-rays and digital technology to produce a cross-sectional image of the body.
   A. X-ray
   B. PET scan
   C. Ultrasound
   D. Computerized tomography (CT) scan

6. __________________________________ machines use computer technology to produce images of soft tissue within the body that could not be pictured by traditional X-rays.
   A. X-ray
   B. PET scan
   C. Ultrasound
   D. MRI

7. __________ are used to image brain tumors and in helping to diagnose disorders of the nervous system such as multiple sclerosis (MS).
   A. X-rays
   B. PET scans
   C. Ultrasounds
   D. MRIs

8. Relatively new, functional __________________ measure small metabolic changes in an active part of the brain. It identifies brain activity by changes in blood oxygen.
   A. X-rays
   B. PET scans
   C. ultrasounds
   D. MRIs

9. ____________________ use radioisotope technology to create a picture of the body in action.
   A. X-rays
   B. PET scans
   C. DEXA scans
   D. MRIs

10. Neuroimaging techniques using ____________ can present a picture of brain activity associated with cognitive processes like memory and the use of language.
    A. X-rays
    B. PET scans
    C. ultrasound
    D. MRIs

11. A bone density scan or ________________ is a special kind of low-radiati X-ray that shows changes in the rays' intensity after passing through bone.
    A. X-ray
    B. PET scan
    C. DEXA scan
    D. MRI

12. ______________ is "a system that transmits, stores, retrieves, and displays di tal images . . . and communicates the information over a network."
    A. PACS
    B. RACS
    C. PICOM
    D. RADCOM

13. On the borderline between radiology and surgery, stereotactic radiosurgery ______________ knife surgery is a noninvasive technique that is currently us to treat brain tumors in a one-day session.
    A. alpha
    B. beta
    C. gamma
    D. None of the above

14. Focused ______________ surgery does not involve cutting, but the use sound waves. Studies involve the use of ultrasound to stop massive bleeding a to treat cancer.
    A. ultrasound
    B. radiography
    C. MRI
    D. SPECT

15. The newer ____________ knife, because it compensates for patient moveme can be used to treat brain and spinal tumors with radiosurgery.
    A. radiological
    B. cyber
    C. alpha
    D. None of the above

CHAPTER SIX EXAM

Name ______________________________

FILL-INS Write the word or phrase that best completes each statement or answers the question.

1. A traditional ______________ uses high-energy electromagnetic waves to produce a two-dimensional picture on film.
2. If a broken bone is suspected, an ______________ is likely to be used.
3. ______________ uses no radiation. It uses very high-frequency sound waves and the echoes they produce when they hit an object.
4. ______________ uses X-rays and digital technology to produce a cross-sectional image of the body.
5. ______________ can be used to locate nerve centers, thus helping in the reduction of pain.
6. ______________ scans may be used in place of coronary angiograms to examine coronary artery blockages.
7. ______________ machines use computer technology to produce images of soft tissue.
8. ______________ are used to image brain tumors and in helping to diagnose disorders of the nervous system.
9. ______________ MRIs measure brain activity by changes in blood oxygen.
10. ______________—unlike traditional X-rays and CT scans—produce images of how the body works.
11. Neuroimaging techniques using ______________ can present a picture of brain activity associated with cognitive processes like memory and the use of language.
12. ______________ can show the specific brain activity associated with schizophrenia, manic-depression, posttraumatic stress disorder, and obsessive-compulsive disorder.
13. Brain imaging techniques, including both PET scans and fMRIs, are aiding in the comprehension of mental disorders such as ______________.
14. ______________ surgery does not involve cutting, but the use of sound waves.
15. Stereotactic radiosurgery (gamma knife surgery) is a noninvasive technique that is currently used to treat ______________ tumors.

CHAPTER SEVEN EXAM

Name ______________________________

MULTIPLE CHOICE Choose the one alternative that best completes t statement or answers the question.

1. Much computer-aided surgery is ____________ invasive, performing surge through small incisions.
   A. maximally
   B. middling
   C. minimally
   D. None of the above

2. Most minimally invasive procedures are done using a/ ______________—a thin tube, which can be connected to a minuscu camera. It projects an image of the surgical site onto a monitor.
   A. camerascope
   B. SurgiScope
   C. endoscope
   D. None of the above

3. The surgeon does not look at the patient; instead, she or he looks at a monit on which is projected a picture of the patient. Thus, much computer-assist surgery is said to be ____________-directed.
   A. picture
   B. image
   C. graphically
   D. None of the above

4. ____________ or telepresence surgery performed by robotic devices co trolled by surgeons at another site has been successfully performed.
   A. Distance
   B. Virtual
   C. Augmented
   D. None of the above

5. With ____________ reality technology, the computer can create simulatio and an environment that seems real, but is not.
   A. augmented
   B. virtual
   C. simulated
   D. None of the above

6. One form of minimally invasive robotic surgery is called ____________ surgery. It does not require incisions. It is also called natural orifice surgery.
   A. augmented
   B. virtual
   C. simulated
   D. endoluminal

7. ____________ is a computer-controlled, image-directed robot that pe formed its first hip replacement in 1992.
   A. HIPDOC
   B. ROBODOC
   C. AESOP
   D. ZEUS

8. ____________ is used as an assistant in endoscopic procedures. It holds an moves the endoscope under the direction of the surgeon.
   A. HIPDOC
   B. ROBODOC
   C. AESOP
   D. ZEUS

9. ________ is a robotic surgical system, which will make possible minimally inv sive microsurgery. It has three interactive robotic arms, one of which holds th endoscope, whereas the other two manipulate the surgical instruments.
   A. HIPDOC
   B. ROBODOC
   C. AESOP
   D. ZEUS

10. ____________ is a robot developed to perform stereotactic neurosurgic procedures.
    A. MINNIE
    B. MAXIE
    C. MARY
    D. MINERVA

11. A new four-dimensional model of the human body called ________________ has been developed in Canada. It can be used to plan surgery and to educate patients.
    A. CAVEman
    B. NEWman
    C. SURGIman
    D. None of the above
12. ________________ is a series of NASA missions in which groups of scientists live in Aquarius.
    A. NIMO
    B. NEEMO
    C. CAPTainNemo
    D. None of the above
13. In the ____________________, images from all sources will be integrated and available to surgeons and other personnel displayed on one central screen.
    A. New Operating Room
    B. Computer Operating Room
    C. Operating Room of the Future
    D. None of the above
14. ________________ using light energy can be used in surgery to cut, vaporize tumors, and seal small blood vessels.
    A. Lasers
    B. Lights
    C. Knives
    D. None of the above
15. ________________ is an eye surgery that uses lasers to correct vision by changing the shape of the cornea.
    A. EYELSIK
    B. CORNEASLIK
    C. LASIK
    D. None of the above

CHAPTER SEVEN EXAM

Name ______________________________________

FILL-INS Write the word or phrase that best completes each statement or answ the question.

1. _______________ is surgery performed through small incisions.
2. Most minimally invasive procedures are done using an _______________—a th tube, which can be connected to a minuscule camera.
3. Distance (or _______________) surgery performed by robotic devices co trolled by surgeons at another site has been successfully performed.
4. One program, _______________, attempts to teach the special skills that a needed to perform MIS.
5. The earliest use of a robot in surgery was in hip replacement operations, usi the robot called _______________.
6. _______________ is a robotic surgical system for minimally invasive mic surgery.
7. _______________ is a robot developed to perform stereotactic neurosurgic procedures.
8. _______________ is system software required to connect the operating roo hardware into a network that a surgeon can control with voice commands.
9. Telepresence surgery (distance surgery) was first developed by _______________
10. Much computer-assisted surgery is said to be _______________-directed; the su geon looks at a monitor, not directly at the surgical field.
11. Computer-assisted surgical planning involves the use of _______________ technology to provide surgeons with realistic accurate models on which to tea surgery and plan and practice operations.
12. With _______________ technology, the computer can create an environme that seems real, but is not.
13. _______________ disease has been treated with minimally invasive techniqu for many years.
14. Through a combination of hardware and software, a _______________ may b able to "see" via video devices and to "hear" through microphones usir speech-recognition software.
15. _______________ is developing flexible, computer-controlled catheters capab of suturing; the surgeon can control them inside the patient.

CHAPTER EIGHT EXAM

Name ______________________________

MULTIPLE CHOICE Choose the one alternative that best completes the statement or answers the question.

1. In the United States, the _______________ oversees the safety and efficacy of new medications.
   A. Federal Drug Administration
   B. Food and Drug Administration
   C. Federal Safety Administration
   D. None of the above
2. PDUFA (_______________) requires drug companies to pay fees to support the drug review process.
   A. Prescription Drug User Fees Act
   B. Prescription Drug and Food Act
   C. Prescription Drug Understanding and Food Act
   D. None of the above
3. _______________ sees the human body as a collection of molecules and seeks to understand and treat disease in terms of these molecules.
   A. Bioinformatics
   B. Medical computing
   C. Biotechnology
   D. None of the above
4. Developing drugs by design requires mapping the structure and creating a three-dimensional graphical model of the target molecule. This is called __________ drug design.
   A. reasonable
   B. rational
   C. graphical
   D. None of the above
5. The application of information technology to biology is called __________. It seeks to organize biological data into databases.
   A. IT informatics
   B. drug informatics
   C. database informatics
   D. bioinformatics
6. The _______________ Project was "an . . . effort to understand the hereditary instructions that make each of us unique. The goal is to find the location of the 100,000 or so human genes and to read the entire genetic script. . . ."
   A. International Gene
   B. National Gene Mapping
   C. Human Genome
   D. None of the above
7. _______________ cells are cells that can develop into different types of body cells; theoretically, they can repair the body.
   A. Stem
   B. Developmental
   C. Both A and B
   C. None of the above
8. The _______________ Project is an international project seeking to create mathematical models of human organs.
   A. Human Model
   B. Human Physical
   C. Physiome
   D. None of the above
9. _______________ (CPOE) can lower prescription errors.
   A. Computerized Physician Order Entry System
   B. Computer Pharmacy Order Email System
   C. Computer and Physician Email System
   D. None of the above

10. Computer warning systems can be used to prevent ______________________ (ADEs).
    A. any deviant event
    B. adverse drug events
    C. Any drug eventuality
    D. None of the above
11. Centralized computerized pharmacies identify medications by th_________________.
    A. color
    B. shape
    C. density
    D. barcode
12. _________________ (RFID) tags include an antenna, a decoder to interpret da and the tag that includes information. The antenna sends signals. When the t detects the signal, it sends back information. The tags can be used to keep tra of anything including medications.
    A. Response frequency identification
    B. Radio pharmacy identification
    C. Radio frequency identification
    D. None of the above
13. _______________________ involves using a computer, a network connectio and a drug-dispensing unit to allow patients to obtain drugs outside of a trad tional pharmacy, at, for example, a doctor's office or clinic.
    A. Telepharmacy
    B. Phone pharmacy
    C. Computer pharmacy
    D. None of the above
14. Some medications can currently be delivered on an implanted ______________ that is surgically implanted in a patient and releases the drug or drugs.
    A. barcode
    B. chip
    C. Both A and B
    D. None of the above
15. Decentralized hospital pharmacies that dispense medications on each unit a called ____________________.
    A. point-of-use
    B. vending machines
    C. drug dispensaries
    D. None of the above

CHAPTER EIGHT EXAM

Name ______________________________

FILL-INS Write the word or phrase that best completes each statement or answers the question.

1. ______________ sees the human body as a collection of molecules and seeks to understand and treat disease in terms of these molecules.
2. Developing drugs by ______________ requires mapping the structure and creating a three-dimensional graphical model of the target molecule.
3. The application of information technology to biology is called ______________.
4. The ______________, sponsored in the United States by the National Institutes of Health and the Department of Energy, began in 1990 and involved hundreds of scientists all over the world. It was an effort to understand the hereditary instructions that make each of us unique.
5. ______________ is one experimental technology used to develop drugs to shut off disease-causing genes.
6. ______________ is a process that cells use to turn off genes. The attempt at developing drugs based on this process is in its infancy.
7. The ______________ has created a virtual heart using mathematical equations to simulate the processes of the heart.
8. Computer warning systems can be used to prevent ______________ drug events (ADEs).
9. According to the 1999 government report, "______________," between forty-four thousand and ninety-eight thousand people die in U.S. hospitals each year as a result of medical errors.
10. Automated hospital pharmacy presupposes the use of ______________ to identify drugs.
11. Some computerized hospital pharmacies are using ______________ dispensing of drugs—a decentralized automated system.
12. ______________ involves using a computer, a network connection, and a drug-dispensing unit to allow patients to obtain drugs outside of a traditional pharmacy setting.
13. Some medications can currently be delivered on an implanted ______________.
14. ______________ are cells that can develop into different kinds of cells.
15. Computers have helped develop drugs for ______________, Alzheimer's disease, and hypertension.

CHAPTER NINE EXAM

Name ______________________________

MULTIPLE CHOICE Choose the one alternative that best completes t statement or answers the question.

1. ________________ is a program that uses virtual reality. Its purpose is teach technical dexterity to dental students.
   A. DentSim
   B. FillingSim
   C. Dextrous Dentist
   D. None of the above
2. The electronic dental chart will be standardized, easy to find, and easy to rea It will include ________________.
   A. administrative applications
   B. the patient's conditions
   C. treatments
   D. All of the above
3. One study traced the high number of cavities in poor children to________
   A. increased lead levels in the children's blood
   B. shortages in calcium and vitamin C
   C. Both A and B
   D. None of the above
4. The fiber optic camera is analogous to the ________________ used in surge It is used to view an area that is normally difficult to see.
   A. endoscope
   B. knife
   C. robot
   D. None of the above
5. Computer-controlled injections are administered by the ________________ It includes a microprocessor that measures tissue density; this insures a stea flow of anesthetic.
   A. computerized injection machines
   B. WAND™
   C. robotic needle
   D. None of the above
6. In dentistry as in other fields, expert systems or ________________ (CDSS) can help.
   A. clinical decision-support systems
   B. clinical dentistry support systems
   C. computerized dentistry support systems
   D. None of the above
7. ________________ is software that allows the creation of medical and dent expert systems.
   A. Dentexpert
   B. FillingEXpert
   C. DentalExpert
   D. EXPERTMD
8. ________________ is currently used to diagnose cavities. An electric cu rent is passed through a tooth, and the tooth's resistance is measured. A decaye tooth has a different resistance reading than a healthy tooth.
   A. Electrical conductance
   B. Current conductance
   C. Electrical dentistry
   D. None of the above
9. ________________ invasive dentistry emphasizes prevention and the lea possible intervention.
   A. Less
   B. Minimally
   C. Maximally
   D. None of the above
10. Teledentistry programs have been developed to help ________________
    A. fill cavities over the telephone
    B. dentists access specialists
    C. Both A and B
    D. None of the above

CHAPTER NINE EXAM

Name ______________________________

FILL-INS Write the word or phrase that best completes each statement or answers the question.

1. ______________ combines computer technology with dentistry to create a basis for research, education, and the solution of real-world problems in oral health care using computer applications.
2. The earliest application of information technology in the dentist's office, as in so many other offices, was ______________, related to bookkeeping and accounting.
3. The ______________ will be standardized, easy to search, and easy to read. It will integrate practice management tasks (administrative applications) with clinical information.
4. ______________ (usually streptococcus) are the cause of tooth decay and periodontal disease.
5. ______________ involves the application of a material to the tooth that can be shaped and polished.
6. ______________ can be used to replace missing teeth.
7. ______________ is software that allows the creation of medical and dental expert systems.
8. ______________ is currently used to diagnose cavities. An electric current is passed through a tooth, and the tooth's resistance is measured.
9. ______________ involves using a digital camera to obtain images of teeth trans-illuminated with white light.
10. ______________ emphasizes prevention and the least possible intervention.
11. ______________ lasers can find pits in tooth enamel that may become cavities.
12. The precision of ______________ instruments helps in performing root canal therapy without harming surrounding tissue.
13. The change in the conditions for which people seek dental care is related to demographic changes. Older adults with their own teeth are more likely to suffer from ______________ disease.
14. ______________ X-rays have some advantages. They take less time and expose the patient to from 60 to 90 percent less radiation.
15. ______________ is concerned with diagnosing and treating diseases of the gums and other structures supporting the teeth.

CHAPTER TEN EXAM

Name ______________________________

MULTIPLE CHOICE Choose the one alternative that best completes t statement or answers the question.

1. The ____________ Project is a computerized library of human anatomy at t National Library of Medicine.
   A. Visible Human C. Human Anatomy
   B. Visible Anatomy D. None of the above
2. The ____________ Project (Columbia University) is creating three-dime sional models (called maximal models) of anatomical regions and structures be used in teaching anatomy.
   A. 3-D Model C. Virtual Anatomy
   B. Vesalius D. Human Anatomy
3. A project called the ______________ is digitizing some of the seven thousa human embryos lost in miscarriages, which have been kept by the Nation Museum of Health and Medicine of the Armed Forces Institute of Patholo since the 1880s.
   A. Visible Embryo Project C. Virtual Human Embryo
   B. Virtual Human D. None of the above
4. ____________ is a computer program that teaches anatomy and physiology.
   A. ADAM C. STEVE
   B. EVE D. HERMAN
5. ____________________ are programmable mannequins on which studen can practice medical procedures.
   A. Human patient simulators C. Virtual mannequins
   B. Virtual human beings D. Human mannequins
6. Expert systems help in diagnosis. Examples of expert systems inclu ______________________.
   A. MYCIN C. Both A and B
   B. INTERNIST D. ADAM
7. ______________________ is a collection of forty databases maintained the National Library of Medicine. Some of the databases in the collection a MEDLINE and SDILINE.
   A. MEDCOM C. MED40
   B. MEDLARS D. MEDONLINE
8. ______________ is a database specifically geared to the needs of nurses a other professionals in seventeen allied health fields.
   A. AHL Line C. CINAHL
   B. MEDAHL D. MEDNURSE
9. __________________ is a collection of data on drug/drug and drug/foo interactions.
   A. Medi-Span C. DrugSafe
   B. Medi-Safe D. None of the above
10. ______________ is a network linking thirty thousand seriously ill childre in one hundred hospitals and many homes in North America.
    A. KIDSNET C. HOSPITALNet
    B. CHILDRENonline D. Starbright World

CHAPTER TEN EXAM

Name ____

FILL-INS Write the word or phrase that best completes each statement or answers the question.

1. The ______________ is a computerized library of human anatomy at the National Library of Medicine.
2. An ______________ is being developed. It will include authoring tools that engineers can use to build anatomical models that will allow students to experience how real anatomical structures feel, appear, and sound.
3. A new project called the ______________ is digitizing some of the seven thousand human embryos lost in miscarriages.
4. ______________ is a simulation program that teaches anatomy and physiology.
5. A program called ______________ helps students learn the skills needed for minimally invasive surgery.
6. ______________ are programmable mannequins on which students can practice medical procedures.
7. A programmable mannequin called ______________ is a virtual child.
8. ______________ refers to learning in an environment where student and instructor are not physically face to face.
9. An ______________ is an attempt to make a computer an expert in one narrow field.
10. An expert system called ______________ aids in the diagnosis and treatment of bacterial infections.
11. The ____________________ refers to the gap between information haves and have-nots.
12. The National Library of Medicine provides a collection of forty computerized databases called ______________ containing eighteen million references.
13. ______________ is a comprehensive online database of current medical research, including publications from 1966 to the present.
14. ______________ contains only the latest month's additions to MEDLINE.
15. ______________ is a network linking thirty thousand seriously ill children in one hundred hospitals and many homes in North America.

CHAPTER ELEVEN EXAM

Name ______________________________

MULTIPLE CHOICE Choose the one alternative that best completes t statement or answers the question.

1. Assistive, or ____________, technology allows some people with disabilit to work and/or live independently.
   A. helpful
   B. adaptive
   C. aiding
   D. None of the above
2. ________________ is technology that involves delivering low-level elect cal stimulation to muscles.
   A. FES
   B. SFE
   C. CES
   D. ABC
3. Computerized devices are used in optometry to ________.
   A. detect glaucoma
   B. make cataract surgery more precise
   C. detect retinal tears
   D. All of the above
4. Glasses that automatically change focus are called ________ glasses.
   A. automatic
   B. focusing
   C. smart
   D. intelligent
5. The ________________ prohibits discrimination against people wi disabilities and requires that businesses with more than fifteen employees provi "reasonable accommodation" to allow the disabled to perform their jobs.
   A. Americans with Disabilities Act of 1990
   B. Health Insurance Portability and Accountability Act of 1996
   C. The Welfare Reform Act
   D. All of the above
6. The ____________ wheelchair stands up on its back wheels if the us needs to climb stairs and raises the seat to allow reaching.
   A. standing
   B. reaching
   C. HuBot
   D. iBOT
7. Head mice and puff straws are assistive ________ devices.
   A. output
   B. input
   C. processing
   D. memory
8. An ________ communication device is any device that helps a persc communicate.
   A. augmentative
   B. diminutive
   C. impaired
   D. None of the above
9. Environmental ____________ systems help physically challenged peop control their environments.
   A. computer
   B. warming
   C. control
   D. None of the above
10. ________ devices are attempts to replace natural body parts or orga with artificial devices.
    A. Replacement
    B. Prosthetic
    C. Artificial
    D. None of the above

11. ____________________ is a technology that allows the integration of living bone with titanium implants.
    A. Bone integration
    B. Bone cloning
    C. Osseocloning
    D. Osseointegration

12. ____________________ uses sensors that detect hand and finger movement and sends signals to the computer. The computer associates the hand movements with a particular word. It can then translate the sign language into text and speech.
    A. Speech glove
    B. Acceleglove
    C. Translate glove
    D. Talking glove

13. The ________________ system, one system using FES (called functional neuromuscular stimulation), allows paraplegics to walk.
    A. Parastep
    B. AutoStep
    C. ParaWalk
    D. None of the above

14. ________________ technology will make it possible for computerized devices to be linked, so that when a pacemaker senses a heart attack, a cell phone will dial 911.
    A. Natural
    B. Bluetooth
    C. Wi-Fi
    D. FiWi

15. __________________ is a new field that may help treat disorders of the central nervous system including chronic pain.
    A. Neurostimulation
    B. Neuropaceing
    C. Neuromodulation
    D. None of the above

16. A computerized program called __________________ contains diagnostic analyses that keep track of specific tests and tasks performed by the stroke patient.
    A. HELEN
    B. MARY
    C. SIDNEY
    D. HARRY

17. __________________ is a "computer-based system [which] gives physical therapists real-time, objective measures of the motion of each joint in the patient's body."
    A. Measuring monitor
    B. Step monitor
    C. Walking monitor
    D. Motion monitor

18. The adult brain can retrain itself. ____________________ retrains the brain of some people who have lost their vision due to stroke.
    A. Vision training therapy
    B. Vision replacement therapy
    C. Sight replacement therapy
    D. None of the above

19. Implants pose certain dangers. Among them are ____________.
    A. infection
    B. rejection
    C. blood clots
    D. All of the above

20. A technique called ________________ attempts to look at the body's response to an implant at the cellular level.
    A. microtesting
    B. Microdialysis
    C. microimplant testing
    D. None of the above

CHAPTER ELEVEN EXAM

Name ________________________________

FILL-INS Write the word or phrase that best completes each statement or answ the question.

1. In hospitals and medical offices, ______________ with embedded mic processors are more accurate than their predecessors.
2. Assistive or ______________ technology allows some people with disabilities work and/or live independently.
3. ______________ (replacement limbs and organs) that contain motors a respond to electrical signals existed prior to computers.
4. ______________ is technology that involves delivering low-level electrical sti ulation to muscles.
5. Electronic stimulation is also being used to relieve chronic ____________ Electronic devices are implanted and send low levels of electrical energy nerves. This does not allow the pain signals to reach the brain.
6. In 2006, a new implantable device using FES—a ____________________—w developed. It uses "low levels of electricity in order to activate nerves a muscles in order to restore movement."
7. An ______________ is a doctor who treats eye diseases.
8. An ______________ examines the eye and prescribes glasses.
9. A prototype of ________________ developed at the University of Arizona w soon be able to automatically change focus. The lenses are two flat pieces glass; between them in a 5-micron space is liquid crystal.
10. A relatively new lower leg prosthesis is called the ______________________ It includes a prosthetic knee and shin system controlled by a microprocessor.
11. The ______________ wheelchair stands up on its back wheels if the user nee to climb stairs and raises the seat to allow reaching.
12. Adaptive input devices include the ______________, which moves the curs according to the user's head motions.
13. ______________ allow people to control the mouse with their mouths.
14. An ______________ is any device that helps a person communicate.
15. ______________ help physically challenged people control their environmen

CHAPTER TWELVE EXAM

Name ______________________________

MULTIPLE CHOICE Choose the one alternative that best completes the statement or answers the question.

1. Privacy includes the right to ________________.
   A. control personal information
   B. own a computer
   C. own a printer
   D. use a computer
2. The unauthorized copying of software protected by copyright is a crime called ____________.
   A. software stealth
   B. software crime
   C. software piracy
   D. None of the above
3. A ____________ is a program that attaches itself to another program and replicates itself.
   A. disease
   B. cold
   C. spyglass
   D. virus
4. __________ theft involves someone using someone's private information to assume their identity.
   A. Personal
   B. Identity
   C. Car
   D. None of the above
5. ______________ is software that can be installed without the user's knowledge to track their actions on a computer.
   A. Adware
   B. Trackware
   C. Spyware
   D. Keyware
6. ______________ includes attempts to protect computer systems and the privacy of computerized data.
   A. Security
   B. SafeComputer
   C. Both A and B
   D. None of the above
7. The ________________ gives law-enforcement agencies greater power to monitor electronic and other communications, with fewer checks.
   A. Health Insurance Portability and Accountability Act
   B. Americans with Disabilities Act
   C. USA PATRIOT Act
   D. Welfare Reform Act
8. The ____________________ is composed of 650 insurance companies. Its database contains health information on fifteen million people.
   A. Medical Information Bureau
   B. Insurance Information Bureau
   C. Medical Insurance Association Database
   D. American Hospital Database
9. ______________________ encourages the use of electronic medical records and requires health care facilities to have privacy policies.
   A. Health Insurance Portability and Accountability Act
   B. Americans with Disabilities Act
   C. USA PATRIOT Act
   D. Welfare Reform Act
10. __________ may display unwanted pop-up advertisements on your monitor; it may be related to the sites you search on the Web or even the content of your e-mail.
    A. Adware
    B. Trackware
    C. Spyware
    D. Keyware

CHAPTER TWELVE EXAM

Name ______________________________

FILL-INS Write the word or phrase that best completes each statement or answe the question.

1. ______________ has many aspects. Among them is the ability to control pe sonal information and the right to keep it from misuse.
2. ______________ measures attempt to protect computer systems, includi information, from harm and abuse.
3. The first federal legislation protecting the privacy of medical records ______________.
4. __________________ is the unauthorized copying of software protected copyright.
5. One common computer crime is ______________—such as using a comput program to illegally transfer money from one bank account to another.
6. A ______________ is a program that attaches itself to another program ar replicates itself. It may do damage to your hardware or destroy your data.
7. The penalties for damaging computer systems have been severely increased the USA PATRIOT Act and the ______________ Act.
8. ______________ is the scrambling of data so that it does not make sense.
9. The ______________ Act gives law-enforcement agencies greater power monitor electronic and other communications, with fewer checks.
10. The ______________ Act expands and centralizes the data gathering allowe under the PATRIOT Act.
11. ______________ of restricting access to computer systems include fingerprin hand prints, retina or iris scans, lip prints, and facial thermography.
12. Electronic blocks (called __________________) can be used to limit access networks.
13. The ______________ has been interpreted to allow employers access employees' e-mail.
14. ______________ are small files that a Web site may put on your hard driv when you visit.
15. The ______________ is composed of 650 insurance companies. Its databas contains the health histories of millions of people.

Test Bank Answers

Chapter One Multiple Choice

1. C
2. D
3. B
4. B
5. C
6. B
7. D
8. A
9. C
10. A

Chapter One Fill-ins

1. information technology
2. program
3. Supercomputers
4. Input
5. Mainframes
6. PDAs
7. chip
8. binary digits or bits
9. hardware
10. RAM
11. ROM
12. Software
13. operating system
14. Bluetooth
15. protocols

Chapter Two Multiple Choice

1. C
2. B
3. A
4. C
5. A
6. D
7. D
8. D
9. A
10. D

Chapter Two Fill-ins

1. medical informatics
2. Bioinformatics
3. 2014
4. cost or resistance by personnel
5. regional health information organization (RHIO)
6. national health information network (NHIN)
7. interoperable
8. The Indian Health Service
9. administrative
10. financial
11. clinical
12. Pharmacy
13. Nursing
14. Picture archiving and communication systems (PACS)
15. Laboratory

Chapter Three Multiple Choice

1. A
2. B
3. C
4. C
5. A
6. B
7. C
8. B
9. A
10. D

Chapter Three Fill-ins

1. clinical
2. Special purpose
3. Administrative
4. Telemedicine
5. balance or bucket
6. database
7. DBMS
8. file
9. tables
10. records
11. fields
12. key
13. DRG
14. CPT
15. transactions

Chapter Four Multiple Choice

1. B
2. A
3. D
4. C
5. D
6. A
7. B

8. C
9. A
10. D

Chapter Four Fill-ins

1. Telemedicine
2. Store-and-forward technology
3. teleconferencing
4. Bluetooth
5. tPa
6. Telepsychiatry
7. telespirometry
8. arrhythmia
9. smart stretcher
10. TeleHome Care
11. TeleHome Care
12. prisons
13. Baby CareLink's
14. teletrauma
15. state

Chapter Five Multiple Choice

1. C
2. C
3. A
4. D
5. C
6. B
7. B
8. B
9. A
10. B
11. A
12. C
13. B
14. A
15. D

Chapter Five Fill-ins

1. WHONET
2. Global warming
3. carbon dioxide
4. Katrina
5. polio
6. AIDS
7. Biomedical
8. SARS
9. avian
10. World Health Organization
11. West Nile
12. Mad cow
13. Syndromic
14. National Electronic Disease Initiative
15. Ebola

Chapter Six Multiple Choice

1. A
2. D
3. A
4. C
5. D
6. D
7. D
8. D
9. B
10. B
11. C
12. A
13. C
14. A
15. B

Chapter Six Fill-ins

1. X-ray
2. X-ray
3. Ultrasound
4. CT scans
5. CT scans
6. Ultrafact CT
7. MRI
8. MRIs
9. Functional
10. PET scans
11. PET scans
12. PET scans
13. schizophrenia
14. Focused ultrasound
15. brain

Chapter Seven Multiple Choice

1. C
2. C
3. B
4. A
5. B
6. D
7. B
8. C
9. D
10. D
11. D
12. A
13. C
14. A
15. C

Chapter Seven Fill-ins

1. Minimally invasive microsurgery
2. endoscope

3. telepresence
4. eXpert Trainer
5. ROBODOC
6. ZEUS
7. MINERVA
8. HERMES
9. NASA
10. image
11. virtual reality
12. augmented reality
13. Gall bladder
14. robot
15. Laprotek

Chapter Eight Multiple Choice

1. B
2. A
3. C
4. B
5. D
6. C
7. A
8. C
9. A
10. B
11. D
12. C
13. A
14. B
15. A

Chapter Eight Fill-ins

1. Biotechnology
2. rational drug design
3. bioinformatics
4. Human Genome Project
5. Antisense technology
6. RNA interference
7. Human Physiome Project
8. adverse
9. "To Err is Human"
10. barcodes
11. point-of-use
12. Telepharmacy
13. chip
14. Stem cells
15. AIDS

Chapter Nine Multiple Choice

1. A
2. D
3. C
4. A
5. B

6. A
7. D
8. A
9. B
10. B

Chapter Nine Fill-ins

1. Dental informatics
2. administrative
3. electronic dental chart
4. Bacteria
5. Bonding
6. Implants
7. EXPERTMD
8. Electrical conductance
9. DIFOTI
10. Minimally invasive dentistry
11. Low-level
12. ultrasonic
13. periodontal
14. Digital
15. Periodontics

Chapter Ten Multiple Choice

1. A
2. B
3. C
4. A
5. A
6. C
7. B
8. C
9. A
10. D

Chapter Ten Fill-ins

1. Visible Human Project
2. Explorable Virtual Human
3. Virtual Human Embryo
4. ADAM
5. eXpert Trainer
6. Human patient simulators
7. PediaSim
8. Distance learning
9. expert system
10. MYCIN
11. digital divide
12. MEDLARS
13. MEDLINE
14. SDILINE
15. Starbright World

Chapter Eleven Multiple Choice

1. B
2. A

3. D
4. C
5. A
6. D
7. B
8. A
9. C
10. B
11. D
12. B
13. A
14. B
15. C
16. A
17. D
18. B
19. D
20. B

Chapter Eleven Fill-ins

1. devices
2. adaptive
3. Prosthetics
4. FES
5. pain
6. neuroprosthesis
7. optometrist
8. ophthalmologist
9. smart glasses
10. C-leg or computerized leg
11. iBOT
12. head mouse
13. Puff straws
14. augmentative communication device
15. Environmental control systems

Chapter Twelve Multiple Choice

1. A
2. C
3. D
4. B
5. C
6. A
7. C
8. A
9. A
10. A

Chapter Twelve Fill-ins

1. Privacy
2. Security
3. HIPAA
4. Software piracy
5. fraud

6. virus
7. Homeland Security
8. Encryption
9. USA PATRIOT
10. Homeland Security
11. Biometrics
12. firewalls
13. Electronic Communications Privacy Act
14. Cookies
15. Medical Information Bureau